LIFE

Before, During & After

May 25/89

L I F E
Before, During & After

Contributing spirit teachers include Abrham, Bartholomew, Crystal Moon Running, Dr. Peebles, Dong How Li, Enid, The Eternals, Hilarion, John, Kunda, Kyros, Li Sung, Master Adalfo, Rahma, Ramtha, Robbyn and His Merrye Bande, Soli, Spirit, Ting-Lao, and Zoosh.

Edited by Molli Nickell

Book Design and Illustrations by Gary Lund

Published by: Spirit Speaks Inc.
P. O. Box 84304
Los Angeles, CA 90073
213-826-9197
Toll free (outside of California) 800-356-9104

First printing November 1988

ISBN: 0-938283-01-4

Library of Congress Catalog
Card Number: 88-92593

This book, like all others in our *Celebration of Discovery* series, has come into being because of teamwork among many individuals who have lovingly shared their time and talents. Thank you and hugs to the helping hands and hearts of Dorothy Compinsky, David, Gary Lund, Bob Mason, Sharon McDonald, Glenn Nickell, Sonia Nordenson, Karen Wellenkamp, Daniel Will-Harris, and Toni Will-Harris.

Grateful acknowledgment is given to a vital part of this team: the twenty channels, dedicated and talented individuals all, who have participated with such enthusiasm.

We also wish to acknowledge the support and loving encouragement from the spirit teachers who have worked so closely with us on this book project. Their dedication and assistance has enabled us to move ever onwards and upwards, despite occasional growth opportunities (challenges).

And special acknowledgment to you, our reader, for your courage and determination to discover more about yourself and your purpose in life. Thank you for inviting us to join you on this fascinating and joyful quest.

TABLE OF CONTENTS

Dear Reader,

Thank you for picking up this book. It has been created to introduce you to the most exciting game in town--the game of life.

The *most exciting* aspect about the game of life is that you create it. You design your own game board and determine who gets to be the scotty dog, the train, or the car. You place Boardwalk and Park Place wherever it suits you. You determine prices on hotels or houses, or give them away if you choose. You make every single decision, including the color and denominations of the money. (How about an orange $10,000 bill?)

You've probably heard that expression, "You create your own reality." This phrase is just another way of saying that you create your own game of life, and it *is* more than simply a New Age phrase, it's a universal reality. The trick to doing it, and doing it successfully, is *understanding* more about the main player in your game, which is you. As you understand more about your choices in life, you'll become much more in touch with *who* you really are, *why* you are a physical human being, and *what* you can do about your life and the lives of others (including the planet).

Believe it or not, you were not dropped into life by a manipulative or angry God who wanted to watch you squirm your way through a quagmire of struggle. Nor are you a cosmic accident, a being created by a random union of ovum and sperm. What you are is a fragment of a universal God who loves you, supports you, and wants to help you win the game you've selected, no matter what it is or how you play it. God experiences your game through you, and appreciates the opportunity to do so. You are also very loved, for not only do God and the universe love and support you, but you have your very own boosters club, a support group of spirit guides and teachers who have agreed to be with you during your entire lifetime. Now isn't that a relief to know?

For many years now, scientists have known that our bodies are not solid; in fact, nothing is solid. All life everywhere is composed of molecular energy--indestructible and non-ending. Those of us in the metaphysical/spiritual field call this force "God/Goddess/All That Is." We understand God to be an indestructible, immortal, eternal, and universal force. You, as an individual human being, are a fragment of this universal energy, of God. You have chosen to experience life in physical form. You, along with your spiritual guides and teachers, have created a game plan which allows you to experience certain aspects of life in physical form on planet earth.

A very important part of the game is that you forget all about the fact that you set it up, and by the time you're four or five or six you believe that the game is real and you begin to function as one of the little scotty dogs or cars or game pieces instead of realizing and reacting to the game of life as if you had created it, which of course you did. Then, when you start to remember *how* you set it all up and *why* you set it all up, you regain memory of your source, your *reason* for being here, and then you begin to radically shift gears.

That is what's happening around the world right now, in case you hadn't noticed. Millions of people are becoming involved in consciousness raising, and are studying New Age this and New Age that. Regardless of how their activities are labeled, what they are doing is beginning to remember their origin, and as they are doing so they are beginning to play the game of life differently. (Among other things, they smile and laugh much more than before.)

They also are winning a lot more. This is not the kind of winning which means someone else is losing. Winning means achieving the greatest and grandest prizes available here on the planet. These include peace of mind, abundant health, bountiful friendships, lasting prosperity, and a real zest for the living of every moment of life.

So just exactly what do you have to do to become a winner? Is there a catch? Do you have to eat 16 cherry pies at one sitting, win $22,000,000 in the lottery, sell your soul to "You Know Who"?

Nothing complicated or catchy at all. To win, you simply make the decision to get more in touch with *who* you really are.

Let's face it, *you* are the most fascinating person you'll ever meet. And getting deeply in touch with the greatest person you'll ever meet is exciting. In fact, finding out more about yourself is like a labyrinthine trail of investigation and celebration.

What this book is about is helping you jump right into this great game of self-discovery.

Speaking of games, this planet who serves as a grand playing field for all of us has her own game plan too! Part of this involves some shifting and changing of land masses as well as attitudes. Because of the more obvious physical changes, many people believe that we are in the "last days" as prophesied by the Bible. And many have great fear because of this.

Well, there's some good news and some not so good news about the last days. In a sense, how we have lived on this planet and the ways we have treated ourselves and each other are coming to an end (and isn't it about time?). What all this consciousness-raising is about is shifting attitudes and actions as a viable alternative to a massive shift of the polar axis. You see, Mother Earth is changing her basic vibration as she evolves to another level of growth and understanding. And it's time for all who live on the planet to do exactly the same thing.

Move on or move off!

Most in the New Age/metaphysical/spiritual community understand the current and upcoming changes as a natural, normal part of life. If there is one universal game plan that you can always hang your hat on, it's that the universe is always changing. Always.

So how can you survive and even enjoy a world where things seem to be topsy-turvy? By understanding yourself. Greater understanding of who you are and why you are a living physical human being will bring you peace of mind, greater enjoyment of yourself and others, and a global perspective you may never have had before. As more and more individuals begin to see themselves as part of an ongoing process of change and evolution, the changes begin to shift and evolve into a less threatening mode than before.

This book, the second in the *Celebration of Discovery* series, has been created to assist you on this most interesting quest. It is designed to give you solid and helpful information about yourself. What makes this book, and others in the series, so helpful is the fact that the material comes from a group of loving and wise beings called spirit teachers who contribute to our bimonthly magazine, *Spirit Speaks*.

The spiritual psychology they share helps you understand more about life as viewed from their expanded perspectives.

The process of communicating with these spirit teachers you are about to meet is called "channeling." It refers to an ancient means of communication, newly revived. Channels, frequently called sensitives or trance mediums, are people with the ability to step aside from their normal state of consciousness, allowing spirit teachers to speak through them for the purpose of sharing information. An example of a channel is Edgar Cayce, whose books of channeled teachings have been sold worldwide since the 1950s.

The spirit teachers we have asked to contribute guidance are compassionate beings. Most of them are very familiar with the game of life we're all involved in because they too have been physical human beings and are acutely aware of the fears and frustrations we experience during our time on Earth. Because they are not, at the moment, in physical form, they see life from a broader perspective than we do as we struggle with the complexities of daily living. Their greatest desire is to offer helping hands to better prepare us for continuing social, economic, physical, and environmental changes.

There are hundreds and thousands of different groups of spirit teachers devoting their energy toward the upliftment of all humanity and the healing of the planet. Each group selects a "spokes-spirit" to represent them all, which is why many spirit teachers refer to themselves as "we."

You may find what appear to be contradictory statements from our contributing spirit teachers. Bear in mind that they are simply sharing guidance from their points of view, which may differ slightly from teacher to teacher. If you will read with an open heart and mind, your inner self and your guides and teachers will help you locate the truths which are most meaningful to your level of growth and development. Should you find some passages which are difficult to understand, just glide right over them, knowing that later you can reread them and they'll make perfect sense to you.

There are three universal principles woven throughout the teachings in this book. Understanding them and integrating them into your daily life will assist you in fulfilling your game plan to its greatest possible potential. They are:

The Loving Law of Allowance for all things to be in their own time and place, starting with self.

Increased communication, with respect, with and for all life.

Taking self-responsibility for how you perceive life and react to it.

All of us here at *Spiritspeaksland* send you encouragement as you move along your path toward greater understanding. We appreciate being a part of your growth and thank you for inviting us.

In light and love,

Molli Nickell, Publisher/Editor-in-Chief
Spirit Speaks Inc.
Los Angeles, California
October, 1988

Reincarnation
Your Plan

"Many on the earth plane
would have less fear if they
could see their form for
what it is--a vehicle which
makes it possible for them
to experience life on
planet earth."

from Kyros

The Birth of Human Consciousness

from Kunda

Over the eons, Divine Consciousness came to the point in Its creative adventure when it became time for It to experience Itself as more distinct groupings. Thus, a stream of consciousness split apart from the main thrust to yield a systematic order of solar entities who, in turn, continued to fragment into smaller and smaller clusters until the soul communities and cosmic souls were born. These hierarchical groupings were given the complete freedom and ability to disperse themselves in order to become different, in order to enable Consciousness to explore creativity more thoroughly by creating the basis from which more diverse characteristics could be originated, experienced, and then reassimilated.

The cosmic soul became the foundation and the birthing process through which evolution could materialize, out of which conscious spirit-entities were established and more individualized characteristics could be asserted. Thus, your essence began as a collective mass of emerged consciousness which flowed into sectors of cosmic soul groupings in order that familiarization be made available. Evolution began its timely course and, to further complete the process of this diversification, human consciousness followed.

Every portion of this fragmentation is linked in consciousness, from the smallest protoplasm just now developing up to the most evolved intelligence grouping in the universe. Even though you are an individual identity with the capacity to freely choose and organize your life structure, you are also a vital part of "another you" that is experiencing multidimensional beingness throughout the entire cosmos. Traces of this will sometimes appear as brief, disconnected images in your most relaxed states of consciousness. Because you possess your own identity, complete with unique characteristics

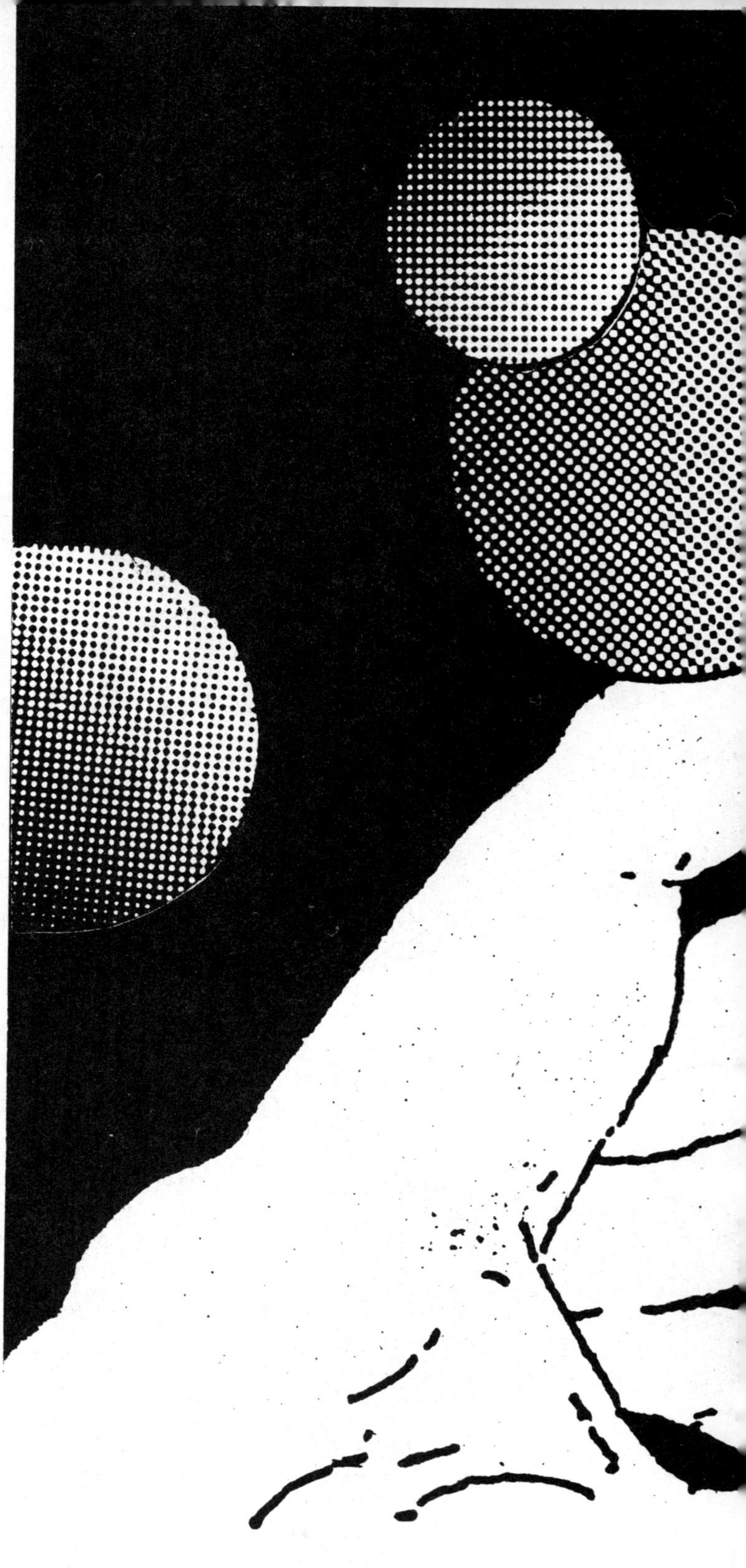

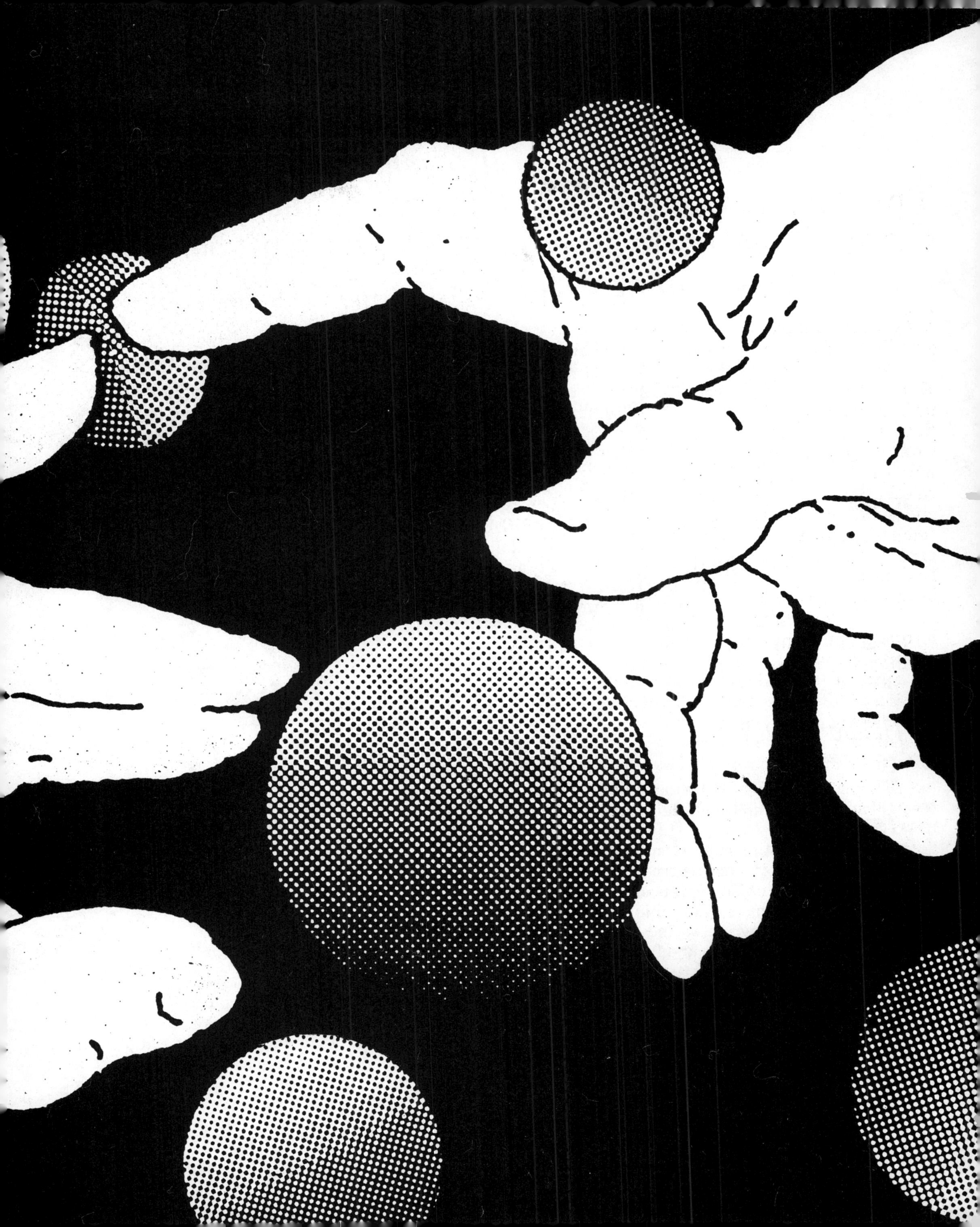

Your existences are truly open-ended; and your ultimate purpose, life after life after life, is to find and to love God--the essence of your being--through your love affair with life.

and desires of your own, seldom are you able to recall your greater self, so fixed is your concept about reality. Your imagination helps you to intersect with the cosmic reality that you yearn to know but can't remember simply because, if you turn your imagination loose, it will reveal spiritual phenomena that cannot be factually proven.

Reincarnation is a somewhat frail attempt, then, to describe the intricate processes by which individualized life could be explored in multitudinous fashion and the consciousness of that exploration returned for a greater sense of unity and oneness within the whole. You are a direct descendant of and participant in this plan. Your existences are truly open-ended; and your ultimate purpose, life after life after life, is to find and to love God--the essence of your being--through your love affair with life.

The flow of life

from Kunda

The natural flow of consciousness is toward the light and unity of all things. Its ultimate purpose is to consummate the joy and fulfillment of Creation itself. So it is that all energy emitted returns to its center, all things created return to their creator, all essence is a part of The Essence, all principalities are governed by the principle. Nothing stands outside of God. All things are of God, and all consciousness eventually discovers and feels its oneness and kinship with God.

This is the natural flow of life, the fundamental principle of the universe and the primary relationship between Creator and consciousness. In other words, it is impossible not to know God on some level of creativity, for God is All That Is.

The primary essence of God is love, the divine energy from which all creativity flows, nourishes, and extends in order to sustain itself. The primary essence of consciousness is spirit, and spirit is the energy of the universe which creates all things. Each person is a part of that energy, a divine being who contributes to the individual, group, and world consciousness on planet earth and is a caretaker for creation.

Many entities think of God as a complex and sometimes heartless being who dwells in an unattainable, faraway place called Heaven. They believe God to be a temperamental God who enforces impossible standards upon His subjects, loving some and rejecting others.

Reincarnation is a part you have chosen for yourself in order to explore the adventure called life.

Know that God is all the simple and beautiful things in life. God is everywhere seen and unseen.

The created were not made to live in ignorance or pain, but to enjoy the beauty and splendor of the Creative Life Force made possible through Eternal Consciousness as an awakened God-Force returning to the Creator Being.

Your natural state of beingness

from Kunda

When you are in the nonphysical realm, your consciousness is united with that greater portion of your being known as the Cosmic Soul. The soul is a divine manifestation of higher intelligence existing as a self-contained energy mass with tremendous creative powers. The essence of your soul is threefold in nature: intelligent, vital, and sensitive. Intelligence is the supreme organization behind the creation. Vitality is the power and permanence. Sensitivity is the awareness that recognizes the act. Creativity operates under two essential principles: the receptive and active modes. The receptive is the female "yin" power, the negative energy which opens the door through which intelligence may flow. The active is the male "yang" power, the visible activity of intelligence. Your soul is a conductor of female and male energies and plarizes its human creations with both.

Your most natural state of beingness is when you are a unified energy-composite resting within the total complex of your cosmic soul. When you are in this state, your consciousness becomes an integral blending of your cosmic mate (your soul), moving freely within the domain of your nuclear cosmic family. However, consciousness cannot help but explore itself, and as such, the cosmic soul participates readily in this act through the manifestation of soul-essence.

Reincarnation is a part you have chosen for yourself in order to explore the adventure called life. You have been treading the path of self-responsibility from the moment you decided to incorporate your essence with human form. You are not only responsible for having created reincarnation as a means of expressing divine energy; you are also responsible for the very fact that you do exist and that you are creating the reality of your own destiny, that which extends far beyond your human involvement upon this plane. As a human being, you will continue to pass through the life cycles until such time as your soul determines that its experience is complete and decides to leave physical existence.

The nature of human evolution requires that your consciousness pass through many different levels and cycles of awareness in order to complete your education here. This is because, as consciousness explores and creates itself, it gradually moves up the staircase of expanded awareness. Similarly, as you unfold along your spiritual path, you will not jump from one rung to another, but will gain inner realization by *degrees* of awareness. It is a profound and necessary cycle of activity and participation, for it is your level of awareness which allows you to integrate the experiences of a multidimensional self in order to perceive the depth of your own understanding.

As you develop, so does your soul, except in a much more expanded way. Your cosmic mate has many other lives going on simultaneously in addition to the one you are living right now. Your soul is a multidimensional being experiencing multifaceted realities. Your human development will take you through many different soul cycles and progressive tests before you can fully join the soul and advance to higher stages of learning. Hence, you are restricted to the physical dimension until

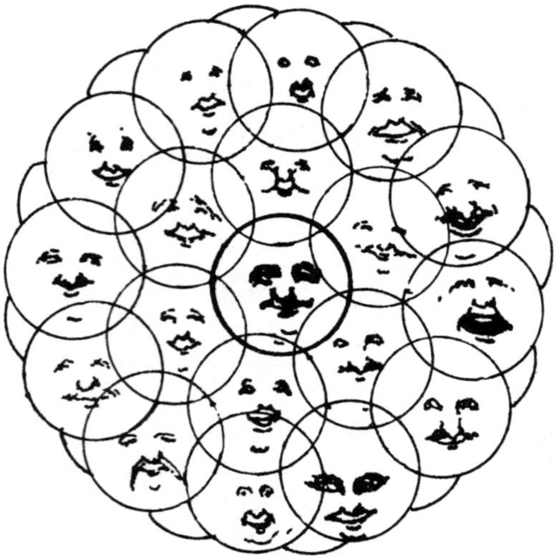

that greater portion of your being is satisfied and fulfilled in its learning processes. However, even though you have temporarily limited your focus of consciousness primarily to the physical dimension, your soul is ever advancing in its capacity to create and explore many other realities. Thus, while you often feel burdened by the human experience and all that this reality represents, all that the soul experiences is also yours by virtue of your birthright.

Why are you here? Quite simply, the purpose of human life is to learn and to grow, and all manner of soul-fabrication will be used to create untold realities and project essence into form.

You registered yourself in the curriculum of physical life; and while you are being human you agree to play by all the rules in order that you may spiritually grow, yet humanly function.

Physically, your body must follow the nature of the physical reality into which you were born. Spiritually, you really are unlimited and evolving in a multidimensional reality with your cosmic partner, your soul.

The Veil of Forgetfulness

from Kunda

The Veil of Forgetfulness allows you to focus a major portion of your consciousness on the spiritual needs of the "resident personality" and to identify with a specific form of manifestation. The Veil of Forgetfulness serves you well because it forces your concentration on a chosen environment and allows you to imagine that you are that person living out a particular life. It helps you to closely relate to the human life you have chosen for yourself and to interpret those human experiences in linear terms.

The Veil allows you to clothe yourself in human flesh, wearing all the limitations of such existence, and to enter the illusion with eagerness and expectation that it is really real, so that you complete the life and all that you set out to accomplish. Your incarnation is a very creative act, and your assumed identity includes the conscious human mind, one that plays with the reality of your unfoldment as only it can understand it in physical terms.

Were your veil to be entirely removed, you would not be able to direct or adapt your consciousness to individual development and fulfill your contractual agreements. Thus, before you entered this dimension and became the in-dwelling spirit, you agreed to abide by all the rules of the physical universe and those that enable you to best perceive existence on a singular level.

When you are ready to assume responsibility for your existence, when you take charge of your person and fully comprehend that you do form what you think of as your personal reality, then you are ready to handle more knowledge, and all else falls into place.

You cannot begin to fathom the extent of your divine reality until you can accept your current reality.

Life without end

from Ramtha

You, my esteemed beloved brethren, are more than that which is termed the creature of the flesh. You are awesome entities taking form to continue the creative ability that is within you. Without it, there is nothing. Without it, the value of thought does not propagate itself to become the next moment of life, or to become that which is termed the eternity that is yet to be lived.

And where, indeed, shall your eternity end? Nowhere. You are ongoing. There is no end to it. When you learn that each moment you live the refinement of your own opinionated self in becoming, then you become one day again the platform from which all life springs.

Life is purposeful happiness. The illusions of creating that happiness are called purposeful destinies. I will tell you:

Your greatest purpose is to live.

To live! Living allows all happiness to occur . . . and all sadness, whatever your discretion be. Your greatest purpose is to live, to express the entity that you are, the embodiment of life.

To you who have made your transition unto this earth plane, it is a wondrous place. But whoever thinks that this is all has seen nothing! For greater kingdoms and adventures are there to come. Life is a splendid adventure! It is, indeed, a wondrous place to demonstrate the creative infiniteness of all that are gathered here; that is the purpose.

There is no mystery to life. If you look around you, you will see all the answers. If you listen to

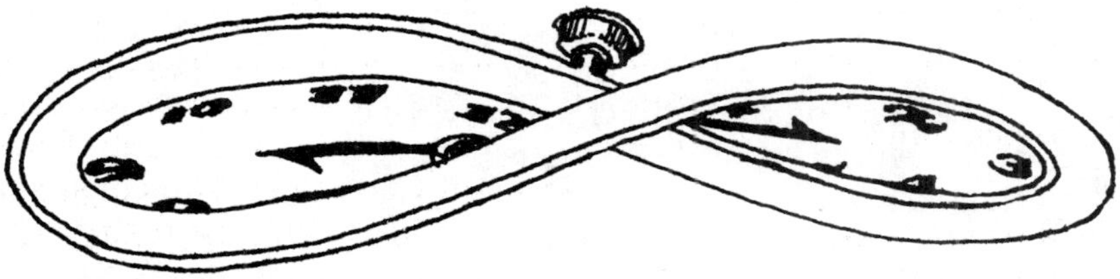

yourself and do what your self tells you to do, then you will soon find the manifestation of that doing.

You are not the same as you were only moments ago, and you will not be the same in moments to come. For life is an ever-evolving consciousness that collects in its moment a totality of refinement, that allows you to bloom. And each moment you become grander, a greater entity unto that which is called a total self, unto God the Father that blooms within your being. Thus, perfection can never be seen, for the Father and life are ever-changing every moment. You only are--nothing less and nothing more.

The Story Corner

The Coin

from the Eternals

There was once a small coin that traveled in the pocket of a man who walked upon the countryside. The small coin spoke to the other coins in the man's pocket, saying, "Where have you been and where shall you go?"

The other coins said, "We have been many places and have seen many things."

The little coin asked, "How many places have you been?"

The multitude of coins answered, "We have been many places. We have seen soda machines, fine department stores, cash registers and velvet-lined collection plates in churches. We have seen the pockets of the rich and the pockets of the beggars."

The small coin said, "You remember the places you have been, yet I remember more distant places. I remember being among the rocks as an unshaped form. I remember a time when as molten metal I was poured forth to be cast. I remember a great die that stamped me."

The other coins laughed and said, "Wretched coin carried to and fro by all of the strange beliefs, there is no life before creation."

The one small coin said, "I can remember. There is a remembrance and I know there was a time before I came into this being as a coin."

The other coins all repeated, "There is no existence before creation."

So the multitude believed not, yet the one remembered.

The Purpose of Reincarnation

The planet Earth was set up as one school of learning where people would have physical bodies which would allow them to have intense and focused learning experiences.

from Robbyn and His Merrye Bande

As you have just read, to incarnate is to embody, to represent or to express a quality or idea in concrete form. And you see, in the whole course of creation, including all the known and unknown universes, and the bridge in between, there are many ways of being, many different ways to express the many facets of the clarity that is the Creator.

To begin with, everything was very etheric--rather vague. But as time went on, and most of the lessons about being spirit and ether were learned, the Creator came up with the concepts of density, gravity, and form, as opportunities for new experiences to grow and learn. Some souls decided to try it. (On the other hand, some very old and wise souls have *never* incarnated.)

The planet Earth was set up as one school of learning where people would have physical bodies which would allow them to have intense and focused learning experiences. Well, beingness was newer then, and the Creator hadn't anticipated all pitfalls. So some of us went along to Earth to see what it was like, and boy was it a shock! First of all, it was very challenging to get a body; then it was challenging to get our soul essence compacted into one (rather small) earthly body. Then, the process of "growing up," etc., was a real Zen grueler in terms of remembering what we came here for in the first place.

So it was decided to let us try to do it a second, and sometimes third, time. Guides and angels and teachers were added to help make things a little easier. After all, the purpose was not for things to be hard, but to learn as an expression of the Creator, and to express. And the planet was beautiful, so people didn't mind coming back to *get it right*. After a while, getting it right became more important than expressing. Well, that's not exactly what it was all about.

You see, souls were (and still are) created for different purposes, to have different forms, and to develop different abilities. Each soul is a creative expression of the Creator who has many, many different facets.

So when each soul achieved independent expression, that soul had a reason to be, a path to fully realize its creation, and a purposeful intent to be and to achieve its full potential, so that it could return, after the full circle of its creation, to the Creator with even more facets and more knowledge, wisdom, and experience than before. As such, each soul, being unique expression, had, as part of its creation, a game plan, a set of lessons to learn, and a general time to report back.

Now don't get us wrong, you still got to pick what you wanted to do; after all, your game plan had to fit into the overall picture, too, so you and the Creator sat down and looked at the overall intent. You probably said, "Well, I think I can do this and this and this, and I'd like to try that, and I'll be back in 80 billion years." And the Creator, laid-back, tolerant being that the Creator is, said, "Great!" And you were off to the races, with only occasional progress reports in between. And lest you think that this arrangement was unfair, an in-depth study and analysis of your soul path would seem only natural to fulfill your curiosity in any event, and is a small price to pay for the privilege of being. It saved the Creator a lot of time as well, because, of course, the Creator could have done all this study alone. Instead, this opportunity was offered to give others a reason to be. (Yep, you guessed it, there is a universal rule which, roughly translated, says that everything has a reason to be.)

Your own personal game plan

from Robbyn and His Merrye Bande

So there you were with your new beingness, your new form, a map of the known universes, and your topic. Maybe it was love, or clear expression, or compassion. At any rate, you knew what you were doing because you had a map, and usually you had many new friends who were learning the same things. Your map probably looked like the one on pages 24 and 25.

Maybe the maps weren't exactly like that, but there was variation, and you were permitted to achieve your discoveries from within any one of those categories, and in your own time, your own way, and so on. Most souls liked it very much. And some of you started out at all levels within your map. And that was fine, too, except the emphasis wasn't intended to be on "Trouble" and below. Then some of you noticed that those of you starting at the "Medium Existence" area and up seemed to be having a lot easier time of it than those of you starting at "Trouble" and under. But you knew that this was the case going in, and that when you got into "Trouble" and under, you were to report your experiences directly to the Creator, and not just stay there stubbornly determined to get out by working yourself out as opposed to turning around and starting at a higher level!

But some of you got very jealous of those in "Higher Calling," and were determined to get out of the "Trouble" area only on your own steam. (This is a little like crossing the Atlantic. There are many ways you can do it . . . planes, boats of many kinds, balloons, surfboards, kayaks, rowboats, or you can try to swim. If you have all the facts about how far it is to swim, and what else lives in the water, and what the weather's like, it doesn't seem very sensible to get mad at the people who chose to take a cruise liner or a plane, does it? (For that matter, you could have, too. In our analogy, the purpose of having the ability to swim is only in case your plane had to go down, or you fell off the ship.) "Trouble" and under is only there to give you occasional, intensely focused experiences of what it is to work through a problem successfully. It was never meant to be the whole journey, or the whole way of life. (Especially not several!)

So now you're probably wondering what this has to do with reincarnation. Well, many of you became so determined to do it your way that you did the same thing over and over again. Training to swim the Atlantic, that is. Instead of buying a ticket to fly or sail--you were jumping off the pier, and drowning every time. Getting mad and wanting to do it again, knowing full well that the logistics haven't changed and won't.

And then 80 billion years passed and the Creator wanted a report, and there you were, still mad that you couldn't swim, determined not to give up, and having learned nothing about compassion in general, much less for yourself . . . certainly not enough about it or yourself to have the compassion to give up jumping off the pier every time. And you're still busy sulking because someone else has it easier, or so you think.

Well, things are changing. While this used to be allowed to happen all the time, it no longer will be. Earth wants new opportunities, and new, different souls want the opportunity to come here to learn. And you may as well get used to the "Higher Calling" crew and accept the fact that there are overachievers everywhere.

We almost wish we could tell you that it really doesn't matter *how* you learn your lessons, but the truth is that some paths are more costly than others. And this doesn't mean that you don't have free will

Understand that you accepted a responsibility when you decided to incarnate.

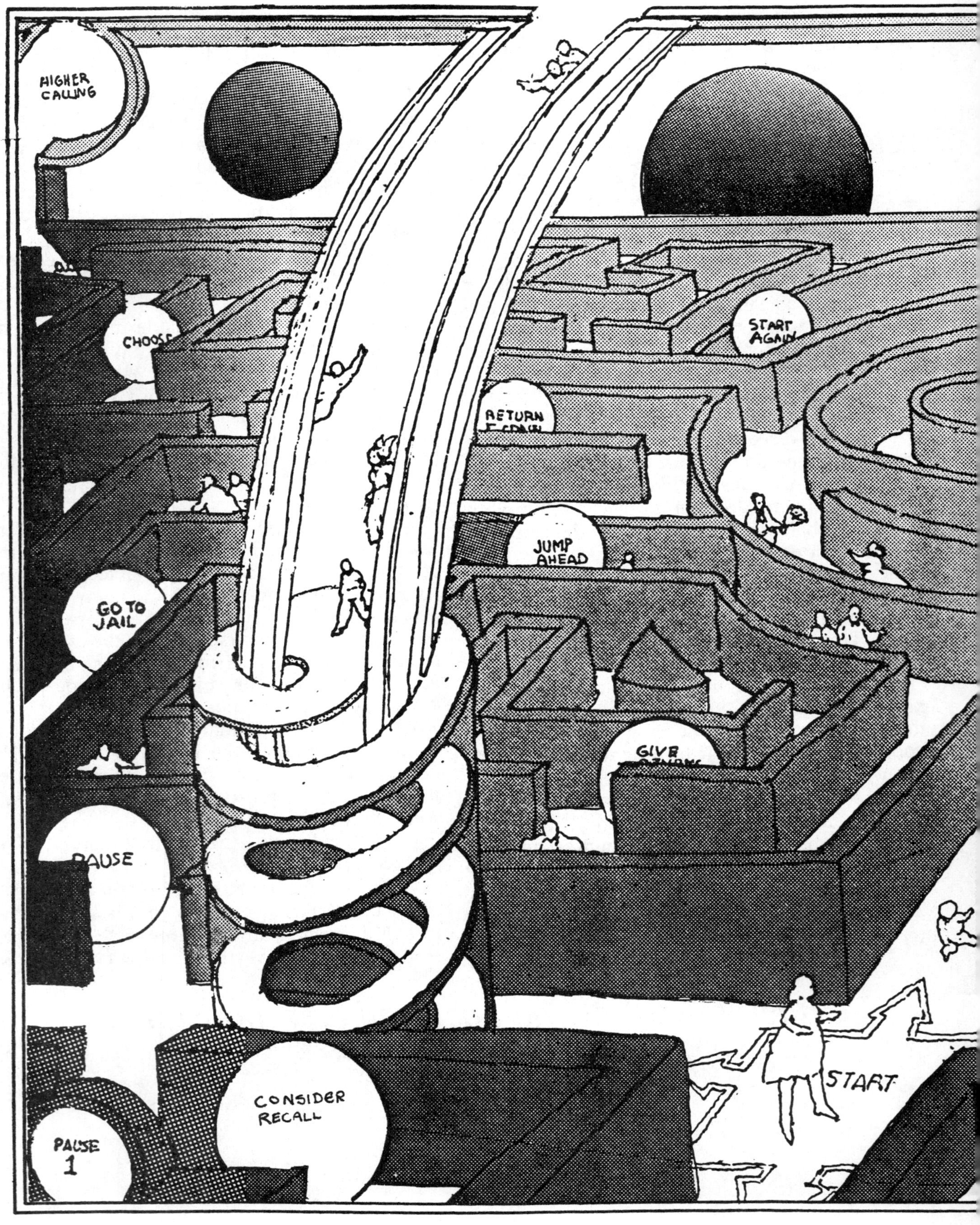

HIGHER CALLING
START AGAIN
RETURN
JUMP AHEAD
GO TO JAIL
GIVE
PAUSE
CONSIDER RECALL
PAUSE 1
START

CLEAR EXPRESSION
PICK 3
FINISH
WAIT
LOVE
MEDIUM EXISTENCE
MOVE
TROUBLE
MISSION MANGLED
RECEIVE 3 TURNS
MOVE AHEAD 2

to do exactly as you wish in the broadest context of things. Understand that you accepted a responsibility when you decided to incarnate. At that time, you agreed on your map. And that map has a lot of latitude. (You don't think 80 billion years is a lot of latitude?)

So every one of you had an opportunity to fulfill every possible whim or individual life purpose that has ever been conceived. And you had every chance to be everything you wished. Now, however, it is the Earth, herself, who has asked for a changing role. And bless *her* heart, she has been more than a gracious hostess to all of us . . . we've learned a lot. But now, she is asking that anyone not in the light or willing to come fully into it within the next two lifetimes (to accommodate those not yet born to those who are still living) leave her energy. So, as we've been saying for some time now, if you do not *fully* incarnate in this lifetime, you may not have the chance to do it again.

You've had your chances, and many of you have done the same things over and over again. Some of you have stopped even trying to learn. And that's not so good, because while it's true that every path will lead you to where you want to go, you must understand and accept that you have an obligation to the universe and also to Earth to be the best that you can--if you want to stay. You have a sacred trust to deliver a report of your *well-rounded* experiences, and that wasn't supposed to mean limiting yourself to being a specialist in "Trouble!"

And that's the first thing you need to know about what not to do in terms of reincarnation. Now you'll probably think that we're contradicting some *sacred* tenet about free will. We're not. The fact that you have a separate existence in the known universe means that you are special and unique, you have a *raison d'etre.* What you learn in your lives means a lot, not just to you and/or the Creator, but to the whole scheme of things, literally. What you learn, what you feel in your existence, has form and substance of its own. It lives and has purpose in the whole complex design of the universe.

Your beingness, forms, and lives will be written (recorded) in what some of you call the "Akasha." This very complex record is woven throughout time, and it will influence things in the future, toward the good and the pure, we hope. (As an evolving universe, it still strives to always be better.)

"Thoughts are things" is not a cliche, but a strong and enduring rule of the universe.

So when you hang out in "Trouble" when everything else is available to you, you attach more importance to the notion that life on this planet is hard than is in any way true. (Truth being, to some extent, what is, and all that.) Once into this way of thinking, you then think that you need to come back to *correct* your *mistakes.*

And not all of you have done that. Many of you have done just what you needed to do. But some of you have become so taken with yo-yoing back and forth to Earth that you don't even take time to evaluate what you are learning. And worse, underestimating what the other person is as a soul and thinking that you have to come back to "balance the karma" with them (let's say you murdered them) is one of the most undermining things you can do to that person. Here's why. You're playing God . . . assuming that you know more about what would be good for them than they do. (You only balance your karma, and they only balance theirs.)

So let's say you've been an axe-murderer. (One of our favorite examples because it always gets your attention!) After this life is over, you're sitting and thinking about what it was like to have been an axe-murderer. (But instead of doing it with your guides and Creator, you are playing the Lone Ranger and doing it all by yourself.) And you're not too crazy about the feeling of having done it. So you check back at your part of the Akashic Record, and you realize that you've had a tendency to be a little brutal on other occasions, too. What to do? Well, what you don't do is rush right back to Earth and ask someone you've axed to axe you back in order to settle the score. (Balancing the karma to some.)

Why not? Well, they figured things out for themselves, too, and they probably realize that they had a tendency to be too passive, or too submissive, or too involved in the troublesome side of life, or whatever, and they chose to correct their behavior themselves (which balances the act). Now they're on to something else. But let's say you're sure that only you can correct the balance, and that in order to do it you must be axed yourself. You ask, they say no. You pester, they retreat. After several lifetimes of you not fully regrouping or reporting to the Creator (who would set you straight on this fool's errand in a nanosecond given even a "ghost" of a chance), you're obsessed with the idea that you must be murdered by the person you murdered.

Eventually, you might just be such a nuisance that you wear them down, and they comply. But what a waste of their time and yours! And eventually you'll have to regroup all your wasted time, *and* understand why you wouldn't take your guides' or the Creator's word on anything!

That's what balancing is all about. Once balanced, you'll see that the person you murdered was perfectly fine without you. (Chagrin, chagrin!) They knew how to fix things all by themselves, and it's really your karma that is dirt. Thinking that you had to fix things is a sure sign of denying your relationship to the Creator, and certainly denying the God within them. (That's what's known as the opposite of letting your higher self shine through you while on Earth . . . letting your [remembrance of] past ego shine through while in the astral!)

That doesn't mean, however, that you never have reasons that draw you back time and time again to learn and grow. It's just that negative karma is not a legitimate reason. Let's say that your original mission was "Watching Beings Evolve and Evolving on Planet Earth." That means that you were a soul created for the love and caring of this planet . . . a real earthling! You've probably been here a long time. Thousands or tens of thousands of lifetimes. You probably saw Lemuria submerge under the weight of all feeling with a denial of the rational mind. You probably saw Atlantis do just the opposite, using the rational mind to deny feelings. You probably saw the weight of confusion in the purpose of reincarnation give strength to the terrible retribution of the Dark Ages. And you probably know that the Earth is undergoing another great shift. (And if you've seen all these things, are a real earthling, and you're reading this, you're probably a whale, a dolphin, a gorilla, or a farmer . . . all currently disappearing species . . .)

If you are still confused about your need to reincarnate

from Robbyn and His Merrye Bande

Are you not sure whether you're confused or on the right track? Here are a few things that may be a tipoff that you are confused!

One common result of confusion is thinking you're John the Baptist, Louis XIV, Beethoven, Joan of Arc, Mohammed, Jesus, or any other great, historic, charismatic leader. With as many of you who think you were *GREAT*, you'd think that every notable person in history was really a group-directed political machine with an ace media campaign! Really, we're trying to tell you this as kindly as we can.

Most of the late greats on this planet were here to help Earth with a very specific project. When their job was done, they went back to whatever their regular job was somewhere out in the universe. They're not you, and you weren't them. It *is* possible that you lived at that time, and were blessed by their energy and have a remembrance of it. But that's all it is. Try to be very, very realistic about this (we know we're going to break some poor little hearts if we're not very careful). Consider. Why would a soul that had the energy to be Beethoven (a brilliant music-composing deaf man) come back and be a spiritual seeker now? (Just think about it.) Please try to believe us: no great historic charismatic leaders, spiritual, military, or otherwise, are here on Earth as spiritual seekers now. If you can accept this, you will save yourself a lot of pain.

You see, some of you think that if you were more important in the past, you will be more important now. Dear, dear friends, *whether or not* you were important in the past has no bearing on what you are now. You are and always will be just as important as Beethoven . . . as yourself. So, please, please try to give up this aspiration to royalty and other historic greatness of the past and do not lose the possibility to be the best that you can, the true and sincere essence of you.

And if it's any consolation, you don't know that Beethoven *really did the best job* he could of being who he was, do you? After all, he looked to Bach as a model. (Just for the record, we're not knocking

You are and always will be just as important as Beethoven . . . as yourself.

Beethoven or Bach: we're just saying that *you* don't really know, do you?) So just be the best person you can be. Be thankful for the legacies of the greats, and use that as inspiration to be as good as you can, and then, you see, they do truly live forever in you.

Another typical result of reincarnation confusion is thinking you're working out your karma over some past deed or act. This can take the form of you thinking that you owe someone something from the past (never the case) or that someone owes you something from the past (never the case). This includes thinking that someone was your father, mother, or in any other particular relationship and making that a major factor in how you relate to that person now. Almost always, whatever that relationship was is over, and now, to bring it to memory and to say "Oh, so and so was my father (or whatever) in a past lifetime and that's why we relate this way" is a way of distancing yourself from whatever the reality is in this lifetime.

However, you may have contracted (in a positive, productive manner) to accomplish certain things with certain people in life. Maybe in love, or business, or friendship, or, well, who knows? It's your business. But let's say the wheels of the universe didn't connect you and that person at exactly the right time, so one or both of you felt that you had to break the contract. You may feel that pull. But it does not mean that that person owes you something. And you can count on the fact that there will be another opportunity to fulfill that learning experience . . . just as soon as you look around and quit following the settling dust of the past (half a dozen opportunities have already sneaked by before you turned your head!). Just remember: *you don't owe*, and *they don't owe*. And you can always fulfill what you want in life, maybe not exactly in the way that you envision it, but you *can* do it.

So what happens if you meet someone from a past lifetime who you really hated and you know you still hate them? So what, indeed? You don't have to love *everyone*, you know. If you have a strong negative feeling about someone from a past life, acknowledge it to yourself and meditate to let it go. Don't put a lot of energy into it! After all, your thoughts will get through to the other person, and if they have regrouped the situation better than you, you may have a very insulted individual on your hands and maybe an enemy now, too!

And the same goes for loving someone from the past. It may not be appropriate to love them and want them now. Really, nine times out of ten, what people think is a past-life attraction is the feeling of someone who could help you to fulfill an opportunity or lesson that you want and need fulfilled. Chances are you've never seen them before in this life or others. At any rate, if you only ever reincarnated with the same people, wouldn't it be boring?

Remember, everyone in your life is probably there for a reason.

Accept people gratefully and reverently for what and who they are *here and now*! (There aren't too many random happenings in the universe, although

The purpose of reincarnation is to learn; to express fully as the creation you are; to help make the lessons in the universe worthy of its

there are some and, of course, paradoxes abound. Isn't life fun?!)

So what's the purpose of reincarnation again? To learn; to express fully as the creation you are; to help make the lessons in the universe worthy of its learners by your free and loving expression.

We're going to close this little communication with a quote from a little gem of wisdom readily available to many of you on Earth right now. It's by a soul you know as Ralph Waldo Emerson.

Yes, he's dead; no, we're not him; no, he's not on the planet; and no, as far as we know, he's not likely to be coming back. *But when he was here,* he said some good stuff that we can still share. And since many of you still look outside yourselves, and since we can't say it better, but since we want you to feel better, to live more fully and richly, here's Ralph's version of success. Take it to heart. Now.

SUCCESS IS

To laugh often and much; to win the respect of intelligent people and the affection of children; to earn the appreciation of honest critics and endure the betrayal of false friends; to appreciate beauty, to find the best in others; to leave the world a bit better, whether by a healthy child, a garden patch or a redeemed social condition; to know even one life has breathed easier because you have lived.
This is to have succeeded.

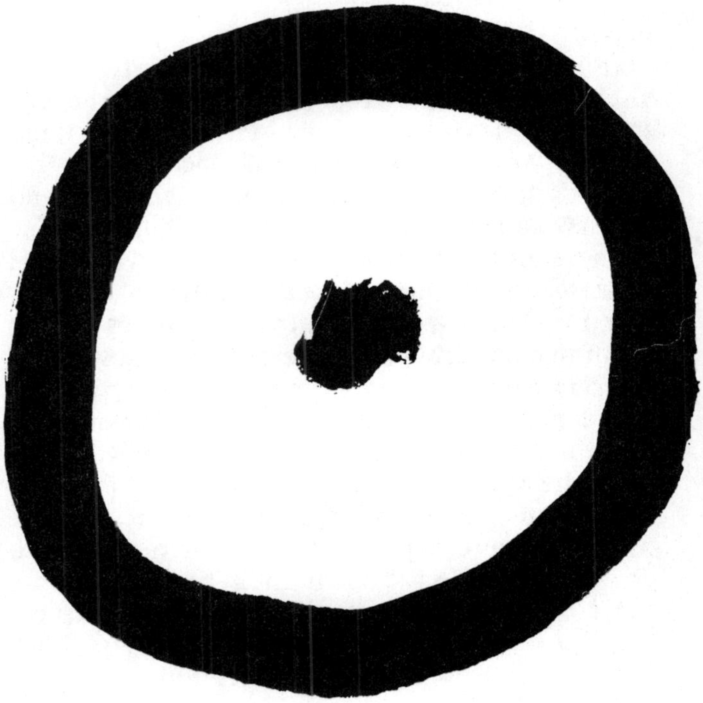

Selecting Your Life Path

from Dr. Peebles

You are perfect souls. You come from the eternal, perfect light, the light of the balanced consciousness of the universe which encompasses the entire universe. It allows life on all planets, on all dimensions, and of all times and spaces to mature, to grow, to experience life according to the motivations of the soul. The Universal God (that God that you would find through all the universe) is a God of pure light, a God that has never lived before and will never live, for this consciousness of the eternal

God is of negative and positive polarity. It is a duality that is so total that it has sensitivity but not emotion. It has free will, but not interference. It has the ability to allow each element, each facet of that perfect self to experience life if it is so *requested* and if we so *desire* it.

There are many elements of the eternal light that never leave, that never take on a physical incarnation, for in their perfection they remain as part of that universal light and consciousness. These souls, and *they are souls,* have no need for a physical expression. They have never bothered following, as it were, the physical attraction to discover what it's like to be alive.

Many of us on the spirit side, the guides and the teachers, have experienced the attraction into physicality. We have taken on lifetimes. There are some who take on physicality. They have experience. They have their relationships, but they remain in a state of objectivity. They don't get caught up in sociological tendencies. They don't get caught up in the pressures of the era that they chose to be born in. They just enter, they discover what it's like to be alive, then they go to that change called death and return to the spirit side, giving up the personality. The personality dissipates, returning to that total, balanced soul.

And they look and say, "Well, that was an interesting experience. So much for that." And they remain in the total light of the universe, for they have had the fulfillment of their interest. But they didn't build it in karma. They didn't participate in any existing karmas. They had *an experience.* The majority of these do not become part of the guiding forces of the planet Earth or any of the other planets. They are in the universal light of protection and balance.

There are others who have that experience and find themselves reacting as *personalities* according to the sociological pressures, according to the tendencies of the moment, the influencing, and the

programming by parents, friends, neighbors, associates. Rather than living within the objective observance, they start participating in the activities of manipulating, controlling, being manipulated, and being controlled. And then, when they experience that change called death, and though they return to the light, though their personality of the incarnation dissipates, they find that they are not in the *total light.*

They are in a density of light, a quality of light, but they are not freed at that point. They have found themselves confined to the cycles of birth and death. And so they begin evaluating how they are going to return to the total light. How are they going to return into that perfect state?

They were not cast out.

They did not fall from the light.

They chose to participate in the earthbinding webs and shadows to such a degree that they were no longer as intricately part of the facets of eternal light.

They find themselves choosing lifetimes over and over again as either male or female, lifetimes at times with tendencies toward a duality. (Now when I am speaking of duality, I am not speaking in any terms of sexual preferences. I am referring to the balanced awareness of the negative and positive available to each and every one of you, that balanced awareness that allows you to manifest all of the elements of the negative or the positive in the physical vortex of physical form.)

Now, before entering each lifetime, the spirits dabble in what I would define as a "meeting." They get together and say, "Well, now we are participating in physical life. We can't accomplish all that we

wish to here on the spirit side for us to return to the total light." And so they plan to return to the physical density again, stating, "We are going to go back to accomplish (in physical form) the balancing and completing of any interferences with right action and the Loving Law of Allowance."

And so the soul says, "Well, I need a body that is going to be a certain physical form, a certain kind, a certain shape. It should be in a certain sociological tendency so that I will have the opportunity to discover and continue manifesting the right action, the objectivity of the higher self." And in the meeting another soul says, "Remember, you participated last time in that particular bit of mish-mash. Are you going into physical density? Well, let's choose the same environment so we can work out not only our experiential karma, not only our participation in that collective karma, but our interpersonal karma as well."

And so two, three, four souls will choose to incarnate at the same time. One might be born in Tinytown, one might be born in Africa, but eventually (and some of you will call it chance) they will be sitting in a restaurant, possibly in London, look upon each other and say, "Hey, let's go and visit," and be instant friends. They will go to a meeting and be introduced and suddenly know, "We are going to work together."

And so you choose densities that in the universal flow of right action will bring you together. It is for the soul, the higher self, to bring you together. It is not for you to go out and say, "Well, I know something's coming. I'd better go out and find who the person is, where they are, what they are." It is for you to be available to allow your higher self to lead you, guide you, motivate you to the involvement for your own fulfillment, and for the fulfillment of all those others that chose to be born at the same time.

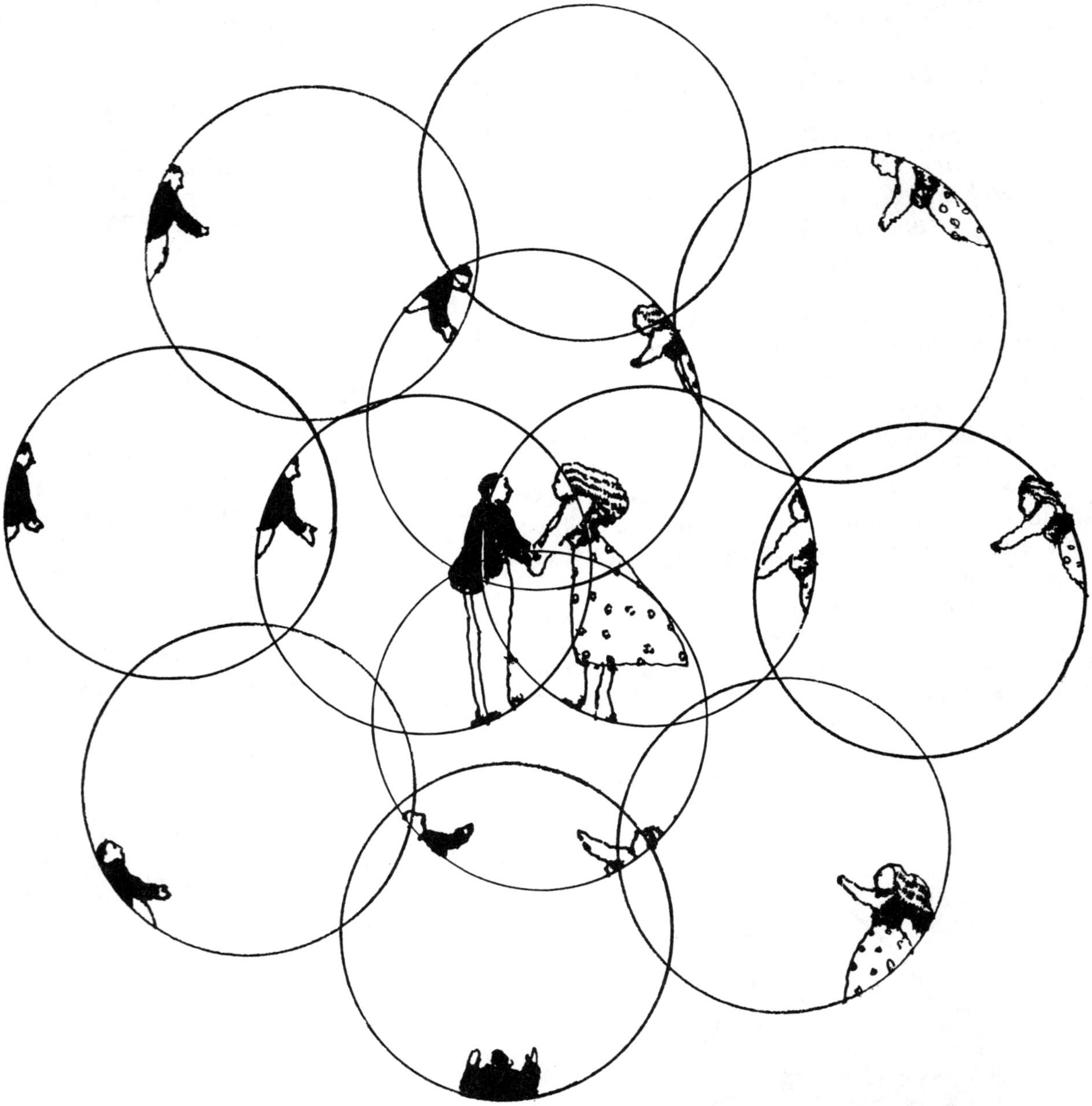

And remember, as you fulfill your karma, as you fulfill your karmic interaction with another, you are actually giving the opportunity for the collective karma of all human beings to grow, to be balanced, to be transmuted from one density to another, from one level of light to another when that is their karma.

It is not that karma can be worked out in one way and one way only. Each and every karmic involvement has many options, many avenues. You can work it out in one lifetime or in many. You can work it out for yourself or you can work it out collectively. One person is capable of being released from the karma and the other ones could find themselves (by individual free will) still caught up in the karma, having to go through it over and over again while you have returned to the light. When you are returned to the higher self, it is important that you see that when you entered these lifetimes, you came for very specific reasons.

Your reasons for being born

from Dr. Peebles

Your reasons for being born need not be defined in specific terms. Your reasons for being born present themselves on a daily basis. Look carefully at your experiences in life, the people you meet, the people you work with, the jobs you do, the jobs you don't do, and realize that these are little more than delightful opportunities for manifesting your spiritual understanding, accepting that there is nothing for you to control or manipulate.

It is only for you to manifest love, light, and allowance, giving the opportunity for all living things to grow in their own time, their own space, their own way. It is for you to see that as you chose your physical bodies, it is most improper to wish for another body. For that body is exactly what you needed, or else you would have chosen another body before you were born. It's exactly what you need. You say, "Oh, but I want to be slimmer." Well then, you would have chosen a body that could eat five times a day and always be slim. And you've seen people like that. Don't try to change what you are. Simply control it, but don't try to change it. Don't wish for something other than what you are.

For instance, suppose you're working and you say, "Oh, I don't want to do this job. I know I can be a teacher." If your higher self had wanted you to be a teacher, if that was really your motivation, you would have studied accounting (for instance), turned around, and suddenly found yourself being offered the position of being a teacher. You don't have to develop your future or your career; your higher self took care of that long before you were born. Rather, you just need to *create* it from a conscious mind level.

It is not yours to understand what you are here to do. It is for each of you *to do the very best you are capable of at any given moment with what has presented itself.* If you do, *then* you will be on the path. Then you will be going about what you came into this lifetime for. And I hear you say, "But if I knew, it would be easier."

If you knew what you were here to do,
my friends, it would be more difficult.

As was stated earlier, before entering physical form, after your meetings on the spirit side, you pass through what I call the "Valley of Forgetfulness." Your higher self manifests its free will up to the point of the Valley of Forgetfulness and there it remains. Your higher self is connected with everything you do, but *it will not interfere.* If you choose a pathway out of ego, desire, sociological influence, and it is not exactly what your higher self had intended, it only observes. It loves you, it respects you. It encourages you, but it will not interfere.

It will not in any way say, "Oh, you're doing bad. You're doing wrong." It will not trip you. You trip yourselves. It loves you if you succeed or if you fail, for on the soul level there is no failure. That is an interpretation according to your personality in this lifetime.

Your reasons for being born need not be defined in specific terms. Your reasons for being born present themselves on a daily basis.

Now, after the Valley of Forgetfulness, you enter the physical body and you have different intensities of free will: on the subconscious level, on the superconscious level, on the conscious level. These levels do not always agree. You consciously choose one direction because you want the new home or you want the new car. You want this new life. You want this, you want that. Using your free will, you choose to do what is necessary to get what you *think* you want, but the free will of the subconscious mind could easily say, "Well you don't really want this. What you really want is this . . ." and in *its free will,* it creates a little battle. It creates a little upheaval, puts a little block in the way, interferes with your reaction to another person, causing you to manifest irritation, anger, and fear in an effort to get you back on what might be a better path. But it is still an interpretation of what a better path is.

Now your superconscious mind observes all of this. But your superconscious mind is not your final step. It is still an element of this, the current life. Now the superconscious mind strives to be always objective, but it is still in physical density. It is still influenced by the conscious mind and the subconscious mind. But if the battle between the personality and the conscious mind gets too intense, the superconscious mind (you might compare it to a parent) says, "Well, I have had quite enough of all this gobbledygook, and we will wipe the slate clean."

You'll turn around and your home will be gone or your job will be gone or your mate will be gone, simply to get you onto the path of the final game, freeing you from the earthbinding webs and shadows of personality-ego interference.

It is then for you to celebrate the day, each and every day, as if it were a new life.

Yesterday is a past life. Tomorrow is a future life. Focus on the accomplishments of today, certainly having recall of what you did yesterday, certainly having inspiration of what you could do tomorrow, but without expectation, without hope, without manipulation. Spend your time not in criticizing yourself, not in judging yourself, but living according to your own interpretations. Spend that time that you use on those elements to the very best that you are capable of today.

And if you say, "Oh, but I could have done better yesterday," my friends, that is not true. For if you could have done better yesterday, you would have, so accept it. Learn from it. Grow from it. And through celebrating the moment, you will do better automatically today.

When you have problems at your job, you will not carry over the problems of yesterday; you will simply say, "It is a problem. It is not *my* problem. It is not *their* problem. It is an existing opportunity to manifest my spiritual consciousness. It is an existing opportunity to bring through the light of the higher self. It is an opportunity for me to balance my personal karma. It will give the people around and about me options."

Yes, if you do the very best in the spiritual light and in the moment, anyone participating, anyone there, will automatically be given choices. Rather than giving them choices of reacting to your irritation, your angers, your resentments, you can give them the opportunity of reacting to something positive, creative, inspiring. Be way-showers. Be light bearers.

Now in this, you're not only then affecting other human beings, you are affecting the atmosphere, the minerals, the plants, the animals, and all of those elements of consciousness--consciousness from the same source of the eternal God that each of you stems from. And so it is yours to acknowledge them, respect them, encourage them.

Manifest, then, your willingness to accept the directions and guidance of the higher self on a human consciousness level. Realize that during those wonderful meetings on the spirit side, you also recognize, "Well, I have a karma with this person, that person, the other person." But often that karma, interpersonally, is connected to a specific event, a specific set of circumstances, and those events, those circumstances, have a consciousness of their own, have a karma of their own. I would even go so far as to say the planet Earth has a karma of its own, with or without you.

You chose, in those meetings, to be born into physical bodies that will join certain organizations, certain companies, certain colleges and schools: an experiential event. You chose to be born on the planet Earth during the tremendous change of energy as we shift from the Piscean era to the Aquarian consciousness. You chose to be born when the planet

is shaking, growing, quivering. It is not something to change. It is not something to fear. If you were not here by agreement with the higher self to experience it, you would have been born on another planet or into another era.

You are here to experience.

My friends, *you deserve everything* that comes your way or it wouldn't come. You would not have any opportunities unless you needed them. You would not have any confrontation unless it was little more than a delightful opportunity to prove to those who are about that you are capable of living up to your spiritual understandings. Don't judge yourselves. Don't judge another. Don't criticize yourselves. Simply say, "Oh, here is an interesting confrontation; how am I going to react?"

You say, "Oh well, it was too late. I reacted in anger and fear." It is never too late, friends. When you have anger, say, "Oh there you are, anger. You are from a level of free will that I do not choose to participate in. Thank you for rearing your head. Now be silent, I'm going about my business." It's not too late.

When you say, "Oh goodness, if that happens, I'm going to be fearful," admit it and say, "Oh, there's that fear, rearing its head. Fear, I recognize you and I am transmuting you into spiritual power. You are now giving me the strength to live up to my beliefs. You are giving me the strength to live up to the *Loving Law of Allowance.* Thank you for coming to me. Thank you for rearing your head. You've given me a reminder to live up to my spirituality while in a physical density."

And so here is another point. You *choose* to be born. It would appear to be, for these moments, a self-motivated reason. You *choose* to be born with certain associates, combatants. You *choose* certain events that are tangents. My friends, you also chose to be born in eras when historical events which were similar to the present ones (as you know history on the planet Earth) were occurring.

Now, many of you lived on the continent of Atlantis and are born again. There are quite a few of you who lived in the spiritual community of the continent of Lemuria. There are many, many of you who existed together in ancient Egypt. There are oh-so-many who trace to the Aztec movement of what you now know as Mexico. There are quite a number of you who also lived in the bodies of dolphins. You come into these physical densities to continue balancing out for yourselves and for the experience of those eras. And so you are not *self-motivated.* That is a concept of physical influences and programmings of this lifetime. You are motivated by *indefinable* energies.

Next time you say "What is my purpose?" think for a moment, for you already *know* the answer.

Your purpose is to go about the demonstration of spiritual acceptance of whatever the event is.

Sometimes you say, "But I know I'm supposed to be of service. I should do it by being a healer. I should do it by being a channel. I should do it by doing this." That, my friends, you must admit, is your ego of this lifetime. If you are to be of service, if that is really part of your inspiration of being born, be of service working in the bank. Yes, be of service working in prison. Be of service by giving healing to the bus driver. But if you need the acknowledgment of, "Oh, thank you," that is your ego.

Give your wisdom. Give your energy. Don't worry how it grows or where it grows. Just *allow it to be.* Visualize your willingness to serve the spirit, to serve God as the planting of the seed. If you were to plant a seed for a flower, would you go out every day and dig it up to see if it is sprouting? You would wait, you would nurture it, you would love it, you would commune with it, and let it grow as it might. You would help it, but you would not interfere with it. Well, the same with your spiritual-mystical capabilities. Give healing to another. *Give encouragement through demonstration.*

Don't wonder if they listen, if they will use it. If you wonder that, you should separate from them. If you must change anyone, rather than try to change them, separate before you interfere with not only them, but yourself. Remember, if you are to manifest your higher self you must learn to accept everything that comes your way. And when you say "But I don't know how," you do. With your intellect, with the power that you use to question and wonder, use that power to say, "Here's an event. It is mine to manifest or never to play at that level and density." Such a delightful challenge!

Why you have chosen the earth experience

from Enid

We come here because there is no other place to find out the things we can find out here.

There is no other place where you can step on a rusty nail.

There is no other place where you can enjoy the feeling of water lapping upon your feet on the beach and feel the sand falling out from under your foot.

There is no other place that you can look into the truest eyes of your lover and bring the bodies together in communion.

There is no other place except on a physical plane that you can do it in quite that way.

There is no other place where you can feel the pangs of loneliness and later come into your own and realize that you were never alone.

The great adventure, of course, is to come back into your own.

The great adventure, of course, is to do what you are doing now--rejoining your spirituality.

Selecting Earth as Your

Your planet Earth is taking a stride forward in its karmic
It expands outward and inward but is not destroying itself.

School of Experience

evolutionary growth. It is shifting, quivering, expanding. Earth is simply preparing for a new level of manifestation.

Long ago and far away

from Robbyn and His Merrye Bande

Long ago and far away there were systems of galaxies within systems of universes near the beginning of time who were struggling toward personal and spiritual awareness. That's right. The world, universe, and substantive mass were not always as evolved as they are today, and at that time they weren't trying to become "more evolved." They were trying to achieve even the briefest glimmer of personal and spiritual awareness, period. (This, of course, stands to reason because something had to kick the whole concept of time, space, karma, dimension, etc. off somewhere.)

Consider a time (primitive in terms of your personal, spiritual awareness) when pretty much anything went in terms of what you would call issues around free will. Ethers, with the intention of manifesting in the flesh, could be enslaved by enslaving energies for "all time." Rational mind and reason had not yet devised ways to reverse decisions. Power could be wielded in such a way that a ruler who cried "Off with your head!" could just as easily and successfully cry "On with your head!" and expect it to work. In other words, cause and effect, ethics, concepts of what you would call fair play, and acts of human kindness, simply had not yet evolved.

Well, after enough really new souls (the kind that are literally fresh off the turnip truck) had lost their way due to the total chaos and confusion, some of us got together with the Creator and asked, "Is this what we really had in mind?" The answer was a simple but speedy and resounding "NOOOOO!" So then we had to do something. (Well, strictly speaking, we didn't have to, but we wanted to.)

What we really wanted to see was that every soul had an equal opportunity to learn and also to grow. What had come to happen was that some of the more experienced souls had begun to exploit the newer souls through use of power, deception, and manipulation (denied will). This came as a little bit of a surprise to all of us, principally because although we knew about all possible actions, we were hardly expecting the creation to reflect them, especially when the "not-so-in-the-light" acts were only mental constructs with us. (We need to clarify this. We weren't acting in ways that weren't in the light. At that point in time, we could only imagine ways that were outside the light. We would say, "Well, theoretically, someone could be really nasty and possibly learn something.")

So we were pretty surprised when so much of the creation took that route. However, what this reflected to us was that many of us were denying some aspect of ourselves, and the results were pretty startling. Not that what we were denying was of such a startling or dramatic nature. The lesson to us was that *anything* denied is not of the light. (That is why we now encourage you to always, always acknowledge your feelings, no matter how dark or bad you think them to be, because that act has the possibility to shed light on the event whereas denying feelings *always* allows them to fester and grow into monsters in the dark.)

Anyway, rather than scrap the project, we decided instead that the ideal situation would be to give the "power-mongers" a chance to learn what it was to be without power, thinking that such an experience would modify their approach to other beings in the future. It would also give the enslaved ethers a chance to exercise their power, so that they, too, could achieve balance in the future. This is how karma began.

Then we decided that maybe we needed several different schools. Some for your basic bullies and disrespecters of will. Some for the basic babes in the woods: souls so new that their ethers were still wet,

There was a need for a school for basic bullies and disrespecters of will and for basic babes in the woods: souls so new their ethers were still wet.

so to speak. And there was one school for the combining of all of the above. That, of course, was Earth!

You see, the Creator said that there was this cute little galaxy coming into being in the outer reaches of space that would have conditions sufficient to meet our school needs, and if we wanted we could put it together. It had a cute little sun, and a number of cute little friends as neighbors in close enough proximity to influence acts and outcomes on Earth. (The rest of the zodiac, of course.) This would give the atmosphere sufficient complexity for the types of inhabitants and learning experiences we had in mind.

So, many different energies from different parts of the known universes got together to develop Earth! (A very joyous little planet with great compassion for us and our learners in what we were doing.) It was such fun! Since we had trouble agreeing on one particular style, we decided to make Earth a composite of our favorite things on our own planets and dimensions. That's why it has such diverse things as palm trees and polar bears; cacti and squid; puppies and pythons; dinosaurs and daffodils; pterodactyls and ponies; different races . . . we think you get the picture.

But the truly marvelous thing was that Earth was developed in such a way as to be self-sustaining! This meant that there were even greater opportunities for the exercise of free will, because within this environment the inhabitants could always find

and create ways to meet their needs. Earth itself had its own consciousness and built-in timing so that it would know when to shift and how much to the right and left, etc. That's why the former dinosaurs and pterodactyls now serve you in your gas tank. And, of course, our old favorite, gravity, created a need for density which created a need for time. Part of the plan was, too, that at a certain point in time the groups of us would leave, taking any of our people still remaining on Earth home with us, leaving Earth in charge of the show. We are nearing that point now.

Gravity performs another very important function which will explain why aliens (and by this we do not mean people not born on the continental wherevers) and extraterrestrials come here, and you don't (yet) go there. Earth, Earth's atmosphere, and you were created in such a way that it would be pretty difficult to get off, thus helping to insure that appropriate lessons would be learned here. And because it is approaching time for some groups to leave, their originators and soul-mates from other planets, times, and dimensions are now coming for them. (Whole groups of them are coming to welcome you back! Isn't that nice?)

Now, as you well know, creation and evolution of Earth didn't happen overnight, in your terms; it took place over millennia, and now, as in any change of management, it is a little confusing to some people who haven't been keeping up with the energy of things. Many of you will be going home to your places of origin, *but mostly not until you pass out of your present physical body.* So not to worry. Some of you will continue to reincarnate on Earth because you're not all leaving within the same generation, and because the Earth asked for, and got, its own beings. Some of you came out of the ethers right here on planet Earth.

Catching the bus home

from Robbyn and His Merrye Band

So, how will you know where to catch the bus home . . . or whether to? Well, most of you, if you do not have some intuitive awareness already of being from another time and place, will (especially if you ask for this knowledge) begin to get clearer and clearer pictures of it. So you will know how and where to orient yourself for this change.

Now, lest all this talk of how Earth was created and catching the bus home and our part in it is a little confusing, we feel it might help you to know that when we say we are "off-worlders" we are telling you that some of us (like many, many others) are aliens who have at times incarnated as human beings. Some of us are beings who are aliens who have never incarnated as human beings. Some of us aren't even from the known universes. Some of us are what you would call "ascended masters." Some of us are even from Earth! But the point is that we are all here to help you now, and so there is nothing to be afraid of. We're here to help everything go smoothly.

What you call UFOs are really for real! They are generally beings who are coming from certain planets to remind their friends and coworkers on Earth who have evolved and reincarnated over time as humans that it is time to begin the preparations to leave Earth. Most of the time, these beings are friendly. However, there are those of you who have experienced having probes stuck up your nose and other places, and who have been very frightened of them. Try to believe us when we say that these beings are just doing their jobs. And their jobs are to remind you that *soon* the bus will be waiting.

So, just in case you are followed or abducted by aliens, ask them if they are the ride home, where to go to catch the ride, etc., etc. If you do this, you'll probably have a much more pleasant experience, and you'll be allowed to live out your earth time with less disruption. (Your nose and other places will probably not suffer any indignities, and you'll probably learn a lot! And we can almost guarantee that your abductors will heave an enormous sigh of relief, too!)

Earth is a very focused and rapid and complex learning experience, so many of your old friends and acquaintances will be genuinely envious of your opportunity of having been here. Many of them will be studying the terrain, food sources, and so on, for enhancements to take back to their own worlds. And some of them will help the Earth through its transition.

Many of you are concerned that the transition will be rocky: that the Earth may shift on its axis, or there may be nuclear war. Neither one is a given, and neither one is a necessary prerequisite to the Earth evolving at this point in time. However, over time, a lot of significance has been put on this time in the Earth's history as one of trial and tribulation, the "last coming," the end of the Earth, etc., etc.

What is really going to happen is that Earth takes over its own management. And because it wants to grow in more peace and light, the beings who are being born now, some from the last 30 to 40 years and those who plan to be born in the next few centuries, are beings from many other planets and dimensions who have not been strongly represented here on Earth until recently. They know more about peace and light and the way that Earth wants to be than many of the souls on Earth right now. They will be great physical teachers and leaders.

So, really, any apprehension you have should be turned to joy! Many of you are going home soon, after having been away for a long time. The Earth is getting what it wants, and there is no ban to coming back, but it is important to check in with your planet of origin in the near future. Remember, as with anything else, the more fear and agony you put into this change, the more likely you are to help create something fearful and agonizing in the change.

Many of you are going home soon, after having been away for a long time.

At any rate, we do want to thank you for your assistance in making the earth experiments such a success, because there are some very important things that we have learned which we will take into consideration when new planets are developed and new projects are undertaken.

Honoring the Earth's Need to Shift and Move

The times they are a'changing

from Dong How Li

Earth changes, to many of you, is a very serious subject. It is my pleasure to try and make it joyous for you because you know, not all your rumblings (Earth and / or personal) are painful, are they? Sometimes laughter too brings great movement. Just as, in your own bodies, laughter brings movement, so also think sometimes of the Earth in her movements. It is not necessarily sad, but joyous.

If you think of the Earth as a body, you can attune to what it must do in these years of changes by watching your own body.

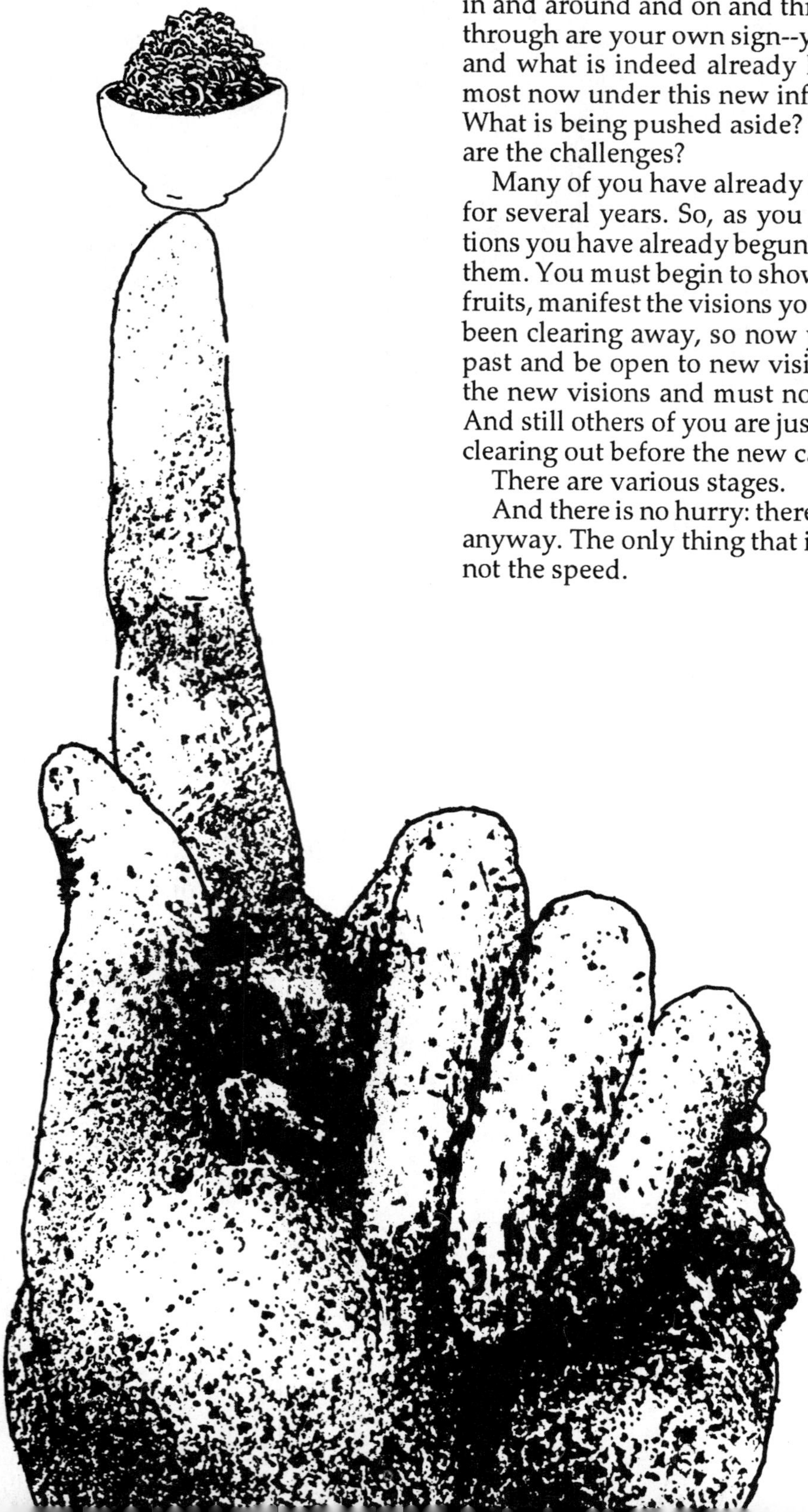

Because you are an expression physically of the energy available in and around and on and through this planet, the changes you go through are your own sign--your own indicator of what is to come and what is indeed already happening. Where are you changing most now under this new influx of energy? Where are the blocks? What is being pushed aside? What is being dissolved? And where are the challenges?

Many of you have already been in the process of transformation for several years. So, as you come into this time--the transformations you have already begun--now some of you must step out with them. You must begin to show them. You must begin to show their fruits, manifest the visions you have been hiding. Some of you have been clearing away, so now you will have to say good-bye to the past and be open to new visions. Others of you have already had the new visions and must now step out and make them physical. And still others of you are just beginning the process where you're clearing out before the new can take place.

There are various stages.

And there is no hurry: there is no timetable, not at the larger view anyway. The only thing that is important is that you keep moving, not the speed.

The planet is playing with how it's going to get back to being healthy again, how it's going to detoxify. And there is both joy in moving in that direction and challenge and fear. It is the same with you. As you are stepping into the future, you are a jumble of emotions (excitement and fear--"kicking and screaming" all the way, as they say). Please don't overlook the fun.

There is no safer place to be than in your heart--wherever that is.

There is no safer place to be than in your heart, wherever that is. You can run to Colorado if you like and get caught in a snowstorm. If your concern is for the physical, that is where you will hurt most. You need to have a balanced perspective about what is to take place. Just as when you go through your own changes, you must work at all the levels of your being: physical, emotional, intellectual, and spiritual. If you get stuck on one, that throws all the energy there--all your eggs are in one basket--you could lose it all. Spread the wealth.

I see for the planet, as well as for many humans, much work to do this year with the heart. I see many schisms in many hearts that are trying to be corrected.

You know, it is no accident that across the world from you people are starving for food when here people are starving for hearts that are true.

You are starving for hearts that are true. You have all these operations with fake hearts. You are trying to find what's true and don't know where to look. Plastic and steel; wrong place to look. Why do you think heart disease is so high in this country?

So, there's going to be lots of work with the heart. The heart is about (in the low form) crusading. There is going to be lots of crusading, not only by born-again Christians. Transforming into high heart (into forgiveness, into allowance): there's going to be some of that too. Your planet is doing the same thing--opening her heart.

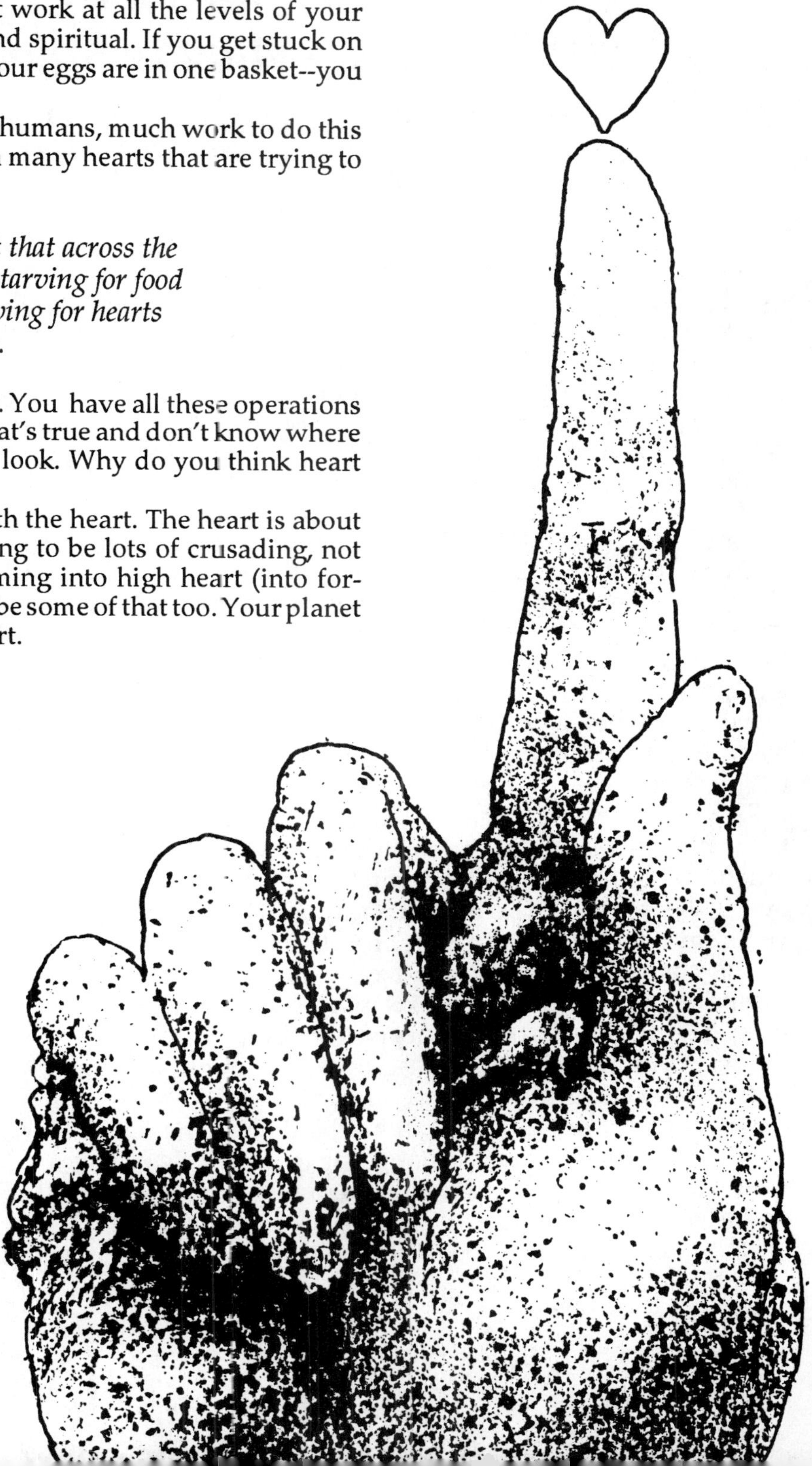

from Dr. Peebles

As well you all know, your planet is experiencing the beginning of a great time of change, physically and energy-wise: a time of fulfillment, a time of release, a time of growth.

You, as individuals, have karma unique unto yourselves. You have karmic experiences that involve other people. You have experiences, karmic in nature, that do not involve specific beings, but involve experiences of events. If, then, there is karma for the human being, there is also karma for the plants, the animals, the minerals, suggesting that there is an Earth karma.

Your planet Earth is (at this time) taking a stride forward in its karmic evolutionary growth. It is shifting, quivering, expanding outward, expanding in upon itself, but it is not destroying itself: it is only preparing for a new level of manifestation.

All life upon the planet Earth is here by its individual soul choice. Therefore you are all intricately involved in the changes of the experiences. You are intricately participating in each and every earthquake. You are each involved in every flood. You are part of the atmosphere itself. You are intricately involved in the masses of illness that are sweeping and will sweep your planet Earth. There is nothing that you are able to consider that you are not intricately involved with.

There is nothing for you to fear with the great changes. There is only for you to involve yourself in such clarity that you do not become obsessed by the changes, but instead become participants (that elevate this time to its highest possible level). In this way, the planet will live its karma in a state of balance rather than being in a state of prolonging the inevitable.

This time of change that you recognize is not new to the planet. It has been a great long time since this much energy of change has manifested, somewhat over 2,000 years --and before that, nearly 9,000 more years since this amount of shift and change.

The changes of 2,000 years ago were minor in comparison to the shift of the axis that is only beginning. You are in a karmic cycle, pattern as it were, that was very important to all growth and evolution 11,000 years ago.

Now when I say that you are in the time of the shift of the axis, your axis is not going to shift suddenly and rapidly. It has already begun (the shift) and it will take a number of years yet to complete itself. Your poles, as you know them, will not reverse totally--they are only shifting. This accomplishes a great upheaval in the physical structure--the physical geography.

I do not see a massive and sudden destruction of any one continent or land mass. Certainly there will be radical changes.

from Master Adalfo

There is a great deal of (what I feel is) very negative focus on the land mass changes, and everyone is talking about all the horrid things that will be happening because of them. That is an invitation to disaster, is it not? I do not like to encourage that kind of thing. The changes from the axis shift were ar-

ranged from very subtle to quite large, but will not necessarily be bad--they will just be changes. There will be changes in weather patterns, not necessarily bad--just different. There will be changes (because of weather changes) in plants that grow in certain areas. Some of that could be very positive, could it not? For example: if we could grow things in the Sahara desert, it would be of great benefit to mankind. Some shifts will be major, but you know mankind has made many adjustments to shifts that we would perhaps not have supposed they could make. You did not have many people die in a volcanic eruption in the state of Washington? No. Very few in comparison to the greatness of that cataclysm. Also, there are constant volcanic eruptions going on in the place called Hawaii. People are not dying.

There will be changes as a result of the axis shifts. There will be volcanic eruptions. There will be some mountains disappearing and others growing, but this will not happen BOOM!

Many people believe that these changes are ordained by God. That is not so. There is no God or God Force out there that has ordained all of this. The planet and the beings on the planet create these things just as you create things in your own lives. That does not mean that they cannot be healed or helped, but that is the process. There is no one out there that says, "When the axis shifts, the following things will occur . . . "--that is nonsense, absolute and utter nonsense.

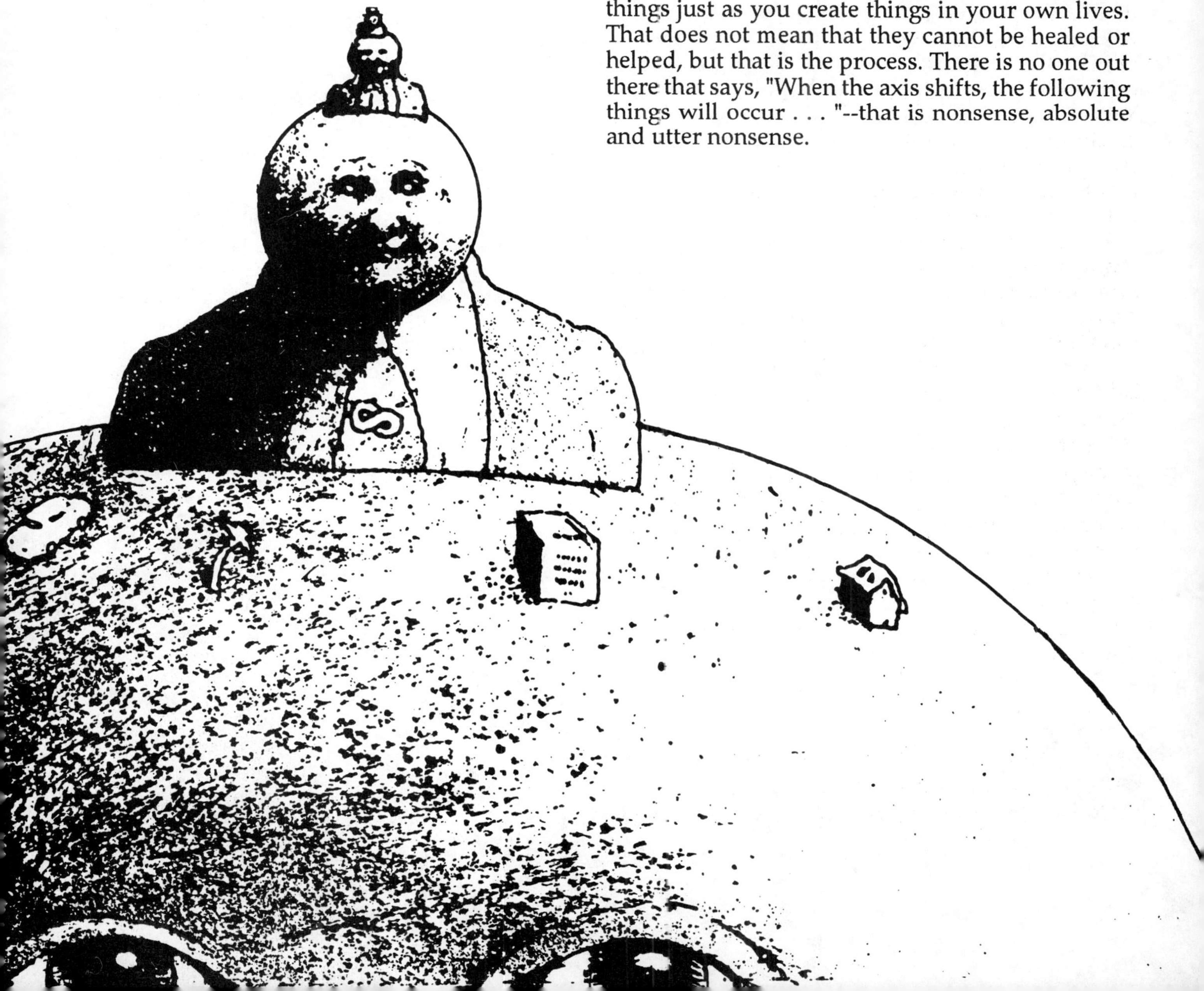

Earth is an organism and she has a consciousness of her own. She also is (of course) affected by the consciousness of entities on her. For example, the bacteria and germs in your body have a consciousness--but it is not a consciousness as you think of it. They are perfectly aware of their path. Often they are more on their path than you are on yours. And in that sense, Earth is also more true to her path. She is still serving all of you--that is her path. She has not strayed, and her consciousness resides on that path.

Assisting the Earth

from Dong How Li

In addressing the question of how to help the Earth, people want to start with the Earth first. I want to start with the person first. I don't suppose it matters either way, except that it's important *at this time* to know yourself in your own heart first.

This planet is working on the evolutionary stage of opening its heart. Then you also have people who are working on their hearts. There are always more directions going on at once than the human mind wishes to conceive of--especially in the Western consciousness. Generally in Western consciousness you want to get locked in--things going one way--righteousness, it's called. This is not so in nature. The most you like to work with is two things like the male/female trying to work together, often with one struggling to get on top. The truth is that many things and variables are operating at once in constant flux, like a wave motion.

If it's true that Earth is going through evolution and initiation at the heart level, it is also true the other way around--that the more you work with your heart, the more Earth moves through her evolutionary stage into the next level. There is an interplay. Most people don't want to deal with that level. They want Earth to get well so they can get well, but they don't want to get well so Earth can get well.

It is important for you to look first at your own evolutionary stage. In doing that you take responsibility for your action and your place and how you affect the environment and the planet.

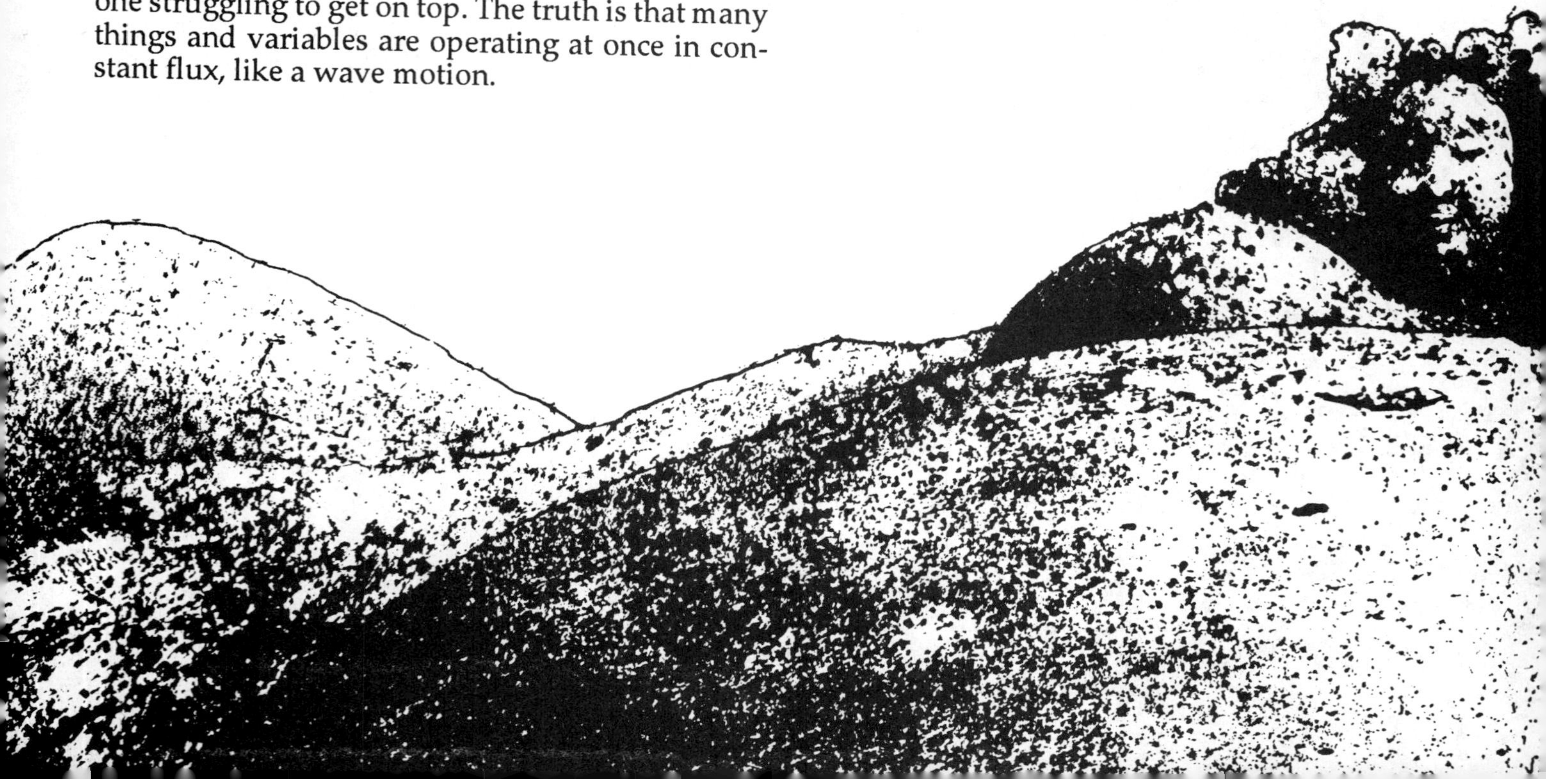

Understand that you are losing energy in not knowing *how* to help the planet because your efforts are scattered. You are going to have to be even more still and more observant to find out what feeds you energy, what nourishes you, what opens your heart. When you do that and you are concerned about an activity like nuclear bans or something of that nature, you will feel from your heart what it is you can do on an outer level (publicly, or as a group) to facilitate that. But it's hard to know what action to take until you know where you stand, until you know where your heart is.

People often feel they'd rather deal with the forms or they'd rather just keep busy because they know they are doing something. But all of a sudden they discover they don't have much energy left because it's been scattered in all these places and they discover that they are unfulfilled and they wonder why. It is much better to go in and get in touch with the initiating energy and let *it decide* what form it wants to take--what action it wants to move in the direction of. When you come from that place, you feel more centered and you waste less.

Usually, when people begin this kind of work, it takes considerable discipline because the temptation is to start in the action and then get stuck there, thinking that is the only way it's going to get solved. You decide, "Let's sign a petition, get more and more people involved, and see if we can stop this or stop that." That's fine, providing people are also working individually and internally on how they are stopping their own violent explosions or not stopping them. Do you see? They are related; they are connected.

If one person pushes a button that shoots off a nuclear war, he is only a physical expression of what everyone else is already doing in their own lives where they are shooting bombs at each other. Now, it would be nicer if some of those people started dealing with their own little bombs and then they wouldn't need somebody to act out a huge one.

The Story Corner

Big Needs, Little Wants

from The Eternals

There once was a little boy who always asked for more than he received. At night he was thirsty and wanted a drink of water before he went to bed. After he was in bed he would call for another drink. Then the lights would have to be turned on so that the child might drink more water.

In the morning the child would rise and eat breakfast, and after all of breakfast was gone he would ask for another slice of toast. If the toast was buttered he would ask for cinnamon.

Always the child asked for a little more than he received. The child received many, many things. He always received all he requested, but he was so busy asking for trivial things that he never thought to ask for the attention he so greatly desired. The child's parents were so busy tending all the requests of their son that they were unable to lavish the attention upon him that they desired so much to give him.

It has become much the same with the world, with the Earth. Many, many people have backed many, many causes, and while they cry out and seek support for the many causes, the one true need that would solve all problems goes untended. Love, pure love in the hearts of all mankind is the answer.

Women and the planet

from Crystal Moon Running

It is important for you women each day to hug the planet as you would hug a friend (to literally see yourself hugging the planet) and exchange energy with her--with Mother. Many of us have not had mothers that we thought did a very good job, but the planet does a beautiful job. And allow yourself to feel nurtured by her, and (particularly as women) for you to nurture her. Healing the planet is going to require the women; the women must heal her. The men must help, but the women must still lead it. That means reconnecting every part of your being with her every day, rejoicing in the dwelling she has given your physical body.

Women must join together in groups to heal the planet. We must sit and do a healing on the planet. Getting in touch with ancient ceremonies that were used by my people will help you, but this is not the only answer. However, these ceremonies will help you to make that connection again. That is the work for your women's lodges. You must dance upon the planet with bare feet--massaging the planet's body.

Being saved by UFOs

from Dr. Peebles

Now, it does seem that there are oh-so-many who are waiting for your brothers and sisters from off the planet Earth to come in their ships during the time of great upheaval and select certain ones, scooping you up and taking you into safety until the change has been complete. Now, it is a wonderful dream; it is a wonderful image. I would not suggest putting too much weight upon it. I do not see these space vehicles, which certainly do exist, coming down to rescue you.

There is no rescue; there is only experience.
That is important for your consideration.

Now, how did this idea come to pass in the first place? Many, many centuries ago, there was a great Earth upheaval. Your space associates (brothers and sisters) were here experimenting, exploring life, exploring the interaction. Recognizing that there was an Earth upheaval approaching, they did not wish to leave so many of their experiments behind. And they did take many away until the Earth settled down again, and then they returned. This is part of the collective unconsciousness. And so for many, sensing that once more the changes are upon them, they are calling out, "You did it once, please do it again."

It is not something that you must pray for, for it's not going to happen. You will only be adding, in your fears, your prayers, your demands, negative energy.

from Dong How Li

Expecting off-planet to do it is like expecting mommy and daddy to save you: that's totally parental. That means you, as humans, are children, and that is not the case. Growing up, maturing, becoming full adult-God beings, that's big work! And as much as you can encourage that, encourage it, please.

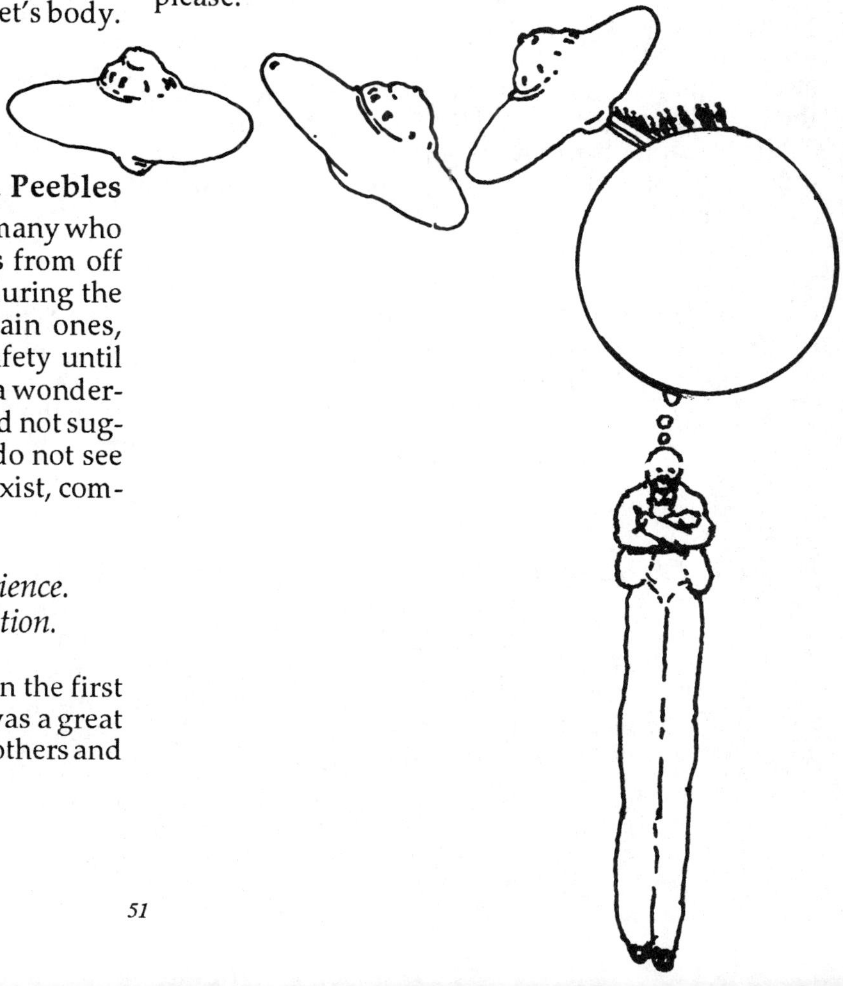

from Dr. Peebles

It is best that you use your prayers, your affirmations and treatments, to uplift all of the planet to such a loving interaction that you are able to minimize the disastrous overtones.

You will not totally avoid the wars that are coming. You will not totally avoid the great mass illness that will sweep the lands. You will not avoid, counteract totally, the earthquakes, the weather.

This is karma for all concerned--including your planet. But you certainly--through your prayers, your affirmations, your treatments, your demonstrations of daily life--have the ability to minimize the negative side effects. That is a most important challenge, and oh-so-few of you are able to embrace that responsibility. I do not offer that as a judgment, just a reminder.

If you want to experience to the utmost (the point of balance--the balance that will ultimately release you from the cycles of birth and death) it is important to minimize, rather than change, that which you wanted in the first place.

Finding safe places

from Dr. Peebles

It is not yours to pack up and run to safe ground. It is yours to experience safety no matter where you are. For if you were to go now to a supposedly safe ground, but your karmic interaction is to experience (witness) the upheaval, you'd find it there, though all around might be safe and secure. After it's all over, your property, yourself, would have been injured, fallen into a hole.

If you are going to have the experience that you designed and created long before you were born, it doesn't matter if you go to part of central Mexico because that's safe. Whatever you need for your evolutionary growth and fulfillment, you will have it there. Might as well then learn to live with your highest soul so totally that you become a beacon of encouragement and light to all, *to all*. Then, during the great times of upheaval, people will be strengthened rather than being caught in the earth-binding webs of the disturbances.

from Dong How Li

If you choose to avoid the movements of the Earth, you might find yourself in a place where you have to deal with the movements of the people, and I mean their violence. Any escape that you would get would be momentary and depend on what level is in operation at that location. But the change is going to be pretty all-involving because the energy coming into the planet (and what the planet needs to do) is all-involving. So watch carefully and see how involving it is. You're going to notice that the people who don't talk about the spiritual (who don't talk about changes in their lives) are going to be up against the wall about changing--and some of them are going to choose to leave, to die to avoid it--not knowing that dying is the ultimate change.

How the Harmonic Convergence Affected Earth

from Robbyn and His Merrye Bande

The Harmonic Convergence is a series of deadlines for Earth's beings to achieve the minimal level of awareness which was required for Earth to take its rightful place as a learning school of substance in the universe. The Earth, being the most ambitious and complex experiment of its kind, aroused much interest around the rest of the universe. So it was with great joy throughout the universe that Earth meeting its deadlines was celebrated.

You see, enough people participated with honest concern and purity of heart, and Earth graduated. Part of this whole procedure was, of course, willingness of the people who were here to leave at the appointed times to go back "home." Hence the spaceships, etc., etc. The process is not over. However, the Earth has speeded up its activity, and this is part of what is causing great confusion to many of its inhabitants.

With the speedup in activities, several issues are coming up for exposure to the light that may seem to some as proof that the world is coming to an end. Shortly after the initial obvious step of the convergence in September 1987, the U. S. stock market suffered a crash of sorts. California, a great financial and learning center, suffered some relatively serious earthquakes. Iran began pushing harder with its religious and racial intolerance. People began fearing more and more that the economy would fail, the Earth would shift on its axis (and all sorts of terrible things!). While it is true that under certain conditions pigs could fly, it's also unlikely.

What is happening, as we've said before, is that the Earth is taking over the management of her own energy in a way that links her more fully with the rest of the universe in a way that no one here has ever experienced. The result is that events in life are speeded up and literally thrown into the light if they need cleansing. So for a while it may seem that racism, sexism, discrimination, poverty, theft, and corruption in high places are indeed getting worse. The gap between the "haves" and the "have-nots" may seem to be getting wider. This is only an appearance. These things are being cleansed, by coming into greater awareness, and what will actually happen is that the energy of society will appear to reverse itself in a number of startling ways.

It will be much more difficult for fortune-tellers to accurately see the future because in the past events moved as if in slow motion. Now they are doing double time, and it will be some time before current seers and fortune-tellers will really be able to master the ability to accurately predict futures, if ever.

It's Time to Incarnate Fully

from Robbyn and His Merrye Bande

Now is the time for everyone to be more responsibly themselves. Now is the time to incarnate fully. Surprising as this may be, most of you have not. You are like big, beautiful Mercedes Benzes and Rolls Royces (with a little red roadster or two here and there) with your engines running and your hands on the wheel, but no one's ever put you in gear. If you don't move pretty soon, you may run out of gas!

Now is the time for you to come into greater awareness of your interpersonal dimensions. Instead of looking outside for the answers, now is the time to look inside. Even looking at things in terms of the victim-victimizer mentality is really looking at things as being outside. So is the other popular concept that somehow your intellect is the villain (while your feelings are the true directors of your best destiny) because it is placing blame on something and separating it from you in some way. (Trust us, your out-of-balance feelings can do as much harm, and more, as an out-of-balance intellect!)

This does not mean that an outside world does not exist, but as we have said, "There is always a solution!" (Yes, even when the Mack truck is bearing down!) And this solution that exists in every circumstance for everyone is what we are trying to get people to look at because that solution lives within the soul, and is simply waiting for a chance to express in the physical.

You see, every moment that you have existed in time in this lifetime or any other has a representation, a "part" that you were at that point in time. To the extent that these parts are in alignment or with each other is the extent to which you are in alignment with your higher self and soul. (And you didn't think being an earthling was a complex way of being! Well, it was meant to be a challenging learning experience, and it is! And a joyous and fun one!) When these parts are out of alignment with each other, you remain in neutral gear because they neutralize each other. The reason that they neutralize (or worse!) is because at different times in your life you had different wants, needs, and beliefs. Everything you have ever thought and learned is still within you now! (And you sometimes don't even think you're wonderful!) Even better, every single one of those parts loves you with all of its beingness and wants to serve you in the best way it can, which is the only way it knows how, whether you still believe in that way or not.

So what happens when you're not just in "neutral," but you seem to be acting with what appears to be self-destructive behavior? (Victimization, unfortunate repeating patterns, etc.) It's very simple: your other-than-conscious parts have a much different agenda or set of beliefs than your conscious mind does, and to change it you need to joyfully and lovingly ask. Just say, "Okay, I know that this part that always causes me to overeat, procrastinate, self-destruct (fill in the blank with your least favorite behavior) is doing this because it loves me, and I know that it is serving me in the best way that it can. However, I'm changing, and I consciously want my life to be different. I also want these parts to be in my life helping me, so I want them to look for some new choices of how to be that will satisfy their need to help me, and my need to be how I consciously want to be."

That may be a little long-winded, but the point is that when you want to change, you must communicate it to all your parts with love and affection. Will the change you want to effect occur overnight? Maybe. But maybe not. At any rate, everything responds to kindness and love, and if you are willing to talk to your inner parts, you'll learn of strengths and self-love that you never knew you had . . . and you'll be a happier and more fulfilled person for it.

Just know that if something doesn't seem to be working in your life, something you believe to be true isn't serving you. The truth is that it doesn't really matter what you believe. What does matter is whether what you believe serves you or not. If not, look very, very carefully both at conscious and other-than-conscious places. If you become too emotionally attached to one belief or another, you can do yourself some very unjoyful damage! So be kind to yourself, and scrutinize your beliefs with a calm and loving eye . . . with an eye to the possibility of change.

As you start an internal dialogue with your other-than-conscious parts, you will probably begin to notice changes in your physical body that ultimately will lead to physical healing. And you will also probably notice that your appetite and what you desire to eat will also change.

We would like to suggest ways in which you can help this process. Eat as many raw and pure, unprocessed (including cooking) foods as you can. This, of course, means mostly fresh fruits and vegetables. This suggestion is, of course, a basic detoxification diet, and will result in weight loss if that's what you need, or just basic detoxification if that's what you need. Of course, you must listen to your own body on this issue and eat what is right for you. Also know that as you do this, you are also helping to detoxify the Earth, its surface and atmosphere.

As you do this, see white light pouring through your body and the Earth, lightening the dark spots, and loving all the parts. Healing your body in the most natural and loving of ways via natural, chemical-free foods is the most loving thing you can do for the Earth right now. Since you are born of Earth, cleansing your "earth body" will result in cleansing the Earth. Honoring your body with pure and natural foods (as nature intended) is honoring the Earth and Earth's offerings in a way that is without equal. And after you cleanse your body, you will begin to strengthen and heal any parts that were weak or tired. In the same way, you also heal and replenish depleted earth resources. Do this joyfully and compassionately. It is the most kind and loving thing you can do at this time.

So take joy in being, for gravity is a rare opportunity! Thank the Earth for being a kind and gracious hostess! Keep your eye out for that bus!

Incarnate fully now to finally drive that wonderful Mercedes that is you.

You can be human without lowering your standards.

Being spiritual is fine (take it from those who know!). You are whether you want to be or not. However, the opportunity to be fully human, with all the experience that that means, is a rare opportunity indeed . . . and a joyous one. Align with your spirit and become One. Now. Here on Earth. In your physical body. By following the path of joy and compassion you will fully incarnate.

Joy and compassion are the energies with which the Earth itself was created. They are the energies with which the Earth school was begun. If you follow that path yourself, you can draw the Earth's energy into you in a way that will make your congruent, aligned conscious intent manifest in a much shorter time and in more fulfilling ways. Why? Because it's Earth's way.

If you are reading this, we want to offer you a special opportunity to help us and the Earth in gently executing the changes.

If you are reading this, you are a powerful and capable being who can envision world peace, and a cooperative, compassionate society that cares about the homeless and the friendless.

If you are reading this, you care that people feel accepted and fulfilled.

You care that Earth has something to offer the greater universe.

You care that disease and disharmony are causing confusion and suffering.

You care that a mass consciousness of fear creates difficulty on the planet that is your current home.

Take time now to imagine a higher and brighter vision where these issues are issues of the past, and do this with us every day. If you do this, you will be walking the path of joy and compassion, and soon you will be dancing with the mountains, soaring with the eagles, floating through the bowels of the Earth through untold sacred mysteries. The flowers will tell you their secrets, and trees will call out your name. The animals will call you friend as you walk in joy and compassion. You will prosper and draw to you untold wealth of all kinds as the Earth says, "Thanks for your help."

Spirit Guides andTeachers:

You are never alone

"Those you call spirit guides and teachers are like gardeners carefully tending to beautiful, growing flowers. They weed, fertilize, provide light and warmth, remove dead petals and leaves--all for the purpose of allowing those flowers to unfold to their greatest potential and beauty in Earth's garden of life."

from Kyros

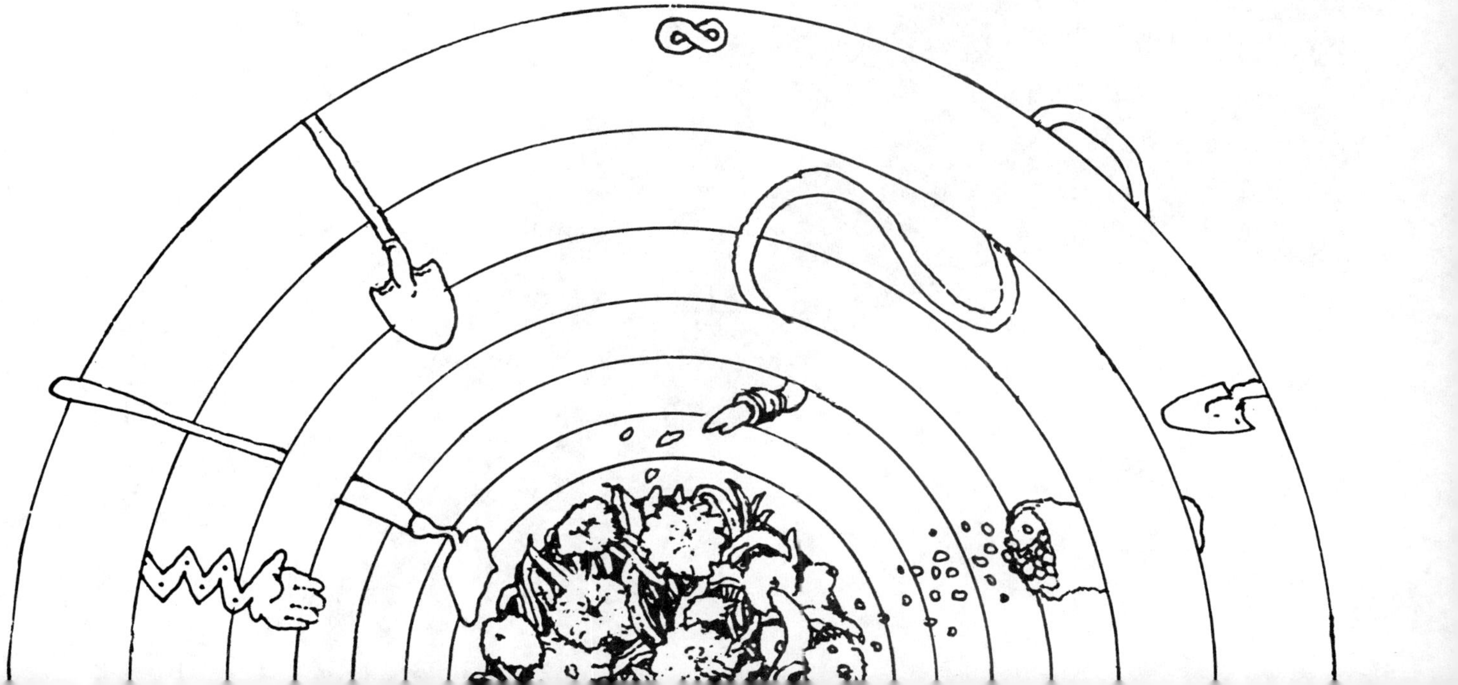

The Earth-School Opportunity

from Robbyn and His Merrye Bande

In order to understand spirit guides, teachers, counselors, angels, and such like, you must be clear on the role of the planet, for elsewhere in the universe are different opportunities.

Here on Earth, we have a school, a school for the evolution of self-knowing and free will, accomplished through the exercise of choice. It is a dynamic and popular school and not so easy to get into! So bless the Earth, for *gravity is a rare opportunity* and one that should not be taken lightly (please pardon the pun). Gravity, of necessity, creates the form of energy in density. Energy in a dense form creates the need for time. When there isn't gravity, the energy that is you can do many things at once. So gravity, through density, forces the need for choice, since its presence means you can only do one thing at a time.

When you are forced to make choices,
you learn about yourself.

So bless the Earth, the star that is your sun, the rock that is your moon, the planets that are your neighbors. They all make up your reality and influence your life on this planet, in this solar system, in this galaxy.

Now, since the system is like that, it was decided that it would behoove the universe to give a little assistance, inasmuch as consciousness takes a much denser form than other channels for evolvement in the universe, and since the experiences here are so intense. Density clouds other channels of knowing. And so, on this planet, we all have assigned guides to help us through. Now, we made these arrange-

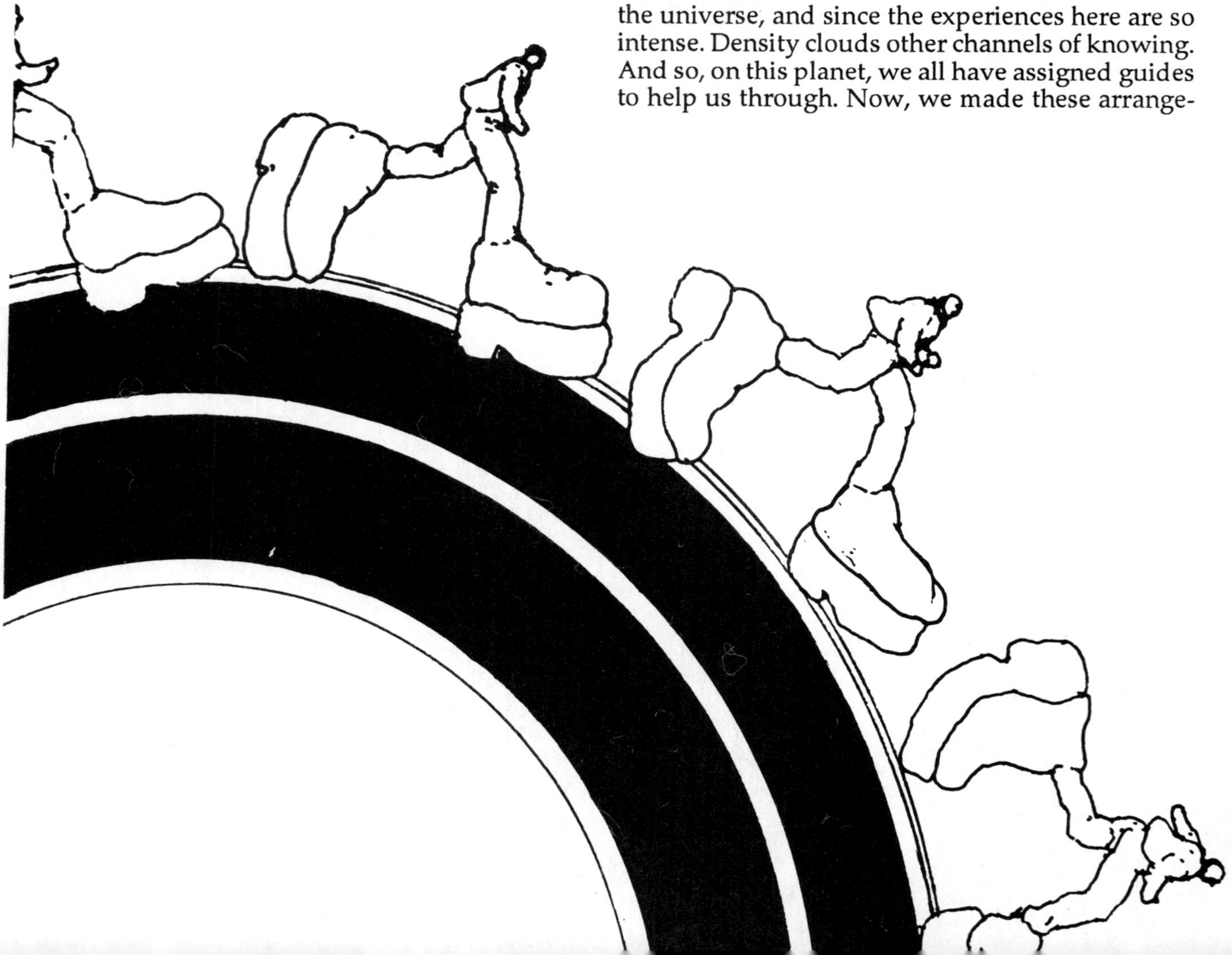

ments, in some cases, eons ago, and in some on the morning of the incarnation. Whatever the case, each person being born had "X" number of guides on his or her team who came along as they started their lives. They stay until the lifetime is totally regrouped (figured out) and sometimes beyond.

The bond between us is love and trust. We want to help you, and *we are learning with you!* We who are guides have made our own commitment to help the planet, just as many of you with your life and vibration have made yours. (Now don't be coy and wonder, "Have I?" Chances are, if you're reading this, you have, so relax.)

We can help you see and accept the parameters and opportunities you chose as your lesson plan (or game plan) this lifetime. We can help you maximize or minimize your karmic choices.

Let's say you've had several lifetimes as an axe-murderer. Now, we love you no matter what. We may not think something is such a good idea, in the whole scheme of things, but we love you nevertheless. And this does not mean that we do not support the idea of creating powerful karma. It's just that at some times, some things are a better idea than at others. Anyway, let's say you want to incarnate amongst your former "victims." So you may have a little fear going in, and understandably so. There are a million ways to resolve it, but in your life parameter, you've chosen possibilities ranging from death by an axe-murderer to a loving, healing relationship with your former victims and everything in between. But let's also say that your life plan includes growth events that extend beyond the moment when someone has time in their life to create the possibility to be an axe-murderer of you.

One suggestion might be that there are other opportunities, so let's release that karma in a gentler way, being of greater service to others. If you listen to us and agree, that's what happens. If you don't listen to us, they bury you, we regroup, and you come back and do it all again. That's all.

We help you manifest things in your life--your clear choices--and we love it. Those things are your life and your lessons. Our vibration is enthusiasm and *joie de vivre!* And that's because the vibration of each one of you is important to the vibration of the Earth.

Because of the density, you get into a planetary mindset from time to time. The thoughts that you have do create form and substance. Sometimes these mindsets are more beneficial than others. We are puzzled that so many of you enlightened beings have a tendency to believe in anything or anyone but yourselves or your guides. You listen to other people's guides, extraterrestrials, or random discarnates, and look for wisdom through flying saucers, dolphins, and so on.

So many of you have been enlightened beings and guides yourselves, so it puzzles us that you prefer to look for wisdom outside of yourselves and your Earth, since many of you lovingly and wisely chose to come back at this crucial time. It is not that we have anything against extraterrestrials or dolphins. Nobody said it better than E.T. when he said, "Be good." Most of you thought it only applied to children. Silly you.

We are also concerned with the growing tendency of you beloved enlightened ones to sit back and say, "Well, you know, so and so created this in their lives"--tragedy and so on. While it is, in a sense, true, we want to encourage you all to collectively leave the idea that lessons of suffering are more powerful or stronger or better or more impressive somehow. They aren't. They're just less pleasant, and more unnecessary. And they reduce the speed at which the planet can grow and flourish in the light. Pain and disruption and disease and suffering take time and energy to overcome. That wasn't the intended role of the planet, just one possibility. Right now, the planet needs your energy in the light. Again, it's your choice, but in case you're ready to give up doing everything the hard way, ask us. We can help. *So ask.*

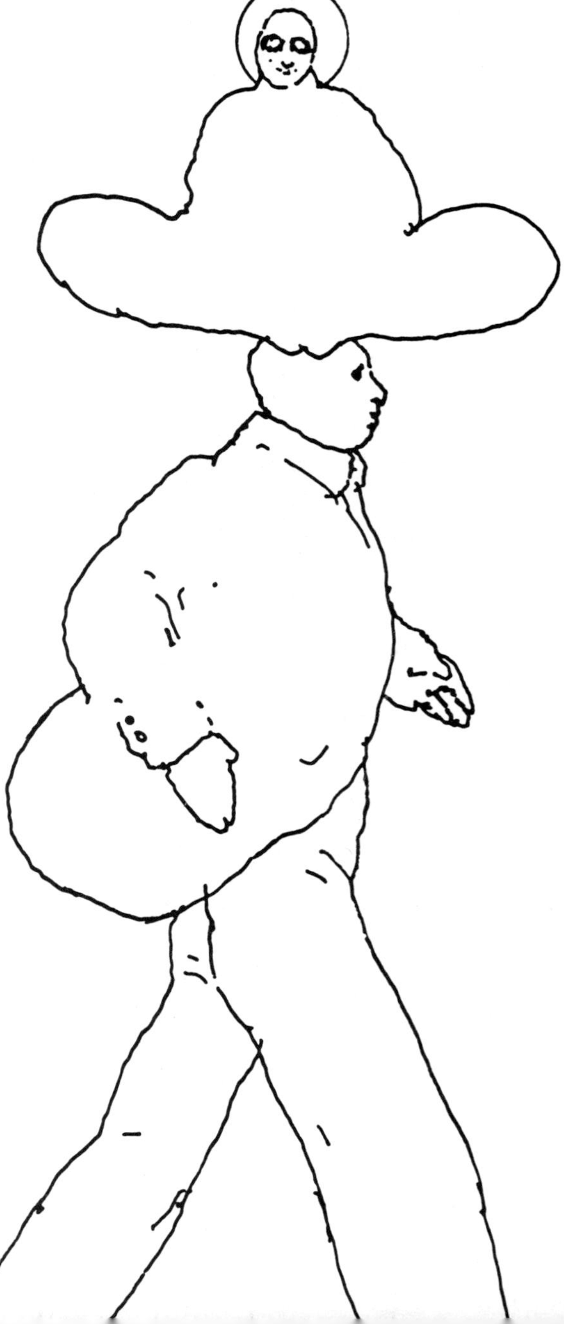

We want to encourage you all to collectively leave the idea that lessons of suffering are more powerful or stronger or better or more impressive somehow. They aren't.

Oh, what joy and enthusiasm when we are asked. We'll drive with you, sing with you, dance with you, we'll even jog with you. And we'll love every moment and hope that you will too. But for this relationship to work its best, you must be very, very clear. We'll never, never help you to do things that are contrary to the laws of a loving vibration in the universe.

All About Spirit Guides

Who we are

from Li Sung

Greetings, friends. We're glad you finally thought to ask us to describe to you our own existence. First, as an example of who we are and why we have come: we have led many lives on your earth plane in which we have studied the mastery of the mind with meditation, philosophy, and good action. In our lifetimes many of us have also been rascals one or two times just to keep things interesting. But it is upon our nobler experiences that we draw in order to bring guidance to you.

> ***In our lifetimes, many of us have been rascals a few times just to keep things interesting.***

In our world we also have school, though not just one school but many schools for training of spirit guides. On the basic level, guides and would-be guides are instructed on how to advise humans, how to give them a bit of inspiration and help when they need it, and how not to interfere in their choices and their own karma. They learn how to bring to humans some measure of help and guidance.

There is a second level of training, a smaller school, in which spirit guides are instructed on how to communicate, how to manipulate the consciousness of humans in order to bring through channeled material verbally or in writing or perhaps just into their minds. We have sometimes quite an elaborate process to do this.

The third school is for more specific training for guides who wish to operate with mediums and to bring through other discarnates, or persons from our world, who have not had the training or experience to communicate directly. This school is a place where technicians are also trained, for like one of your movies or television shows, there are many people behind the scenes in order to bring you the picture. It can be quite complex.

Above these are not exactly schools but something more like select academies in which persons higher in the spiritual hierarchy are becoming versed in philosophy, especially in worldly philosophy. And here we mean speaking about and debating on the future of your world. There are considerations of the various plans, blueprints, or ideas which are to be expressed in your world. There is some discussion and continual revision going on.

And still higher is the angelic realm in which beings who have never incarnated bring through the Holy Spirit. They are more in charge of the larger divisions of humankind. And above them there are numerous religious figures, such as your Jesus, who have established themselves as gods in the eyes of men, and to whom prayers are often sent. Near them are their saints and related religious figures. Each religion has its own garden in which the mighty stroll. And so in this hierarchy or multileveled condominium of spirit beings there is much concern at all levels for activity on the Earth.

Those who are assigned (and this is done by consent) to individual humans are often so assigned by prior agreement.

It is not unlike some of your sports events in which the players team up for one game, and then later they have a rematch in which they are reteamed, and so on. But there is a continuity there. The spirit guide and the incarnate, the human, often have had a prior relationship, although this is not always true. But there is certainly an affinity between the human and the spirit guide.

Now in our own case, we have known Vaughan (the channel) in two lifetimes on the Earth, and have agreed to help with a plan (that has interested us and interests him) of bringing to the earth plane the plans and concepts for a united consciousness, during the latter part of the twentieth century and the first part of the twenty-first century. We are working in concert with many other spirit guides and their mediums to plant new seeds of thought into your society. We already see some progress, and soon, we believe, more and more persons will be looking into their own hearts, into the inspirations from us and from their higher selves.

For you live in a time, my friends, when there is great excitement upon the land. There is fast movement. There is fear, but there is also great promise of brilliance, a promise of a society that will equal, or even surpass, those that have gone before. A sort of Golden Age of Consciousness. That is what we are striving for.

Many of us attracted to working as spirit guides have had for this purpose some prior training in earlier attempts at bringing golden ages of the mind and of life into being. And so, you may find that there are a lot of Atlanteans about.

That was a brave, bold attempt to bring technology and mind together. But the Atlanteans didn't quite get it right. Of course there are the ancient Greeks, who also tried very valiantly for a time, and many of us are coming back from that for a rematch in the twentieth century. There was an age of brilliance in Japan and in China and in India and in Tibet--in many places. And those sages from those times are returning now as spirit guides. Indeed, a few are also incarnating into your physical world, too, to bring the benefit of their knowledge.

But the largest group of spiritual beings here are Atlantean, and many of them are so terribly disappointed that their brave plan failed that they have resisted incarnating ever since. Now they see once again the promise of attaining their ideal in reality, physical reality, and so they are returning in droves.

The selection of spirit guides is by agreement between the human and the spirit, but it fits into a much larger plan of what is to transpire, we hope, in the manifestation of the physical universe. And soon you will see, or perhaps you have already begun to see, spirit guides from other galaxies, other dimensions, who have not been in human form at all, but who are beginning to interpenetrate your world to prepare for a meeting of consciousness, a meeting of beings, from other worlds. And their presence will be announced by some of these guides. We have heard you call them space brothers. To us they are not spacey, but they are more distant from our vibration. The Earth people are exhibiting great abilities now at altering their mental vibration to accommodate these beings of other galaxies, other stars. So this also will be a form of progress in a surprising direction.

We know that in many of your religions there is talk of guardian angels, and by that is usually meant us--spirit guides--who operate not to channel through, but to inspire, and to guide, and to protect. Yes, that is what we are. We do not wear wings. (A *few* do, but they are considered rather too flashy, in bad taste.)

Most of us have sincerity in our hearts. However, we must also protest that you human beings have the most fantastic concepts of life in our world. You think it is peopled by demons, by great fantastic savages, or by huge beings with white fluttering wings and playing harps--all sorts of nonsense. Of course it is not true. We create our worlds in a most civilized manner. They are lovely and have beauties that are not experienced in your physical plane, although we must say they do lack the erratic excitement of earthly life. There is a certain serenity and a feeling of love here that makes it quite pleasant, really.

You, my friends, are about to be born again--after you pass the physical transition--be born again into our world, and there you will have the choice of working as a spirit guide to help the next generation of humans or to incarnate yourself and go forcibly into the fray, into the battle of life. There are many choices to be made.

We are not trying to sell you on the idea of becoming a spirit guide, for it is often a thankless task.

Too often humans not only ignore us, they do exactly the opposite of what we advise. It is very off-putting. But we tend to be somewhat tolerant. Yet we are most delighted when our human friends do understand our guidance and do find it within themselves to contact their own higher beings or soul beings to make their beautiful and positive promised reality a true manifestation.

The grand difference

from Abrham

Spirit guides have no time. Spirit guides have no patterns of emotions because they are emotional energy as you are emotional energy. There is one grand difference between you and your spirit guides. They realize in all ways that they are *their own emotional energy,* and only at times will you people realize that statement.

When you are feeling very good about yourself, about your lifetime, you are functional in a free way, in a free sense. You have no limitations, but you know that you can create them when you wish, as you wish, how you wish. You can create limitations for your spirit guides. When you become hardheaded, not willing to listen, when you shut down your emotions, when you are not willing to express yourself, you create a barrier, a wall that is highly functional between yourself and your guides.

There is no end to your imagination.

Now, as you have your own identity and your own personality, your spirit guides have their own identity. They *are* of their own identity which is fully and totally functional all the time. There is no time in their reality because they are not *in* a reality. They are only *within* the experience of what they are at any given moment in time. That allows them to enter dimensions of your reality and guide you along within your subconscious mind, within your unconscious mind. And at times, as you are frying bacon, they are within your conscious mind!

And when you are hearing your spirit guides consciously, whether or not you are frying anything, sometimes you think it is only your own imagination working a bit overtime. But truly, when you examine your imagination you will find one thing. There is no end to your imagination, and that does not mean it is empty. That means it just exists with its own continuum. And in other words it keeps going and going and indeed you find yourself in various points of your own imagination during your day, during your night.

In your dream state, *you become your imagination.* And when you are allowing yourself to become your own imagination, you have that face-to-face communication with your spirit guides.

If you are thinking that your own spirit guides are either male or female, why do you wish to limit yourself to thinking only that way? Maybe you have a little dog spirit as your spirit guide or a plant spirit as your spirit guide, because life is only consciousness, only energy. There are many times during your life when you will actually merge with the consciousness of animals, the consciousness of plants. Your form of reality is a change unto its own self. And that means purely and very simply that no idea will stay the same. As you take an idea, you break down the structure of the idea only to rebuild a different structure of the same idea. And as you are doing so, you wind up with a brand new set of probabilities and possibilities that will enable you to have more ideas so you can only break them down again, only to rebuild them and wind up one more time with more probabilities and possibilities, only to do it all over again. And you create your spirit guides in that way also. It is you who will give your spirit guide the majority of its, his, or her own identity.

School is never completed

from Dr. Peebles

The way you live as individuals, what you do with your experiences, your emotions, how you evolve with your faith, how you evolve your conscious interaction with guides and teachers, the angels, the deva, the nature spirits, these all help other human beings grow. Not your words, but your attitudes, your vibrations, your frequencies. And so *you are guides to other human beings.* If you deny the spirit, if you deny yourself, you are guiding them into darkness. If you live in light and love and harmony, you are guiding them into living in light and love and harmony.

We on the spirit side, we are responsible to help you grow if you are ready. And as you grow, as you evolve, as you develop, as you trust, you are helping us *take on even more responsibilities* that we are capable of attaining. You help us, as you grow, to continue growing ourselves. We will grow with or without you. But as you grow as individuals, you allow us to grow more swiftly, more clearly, more quickly. We will grow without you. We just grow more quickly, more gracefully, as you grow on the Earth side.

As you study the spirit, as you study communion with the guides, you are also guiding those on the darker planes who are searching for the light, for you become beacons and flashlights that shine into the darker planes. In short, you are helping us on the spirit side as you are helping those on the Earth plane. You are helping those on the darkened levels of the astral in the way you live, in the demonstration of your spiritual attitudes.

Rules and regulations

from Li Sung

We are like umpires in your sports games. We cannot go out and play the game itself. We cannot grab somebody's bat and hit the ball. We cannot go and take the ball from the pitcher and throw it ourselves. No, we must remain on the sidelines to give inspiration, and also, of course, to give some judgments about what is proper and what is not proper. We cannot directly interfere; that is forbidden. We have to wait until it is time for us to play the game, and then we can do as we like. When we incarnate in the flesh, it is then our turn to play the game, and perhaps your turn to be the coach. So we are restricted, and I must confess that there are a few spirit guides who are a little soft in the head, and sometimes they do transgress these rules. They get so very fond of someone and they hate to see him suffering. Perhaps they don't realize the suffering has a purpose, and so they do some foolish thing by stepping into your world for a time, materializing, just to give consolation. That is not considered good form at all.

from Robbyn and His Merrye Bande

Now to be clear, we never, never (1) do things for you, or (2) decide things for you. You must make up your own mind, make your own choices, *and* if you want our help, you must *choose* to ask us. We never, never interfere. Not that we won't try to drop hints now and then like, "Excuse us, but did you know that a herd of buffalo is about to stampede over you?" or, "That fellow in the black leather jacket with brass knuckles and a knife may not have the best of intentions concerning your welfare, so be alert." Realistically though, because you are so dense and we are not, we can only do so much to get through to you. You really must do the rest.

Question: Is it fun to be a spirit guide?

from Li Sung

We would not call it particularly fun. It is a job. It is an agreement. It is a relationship. Understand that while you are in earthly life you have many relationships with others, but none quite the same as what you have with spirit guides. For here there are no jealousies, for we cannot compete with you. We do not want to. There is no erotic love for we cannot make love to you, nor do we. We are not your fathers nor mothers. We are not your children nor lovers. We are friends--friends who exist because we want you to succeed in life. It is a partnership. We on the spirit side, you on the physical side, working toward the same ends--a fulfilled life for you, a fulfilled society on Earth that breathes and loves and celebrates. If you can do that, then we are most happy. What we get out of it is the love that we share, the joy that we share.

Spirit guides are friends who exist because we want you to succeed in life.

There are a few guides who think they are doing prison time in this work, and that is because they are working with mortals who do not cooperate. So they do feel frustrated. It is part of their karma, we suspect. They have to put up with it. But, you know, most human beings do follow the guidance, do appreciate the protection from our realm. And we ask only that they accept our love and remember that we were once human, too, and we understand.

There are some of your religious traditions that have convinced people they are terrible sinners, so they always feel guilty or worried or upset. But understand that these so-called sins are trivial nonsense. They are merely little pebbles under the foot. They are not boulders that obstruct justice and light. So, we *do not judge our humans.* We are with them in all they do and all they ask for. We bring them good will, for when they are successful in their accomplishments it is time for us to celebrate.

from Soli

You may sense that there is some frustration in being a guide, but it is not quite the same as you would see it from your ego point of view. And yes, there is a certain amount of truth in that, nonetheless, because from the spirit point of view it is not always that easy to get individuals on Earth to listen or to take action. And so there can be frustration because there is a certain element of personality involved in the guide.

Understand this about guides, my friends. They are at various different levels of evolution within themselves. Ultimately all is spirit, but spirit has had many, many different lifetimes. You, my friends, are not who you think you are.

You are infinitely varied experience in all kinds of time and space and dimensions.

You have had lifetimes in many different places. So you are not who you think you are, even though you use your name and think that that defines who you are. All it defines is your current personality expression in this, your current life. But you are infinitely living spirit, and so are your guides and teachers. Some of them are more aware of that fact than others, just as on this Earth dimension some are more aware of that fact than others.

Why have spirit guides?

from Soli

You all have guides and teachers. You do not incarnate upon the Earth dimension as a human being without having guides on the other side.

Understand first and foremost, my friends, that when you come into your physical bodies within this life, you come in through what you would call the Valley of Forgetfulness. You cut yourself off from your spiritual understanding. In a very real sense you forget *who you truly are.* You forget that you are the infinite I Am, the All That Is. You forget that you are God. And in the process of becoming the present personality, the present ego that you are, the new subconscious mind that you bring with you, you cut off even more memory of who you are. When you first come into the physical body there is very often a carryover, a memory of who you are and where you have been before. But as time goes by, with parents and teachers around you, you very soon learn to realize that such stories can't possibly be real. And so they are closed off. You close off those memories.

While you are within the physical vehicle inhabiting this Earth dimension, you need some assistance in finding your way around, for you do not have the overall picture that you had before you came into the physical body. Before coming into the physical body, you could see exactly the probability pattern laid out in front of you of all the events in your life that you intended to experience.

But when you get into ego with your own free will and choice, the ego wants satisfaction, wants gratification, wants the easy way, wants the life of grace and favor, and does everything in its power to create that circle of reality for yourself. And so you need guidance to keep you on what you would see as being your "spiritual path." In truth, there is no spiritual path, but you see it in that way. There are, however, events, circumstances, experiences that you have laid up for yourself in probability that you do wish to experience. And you might call that your spiritual path.

And so you have those guides on the other side in the spiritual domains available to you to assist you, guide you. And most importantly, my friends, understand that a guide is just that. A guide can never do anything for you. Well, they can, but if they do, they may create karma for themselves. It is an infringement on your right to your experience. The guide is a guide.

The guide can take you to the light switch in the darkened room and put your hand on it, but you must make the action in turning on that switch.

Understand that guides and teachers around you the most are your brothers and sisters in soul. You have had many lifetimes together. You have been a guide for others when they were in the physical body and you were currently not in physical form. And so you mix, you change.

You might liken it to being within a travel club. A group of you get together and form this club and some of you decide you're going to visit Spain. And so a group of you get on an airplane. Some go directly to Spain. Some take a bit longer and leave at different times, but ultimately they end up in that country. Some of that group might stay behind at home to staff the telephones in case you get into trouble in Spain and you want some assistance, to be able to relay messages to you over there. It is very much like that.

You have a soul group, a soul family, entities who are a spiritual core group, if you might call it that. Many of you incarnate at the same time and many stay out of incarnation at any given time. And you agree with certain members of your immediate soul family that you will be incarnated this time and that they will assist you from the other side. And sometimes you stay there and assist others. And those that are assisting from the spirit dimension are learning at the same time that you are. In many ways they are living vicariously through you by experiencing your experiences. They are seeing how you handle the vicissitudes of life. And therefore, they have further knowledge for themselves when they incarnate into their next existence.

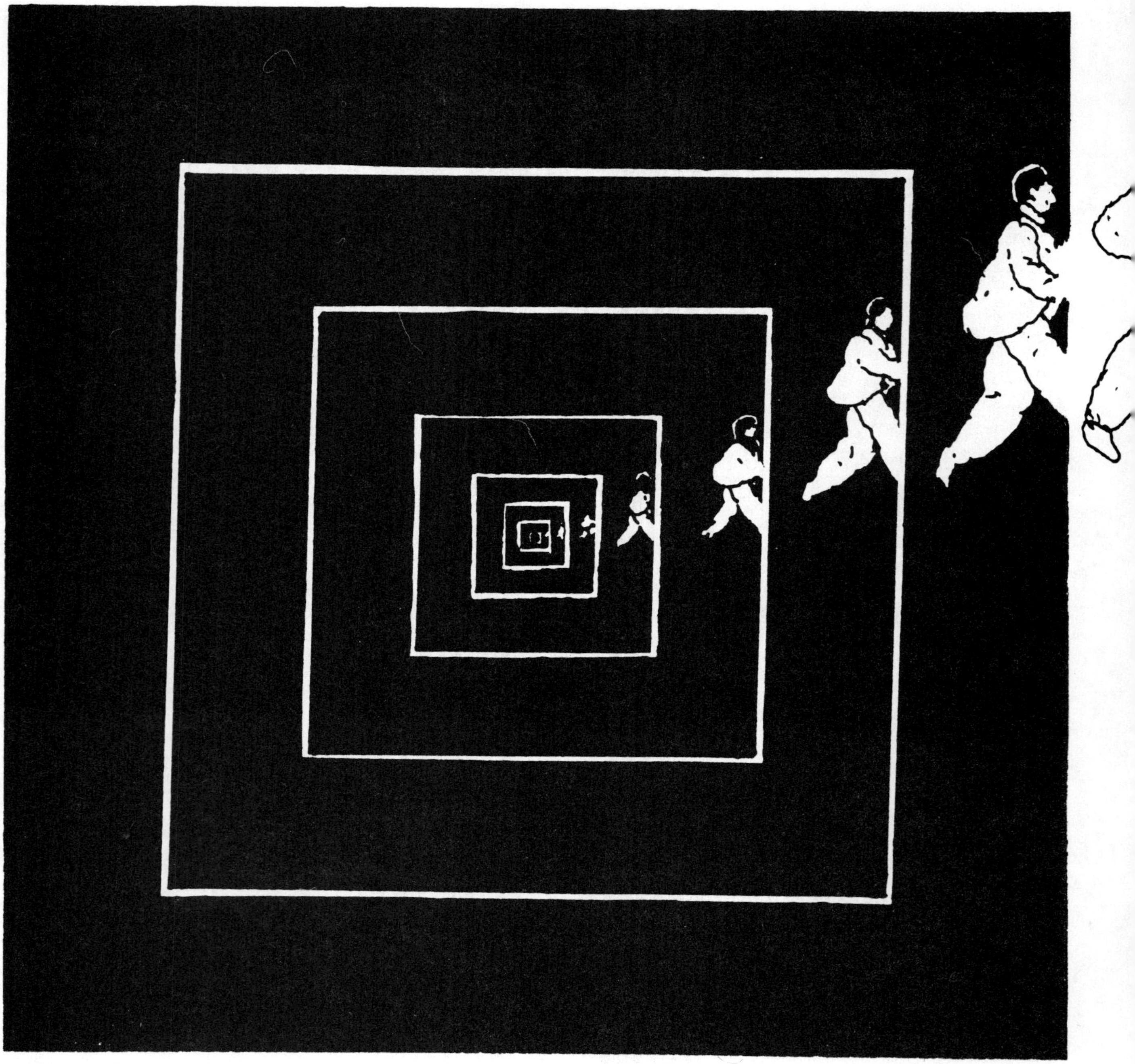

Oneness, temporarily separated

from Kyros

With respect to that which is termed "spirit guides and teachers," it is important to remember that *nothing is beyond your own being.* Nothing is, in truth, external to yourself. It appears this way only because human entities have a tendency to separate and fragment life. As a subject in your world, you perceive everything which you observe as external to that subject called you. When you perceive things as external to yourself, you are separate from them; you are not in oneness with that which you perceive. Externalizing beyond your own being is how you create your illusions. One of the lessons upon your journey is to understand your oneness with All That Is and to reach this awareness of oneness. The path seems to lead you through illusionary separation.

Nothing is outside of the subject or the perceiver. In truth, it is one's perception which creates the illusion of things being external and apart. I, Kyros, am not a spiritual energy existing in a space or a time external to you. This truth is difficult to explain to entities who live in a space-time dimension of form and who create illusionary realities of separateness. You see, all there really is is the One Mind or the Life Force or God or whatever else you may choose to call it.

Let's use a simple example--a balloon. If you blow up a balloon, that which is in the balloon is the same as that which is outside of it. That sameness is separated by the balloon itself. Release the air from the balloon and that which was within becomes one with that which was outside of the separation line of the balloon.

In communication or in channeling, the separation line dissolves (for lack of a better term) and oneness occurs. That which you term "individualized mind" is the One Mind when the subjective line of separation is dissolved. There are seven levels of consciousness in mind, and the human entity is operating on all of them, including omniconsciousness, which is the One Mind and cannot be individualized.

That which you term "your" mind is the One Mind and recognizes no separation. However, that which you call the level of present consciousness within "your" mind does recognize and create the illusion of separation, and this occurs for your work and learning within a space-time dimension, which, I might add, is also illusion. The present conscious level then offers you the illusion that higher guidance is coming into conscious awareness from some "place" beyond you. And because of this you fragment, separate, compartmentalize spirit guides and teachers.

No human entity is ever without guidance or direction on their walk.

Sometimes you separate and say the direction is coming from God or Kyros or intuition or a gut-level feeling. It is all true, for regardless of whom you give credit to, it is still issuing forth from your own oneness with universal intelligence or cosmic consciousness. The human entity's choice, of course, is always whether or not to follow the guidance. Other aspects of nature tend to be more attuned to oneness and thus are more obedient to inner direction. Do not think that something as natural as a tree upon your planet receives no inner direction.

Let's make things more simple and begin to follow the human entity's belief that spirit guides and teachers are separate from you, for it's really all right to believe this, too. When you exit third-dimensional life, you will understand what I have tried to explain about One Mind and oneness with all. You will understand that your line of separation was your vehicle of form for expressing on planet Earth, as well as the ego programming of your brain computer. And, you also will understand that what you really are is spiritual energy with absolute consciousness.

So, given your belief in separation, why are we part of a human entity's life? For the most part, our purpose is not to protect the material form except in the very highest sense of the word. The survival programming of the ego operating from the organic brain computer has been magnificently created for the maintenance and protection of the physical vehicle. Part of our purpose is to create the awareness that you have reached the evolutionary point where you don't need to rely so heavily on survival programming. In other words, part of our work involves teaching you higher truths so that you will change your own programming. A change in programming results in a shift in individual consciousness which feeds into collective consciousness. In time, this will produce a higher order of life for entities upon planet Earth. Collective consciousness will not shift until individual consciousness has shifted, and so the work must be done first upon the individual level. This is why I always say that everything begins with you, the individualized God expression.

All human entities receive guidance or direction whether they are aware of it or not. The greater one's awareness level is, the easier expansion of awareness becomes. All is truth on your planet at some level of awareness, but always it is relative truth and is in accordance with the one holding that truth at a particular level of awareness. For the seeker, for the one who is open and aware of guidance, truth will always be expanded and greater knowledge will be given. One's level of truth will always parallel his level of awareness in the conscious, present state of being.

Our purpose is to guide those who are willing through the process of soul evolution, which is essentially movement into higher consciousness. I do not use the term "spiritual evolution" because the spirit and the soul are not the same and because the spirit is already in a state of perfection.

Part of our work, through that which we teach to those who will listen and hear, is to assist you in making the Earth phase of your journey happier and more fulfilling (which is how it really should be). When you release from your attachments to old programming and are able to see things with an expanded awareness, your perception changes and your consciousness shifts. When this occurs, you begin to think differently.

As you know, empowered thoughts are what you bring into your manifested illusionary reality. In the movement in the process towards higher awareness, your thoughts will be aligned to your awareness level and your outer world of reality will reflect what you are in present consciousness.

Therefore the more highly aware you become and the more attuned you are to higher guidance, the higher your thoughts will be.

And the more aligned you are to Universal Mind, the greater your ability to empower these thoughts, because this alignment means connection with the greatest power, Love. This, then, fills the Earth phase of your journey with joy, thus making your particular mission much easier to achieve. If your inner world of being is rich in joy, this is what will be reflected in your self-created outer world.

Your outer world will always reflect what
you are in your present consciousness.
It is a mirror of your inner self.

So, essentially, our work involves teaching you, through guidance and direction, higher truths so that you can move continuously upward in consciousness. Yes, we offer a lot of knowledge, and some of it oftentimes seems a bit mundane. Knowledge is given only to be converted into wisdom. Wisdom is knowledge used for the higher good, and without wisdom, knowledge is of little value. Many human entities have an abundance of knowledge, but unless that knowledge is transformed into wisdom, it is meaningless. As you ascend in consciousness and awareness, you will use your knowledge with wisdom. What matters is not *what* you know, but rather how you *utilize* what you know on your journey.

When you're looking in the mirror (and a number of you have had this experience), suddenly you see something that isn't quite you. And you blink your eyes, you rub your eyes and you take a deep breath to get your focus back. You will say that was the spirit. At times you are even seeing one of your own past lives.

You are all capable of seeing
and talking to the spirit.

I wish there were a formula that I could give that all of you could practice and suddenly become directly in touch with spirit. I cannot do that. There

Communication Glitches

Trained against communication

from Dr. Peebles

To be born into physical density (in this case human), you each come into the body with the potential to commune with the guides and the teachers in the spirit world. Those of you who chose to be born in the Western world, particularly, have been trained *against* such communication. And the majority of you who have communed with the spirit, even on a conscious level, will call it other things to justify the communication. Each of you reading these words has heard the spirit. Each of you has seen the spirit. Each of you, in your own way, has denied it. And that is not wrong, that is not bad, for that is part of your experience.

Eventually, by being with others in the same experience and by appreciating each other, you get the strength of character to say, "That energy I saw in the cloud the other day, that energy, that was spirit. That face I saw in the cloud, that wasn't my imagination. That really was the spirit." You may say, "Oh, when I was sitting quietly on my patio, and I felt the breeze when there was no breeze in the air, that was the breath of the spirit."

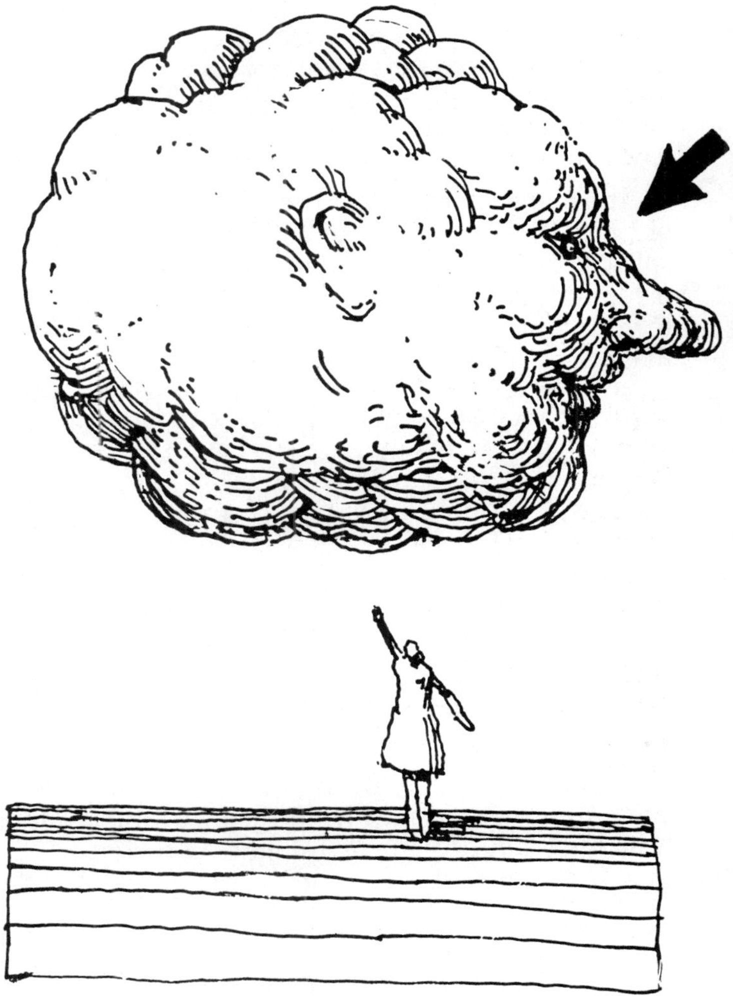

is not one formula that works for everyone. For each of you came into your bodies for *very specific purposes and reasons.* Your greatest effort to find your individual formula is made possible simply by your interest, by your reading these words. You have opened the door; you are already discovering your own answers.

You could all sit and chat for an hour each day. One would bring the spirit forth consciously. For another, the spirit would be there, but not on a conscious level. You could all do exercises in front of mirrors, and some would see the spirit and some would not. For it is *not* the exercises that make it happen. It is your *willingness* as individuals to move beyond your programs and your trimmings of this life. Most of all, then, the greatest formula is very, very simple.

Continue believing that you have the right to look into the eyes of the spirit, that you have the right to and deserve to hear the guiding voice.

And above all else, dear friends, when the voice of the spirit comes, and all of you have heard the spirit say, "Turn right, not left," you must turn immediately, even when it doesn't make a lot of sense to your mind. Each of you have heard, "Don't take that project over there," but because you've worked on it, because you think you want it, you take it anyway. You're missing the miracles that your higher self has waiting for you. Most of it then is trusting, willingly accepting the responsibility of listening beyond the interferences of your earthbound personalities and egos, listening to the voice and the guidance of your higher self.

Now that is very, very difficult, dear friends, and I understand. None of you like to hear that your personalities cannot control the universe. But each of you, in your own heart, knows that this is true. Each of you needs to keep your intellect, certainly. Keep your opinions, most assuredly. But allow equal time, equal space within your own heart to hear the truth of your own higher consciousness that put you into this body in the first place.

None of you are here by mistake.
None of you are here by accident.

Fear of communication with spirit

from Dr. Peebles

The question of the "dark forces" is a very complicated one. There are human beings who hear the spirit from the darker planes or the earthbound (dark forces). They are channels who have not taken on the responsibility of *only* hearing the light. They are channels that enter physical densities for *their* experience, and also to *give* other people their experience.

It's hard to accept that those who were murdered wanted to be murdered. If they did not want it, they would have chosen another body. Now, that does not *justify* such experiences. You are all working to uplift the consciousness so such will *not be necessary.* Your planet just will not be equipped to attract souls who need that experience. But all of you needed to be in this world during times when such phenomena could take place, to remind you of what you *don't need* in your life any longer.

But quite possibly you participated in these experiences in another life and part of your balancing is to observe it, without magnetizing it to you. There are many who hear the darker forces. There are those who come into the physical density to do very specific things, but society says, "These things cannot be done. These are bad. These are not to be accomplished," and yet they are driven by their own experiential needs to accomplish the act, whatever the act is. To justify parts of the brain and what you would call distortion or insanity, they create voices or guidance to justify what they have to do. However, this is not on a conscious level. A body that is equipped to murder, that is destined to be in an environment where such will take place, will attract a soul that has to do that job. And so I'm saying, yes, on a soul level, that soul, for its experience, chose a body that would allow it to do its act. That's a big one, isn't it? Perhaps a bit hard to take. You may be saying, "Oh, but that's bad, that's bad." It is not your right to say that.

All of the experiences are necessary to the soul's evolution. That does not mean that all of you should go out and murder and steal. Then you would be forcing that experience. But those who are driven to it, you can help them. You can love them. You can work with them more productively if you don't judge and criticize them.

You may say, "How come that person over there always gets beat up?" They are experiencing something that, on a soul level, they need. Now personalities don't like to get beat up, but you have the job to help personalities grow to such a degree that they will accept their experiences. And once they

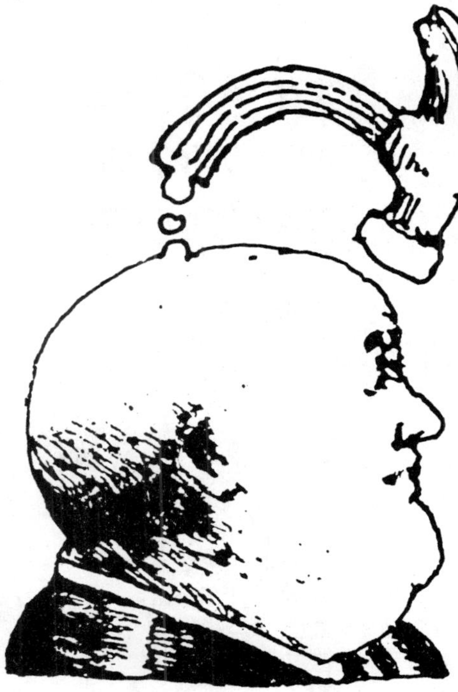

are accepted, and once they are faced--not on an ego level, not on an intellectually defined level, but on a soul level--the experience will complete itself, and they will no longer get beat up. *No experience comes by chance.* They are all part of the evolutionary process.

from Li Sung

There are spiritual elements, or elementary spirits, who dwell on the lower level of vibration around your Earth. They are not assigned to be spirit guides because they have not gone to the school. They are generally mired in materialistic values. They seek merely Earth experience. They have not accepted the fact of their death or the fact that there lies above them a magnificence to be obtained. So these are very backward elements and they will occasionally sneak in and cause havoc. They will get into somebody's head and the person will think he is hearing voices. Well, of course he is. And so one

Stupidity was never ruled out as a growth experience, but it is rarely directly helpful to anyone other than the individual exercising it.

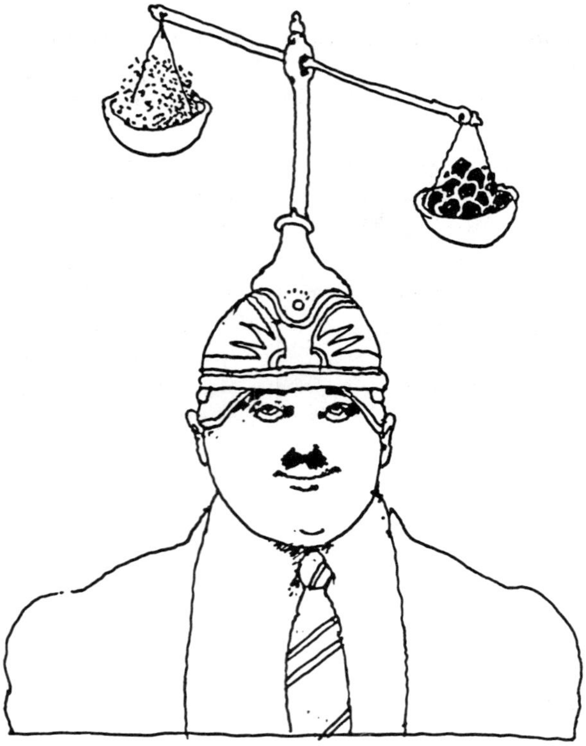

must guard against these rascals who have no manners at all. Understand that they are not assigned as spirit guides. They are more like a band of marauding, naughty children. But you need not have truck with them.

As to whether there are official spirit guides who have bad judgment--well, unfortunately, that does sometimes happen. They think they know better than they do, in fact, know.

You must weigh inspiration given from our realm with the same judgment that you would use to weigh comments from any human being.

Do not assume that spirit guides always know better than you, for after all, it is *your* game, and we *can err.* Although we are looking often at the proposed program of your life, sometimes spirit guides have bad judgment or bad information, or outdated information, and so you have to keep your own wits about you. But, for the most part, we have your goals, your plans, your love at heart. We wish you well.

For the most part, we have your goals, your plans, your love at heart. We wish you well.

from Robbyn and His Merrye Bande

If the feeling, advice, or information that you get from communication with any guides or teachers makes you feel mentally or physically bad, you're talking to the wrong being and *not your guide!* You may not always *like* what we say, but we will say it in as loving a way as possible. We never seek to control, save, browbeat, or force you to do anything, nor do we seek dedication from you. If any discarnate makes you feel bad, just yell, "Help! Will my real guides please stand up?" They will--with pleasure.

If the discarnates that aren't your guides persist, just tell them they're dead and they must go out into the universe to regroup (figure out their lifetime). They may not know how to contact *their* guides, especially if they've spent a whole or several lifetimes ignoring their guides in the first place. In fact, they may be as scared of you as you are of them! So, just bless them and love them for trying to help. And be careful of their advice. Just because they're in spirit form doesn't mean they aren't idiots. Stupidity was never ruled out as a growth experience, but it is rarely directly helpful to anyone other than the individual exercising it.

So you can see that loving them and clearly communicating with them may be all that it takes, because love is such a powerful tool. If they see you talking to your guides, they may try the same thing! And then what a wonderful thing you will have done, introducing them to their guides.

Communication Techniques

from Li Sung

Often, when there is poor contact between human beings and spirit beings, we get the blame. But understand that we are rather like a fisherman standing on the bank of a river, with a long pole in our hand, trying to gauge through the water how to put the pole to the fish. This is very difficult to do. It takes a lot of practice. And if the fish stays still it is easier to contact. Now most human beings in your country have not learned to still their minds. The mind wiggles, it squiggles, it goes all around. It is very hard to grab hold of. But those who have learned to still their minds, to keep them in one place, and let them radiate the radiance of the soul, make for us a much easier target. And then we may draw closer to them and communicate by merging our energies with theirs. So, to put it simply, if you keep your mind still for a time, it is easier for us to catch it.

Now there are also matters of attitude which are important. Of course, you must open to us before we can come in your door. If you have locked your door, we do not try to bang it down. If you please, when you go to bed at night, think of us with love in your heart, open your door a little bit. We will come to caress your cheek, and to sing you a little lullaby. We only have harmony in our hearts to share with you, and certainly there is no need for fear.

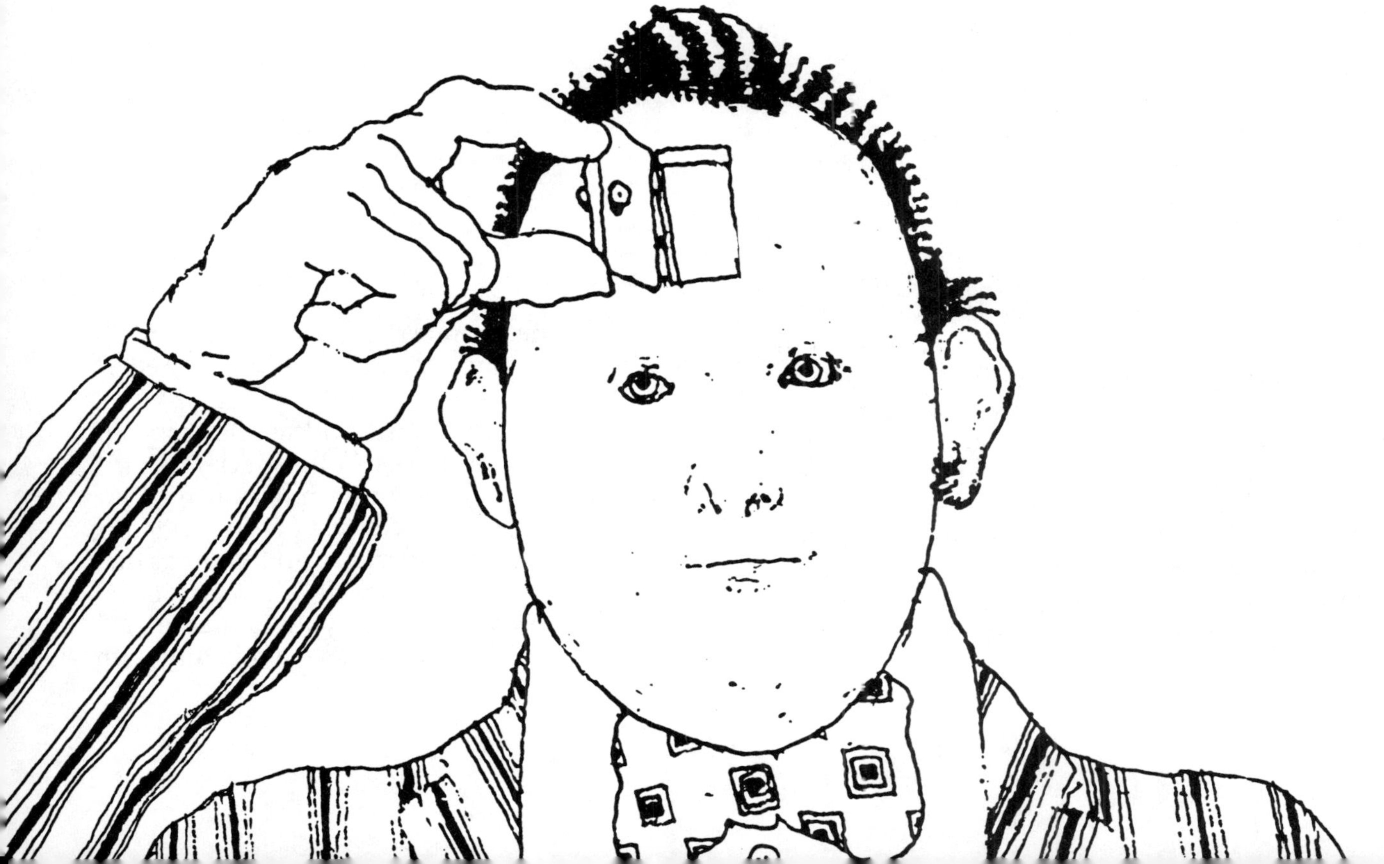

from Ting-Lao

The basic reason for a person in a body here in this world to contact one's spirit guides and teachers is to learn to live life well. We can get lofty and tell you it is to *evolve as a soul,* but that will happen if one lives life well. Helpful guides and teachers always are available to everyone.

Spiritually, to contact one's spirit guides is easy because there is already a connection. There is already the knowing. So just surrender and feel the safety of one's body, and feel the safety of the emotion of it. Feel the openness and the willingness. It is not difficult. Let me go on to give some practical exercises for contacting one's spirit guides.

First of all, you can make a little altar in your living space. An altar consists of a special cloth, a candle, and anything that reminds you of your sacred self or of your spirituality: a picture, a statue, a special rock from a power place, pretty things that you like, that make you feel special and that remind you of your powerful self and your centered self. You pick a time every day to have a meeting with your guides. It is best to pick the same time every day or every other day or once a week.

You sit and you just say, "Beloved one, be with me. Talk to me, touch me, heal me." Whatever you want to say, you can say, but have time with them. It is just like building a relationship with any person in a body. *You need to have time together.* You need to get to know each other. You need to do things together. It is important just to invite them to be with you, and you can work on your issues of fear or acceptance or whatever your individual issue may be. This is a good time to practice meditation or quieting the mind so that you can hear and receive and feel all that will be coming from your guidance.

You can begin by just feeling your breath and bringing silence inside and darkness inside. Oftentimes people cannot hear or perceive their guidance because their minds are chattering so. That is a good way to begin. And then you just invite them to be with you, and it is important to keep the appointment. And that does not mean that that is the only time that you can ask for connection. For example, if you are relaxing in a park or something, you can have extra time. But it is honorable to be prompt in your discipline of having a meeting. Every other day, at the same time, is a good way to start. Then you can change this as you progress.

from Master Adalfo

The best way to develop a relationship with spirit is just to do it! Many people want to have this relationship, but they set aside no time in their lives for it. It would be like saying that you want to have time in your life to eat, but you never set aside any time to eat. So you never take in any food. So, if you go around and lament that spirit doesn't talk to you, and you don't have any relationship with spirit, but you also make no time for that in your life, whose problem is that, spirit's or yours?

So it is necessary for people to set aside time. Especially for beginners, the more regular the better. At first it should be at the same time every day because that gets the body used to whatever the process is, whether it is prayer or simply sitting and saying that you would like to communicate with spirit and that you are open to that. And at first, to do this not only at the same time but in the same place is helpful because the whole vibration is set up then.

You don't have to sit for hours hoping spirit will talk to you. You can say, "I am going to set aside 15 minutes every day. This is the time, this is the place that I will do that." And you make yourself available to spirit at that time. Say a prayer and wait. If you don't get a message or you don't hear spirit or you don't get an answer or whatever you think you ought to be getting, that does not mean that you should believe that this doesn't work, and never do it again. Sit again the next day and the next and the next because your intent is important. Also important is your willingness to accept things that come in different ways.

Sometimes people expect the communication to be a certain way. So if it isn't, they are completely blind to what they are getting elsewhere or in some other way. So there has to be an acceptance of how this happens, how this relationship can be, how the experience can be. Let us say that you ask a question of spirit. The answer could be given to you later in the day by a person. That does not mean that you *are not communicating with spirit.* You must not limit yourself; you must be open. You might see a picture in answer to a question. You might receive a mental picture. That doesn't mean spirit isn't talking to you. What does the picture look like, what does it tell you? People need to make time for this process in their lives. They need to set their intent about what it is they wish to accomplish. And then they need to be open to having it happen in whatever way it happens.

Recognizing your guides

from Dr. Peebles

You are recognizing your spirit guides and teachers just by talking about them. They say, "Oh, he knows me, he knows we're here." Then they'll be having a little party. Now, as you get to know them more personally, they just celebrate more because they are getting all the acknowledgment that they expect.

It is you who try to give them *more* than they are really needing. Certainly they enjoy it. We enjoy

being acknowledged, but we are quite content with the acknowledgment that we get *vibrationally.*

It is you who say, "I must know their names, and I have to say them over and over again." If you were to say the name of every guiding force, you wouldn't have time to go to work. Understand? But when you say, "Thank you, guides and teachers, for being there," we all celebrate because you have acknowledged us. When you say, "I believe in you," not just when you want us, but all the time, we are so ac-

knowledged. But when you say, "Oh, I think I'm feeling miserable, I better call upon the guides and teachers," at that moment, dear friends, we are rejected. The acknowledgment that we need is the constant faith, truth, and awareness of our presence. When you say, "Oh, I'm having a problem. I'm calling on the guides and teachers," you have just rejected us for you have rejected *yourself.* It is manipulation. It is interference.

The acknowledgment we need is not for you to call us by name (though that is most enjoyable too) but that you know us, know our presence, know that we exist whether you see or feel us around you or not.

from Soli

Talk to your guides and teachers when you are walking down the street enjoying the sunshine and the flowers around you. Talk to the guides about how wonderful this is. For although they are no longer in physical form, there is memory of the delights of the physical Earth. Give them back that feeling. You are now currently in physical form. Help them remember what it is like, let them *feel* your feelings. Just talk to them. Say, "Isn't this gorgeous? Isn't this beautiful? Can't you just feel the vibration of this flower?"

And then, of course, when you need guidance, talk to them, ask them, "Hey, friends, I need some information. I need some input on this. I need to know which way to turn right now." And then *be open* to the communication when it comes. It may not come immediately. It may not be even that day, it might be the next day.

You walk into a bookstore, and you are guided to go to a shelf of books that you would never normally read. And you pull down one book idly because you've got nothing better to do. You open it at a page and a paragraph leaps out at you. It's the answer to the question that you posed. You've been guided to that book because it was the only way that the message could come through. You wouldn't listen to it if you heard it in your head because you'd think it was your own imagination. So you were guided to a certain book to read the answer.

When you recognize the response from your guides and teachers, accept it and thank them for having brought it forward for you. Be open, my friends, to communication from wherever it might come. It might come as a breeze that comes up around you on a still day. It might come in a sunset or the special scent of a flower that simply affirms within you total knowingness. Be open to communications. They can come at any time, at any place, my friends. And usually they will come when you least expect them.

When you are expecting an answer, you are so focused on trying to receive that answer that you literally squeeze tight the doorway. You cannot allow it through. For the mind tries to do all. It tries to analyze what's going on, and that prevents the communication from coming through. So allow yourself to know that once you have thought of the problem, you can simply *let it go.* Don't keep worrying about it--easier said than done, of course, we know. But, nonetheless, try to release that and know that the answer will come in its own good time.

Question: Are there spirit guides with particular specialties, and how might we contact them?

from Li Sung

Indeed, many of us have areas of specific interest. But understand, these are not the primary spirit guides of the person. They are more like secondary ones, committees, much like a faculty at college who have expert knowledge and can be called upon. There may be, for instance, one in medicine or one in law, one in mathematics, one in philosophy, one in communications, and so on, much as in your Earth life. And individuals also may wish to call upon certain guides (the Greeks called them muses) who each have a creative specialty. They can work with you to open up your own channels of inspiration and creativity. So there are many specialties here. We are like a vast reference service, but questions *must be asked* before we can become aware that we are needed.

We, Li Sung, work more as a general philosopher. We have not a great deal of specialized knowledge, so when we are asked about such things we call on a panel of experts. It's like making a telephone call, you know, to the person who will have the answer, and who can look it up in the records. So we are highly organized here, though a tad slow sometimes.

Through your own higher self you can make this request for specialized information, and certainly through your guardian spirit or guide. It is rather difficult to make the request directly, for you have to be somewhat in our realm and to be somewhat accomplished in our realm before you know how to dial the spirit telephone.

First, put in your mind the thought of coming into our dimension. Next, raise your vibration so you join more closely with us. Then visualize the face of the person you may wish to call upon. In time you may find that person is drawn to you, and is conjunct with your higher being, if you know who has the knowledge that you seek. But there may be times when you do not know who knows what. So, in such cases, it is better left to your spirit guide to go and find them.

Contacting the guides of others

from Ting-Lao

It is very useful to use contact with the guides and teachers of others to help you with others: your children, spouse, significant others, and also with the people in your daily life. This helps others live better, develop into their soul's way, and unfold their soul's purpose , expressing it in their lives.

Sometimes it is much easier to contact the teachers of others than it is to contact your own teachers because you have an emotional body that often gets in the way of your perception or your hearing of your own guides and teachers. It is good practice because it exercises this muscle of communication and clears out the channel of communication, just like being roto-rootered. It keeps the energy flow going. All you have to do to do it is to do it.

First you can ask to have contact with your beloved one's teachers or with your associates' teachers. Have your meeting at a regular time.

Working with the spirit teachers of children is very useful. You simply go in each night and sit on the child's bed when the child is asleep, and ask that their guidance come and help you with the rearing of this beloved child. And you can ask them questions or you can just invite them to be around, invite them to be active in the child's life. Ask them to be active in the family life and give you guidance as the parent. You also can talk to them about specific situations and problems.

It is much like mental telepathy. You just *believe* what you intuit inside or hear inside. This is the most important way to communicate. Ask the spirit guidance to be active in the other's life. Oftentimes, if a person is not interested in their spiritual development, they may not have invited the guide to be active in their life. So, it is all right for you to intercede on their behalf and ask the guide to come and guide them in their life.

It is good to use guidance even in mundane situations like the work place. It helps if you can have some kind of little altar in the work place, even if it is just a plant. A candle is best, but sometimes candles can bring too much attention, which is not wanted. Use anything that reminds you of the lighter side of life, remembering that work is not such a big deal.

You just invite the guides to be present in the work place. Ask them to heal relationships between people there. Ask them to help with ideas. There are many guides of ideas. There are many guides of inspiration and motivation, and just of sources of energy if things get bogged down in the work place. So you ask the guides for what you need and then just be receptive to what they may say, or be receptive to feedback from them through situations. Situations may change and new ones may arise, and this can be their communication to you. It can come in many forms. It does not necessarily come only in a verbal or telepathic form.

That wee small voice is you

from Rahma

To hear that so-called "wee small voice" is to touch a state within that provides moment-to-moment guidance in all of your daily activities. Some choose to call this subtle communication their spirit guide and then they proceed to assign a name and a personality to this guidance, thus creating an individual entity separate from themselves. Others of you peoples imagine a discarnate teacher, a wise old sage who directs them step by step in the ways of enlightened living. Be all this as it may, the truth is that, in most instances, inner guidance comes from the soul of each individual.

Know that your beingness is vast and grand indeed! This little self that feels trapped in a physical embodiment is merely experiencing boundaries of its own making. There are many aspects to this self that you know as you, and this personality who expresses in dense matter is but a small portion of that whole. This is a truth, I assure you.

Now, to further illumine the nature of your guides, consider this, if you will. In your total being are others of your physical lives, lived and expressed at once and moving out from what you think of as your present multidimensional aspects which encompass vast reaches of your own consciousness. Within this network of expressions, which is your totality, knowingness filters down to you in many ways from a larger source than you can now imagine. Know too that the events and challenges, so termed, which you draw to you for your learning often have their origin from guidance received in your dream states.

Contained within each physical structure on the Earth plane is a guidance system. It is up to each of you to dust it off to cleanse it of the eons of encrusted layers of density that have held you peoples to a belief in the bondage that you have created for yourselves.

Freedom is realized when you trust
and allow the outworking of
information and knowledge
to flow in through your guidance
system and out into your
conscious experience.

So, your spirit guides and teachers need not be an entity, as you think of one who possesses an individual identity. Working exclusively from what is termed left-brain linear thought, as you do so much of the time in your world, is to categorize, to name, to pigeonhole, to limit. Your tendency is to do this with what you think of as your inner guides. Is it not so?

They are, indeed, overlays of reality that exist as streams of consciousness throughout all of creation in your time-space world and beyond into other dimensions of being. These streams are not individual entities, but rather what you might think of as free-floating informational sources that group together to create points that intersect with your physical reality. For those who have shined up their guidance systems and who have made clarity of mind a priority in their lives, these sources of which I speak are readily available.

Now, it is true that souls do work in cooperation with one another in what you might call a chain of souls. And there are those entities such as myself, Rahma, who have dedicated themselves to maintaining a certain focus in order to assist in the transformation of mankind on the Earth plane. These souls do display a certain personality of character so that they might elicit an identification with the wisdom they desire to impart.

In truth, each one of you people are teachers to one another as well as to other forms of life of which you are not presently aware. So, the only difference between you and the nonphysical beings who are currently being channeled in your world is that they are consciously reaching out to others to share of their light while often you are not.

In a more refined understanding, there are not two beings in all of existence, but there is One Being and that is you! So do not take the word of another, but experience for yourselves the vastness of your own expansive being by tuning into and listening for the grand wisdom contained within your own souls.

To come to realize your totality and what has been termed superconsciousness, it will do you well to take the restrictions off your imaginings and to know that your own highest calling is to channel not another entity that you might create, but to consciously channel from *your own* inner knowing. That is, do not feel you have to put a name to your guidance so that others will sit up and take notice.

It is akin to the many on your plane who have taken the one known as Jesus Christ as their personal savior, when in truth one can only save oneself. That which Jesus personifies is a consciousness that none could perceive unless it were already a part of their own being. Christ was, indeed, one

of the great teachers on your plane and he continues to assist all those who will listen. His main thrust, however, is not about the worship of his Godship, but about the worship of self, which is to be found in each and every one of you.

For those who still require the so-called "crutch" of naming their guides, whether calling them Jesus or Ramtha, this is all right. Often, waking up to who you truly are necessitates steps in a process. During that process many put their power outside themselves and onto another entity. All will come to know their own Godhood and the interconnectedness of all life when they are ready.

But do know that guidance and direction for one's life has never been so easily accessible as it is now on your plane. As most of you know, your world is ready to take a grand leap into a whole new way of being. Many from inner realms are "hanging out" in your corner of the universe to witness and assist with this transformation of your planet and its peoples. With much light and goodwill in close proximity, your own unfoldment can be enhanced and your guidance reached more easily than ever before in what you think of as your history.

So, for practical application of what I have shared with you about your guidance, may I say that if any of you have not made this conscious contact with your expanded selves, then I will give you assistance now.

You are often counseled to be still and centered and then told to listen. Yet many of you dear people do not know what you are to hear or how to recognize your guidance when it does come through. To be still means to quiet the mind from all outside disturbances. This necessitates that you take time each day for a period of contemplation.

I do not use the term "meditation," which is widely practiced. Many who sit in this state waiting to hear the voice of God never hear it. This particular form of discipline, in truth, can be a trap in which certain altered forms of consciousness are achieved, but often those meditating stay locked into visions of color and light that move back upon themselves, and these people never break free into higher states of receiving.

To contemplate is to allow divine thought to move *through* your mind so that guidance and ideas may come into your conscious musing. When you try too hard to shut down the outer nagging of anxious thought patterns and you accomplish this, it is akin to throwing the baby out with the bath water, as they say. To contemplate is to allow all thought and then to know you have the choice as to where to put your focus of attention. When you judge some thoughts as acceptable and others as not so acceptable, then you shut down those centers from whence springs your guidance.

Now on this particular point I wish to elucidate. Many of you dear ones have learned to withhold judgment of your fellow beings, but still you continue to judge your own thoughts. When you do this, then divine assistance through your guidance system is inoperative, so to speak. To allow all thought to flow is a most powerful way of accessing grand reaches of knowing. This is a point to ponder for those of you who have not yet realized the moment-to-moment direction that is your true birthright.

It is important for you to know that your guidance does not come in words per se, for this is something you do in a translation from feelings, which is the manner in which all knowing is received. You see, nonverbal communication can be a feeling. So, as you sit in contemplation, take heed to listen at other levels than that which is linear. Allow your body to relax enough to feel the energy in and around you. It is within the vibrations of that which is your vital energy that divine thought resides.

One other suggestion I desire for you to ponder is that when you go out into your woods, allow yourselves to feel the flow of Mother Nature all around you. She can be the grandest teacher of all. Wondrous guidance abounds when you listen to the winds that blow across your land, when you realize there is consciousness in every rock and tree, when you truly hear with your heart the song of the birds and the rustle of the grass, when you take the time to savor the fragrance of a single rose.

Your spirit guides and teachers, then, are you, perceiving your experience from the truth of your own beings. Heed the splendid selves that you are. Do not entrap yourselves by putting a limit on what you can know, because your unfolding Godhood is, indeed, at hand.

Create Your Own Reality

One Day at a Time

"The universe is a dream in the mind of God, but it is also a dream in our own mind. It is a very real dream that plays out its drama of purposes, for you have not come into this world by chance alone. You have chosen to incarnate, to extricate your soul's journey, to discover your reasons for being, to paint on the canvas of life the vast variety of love and of attainment, of sensibilities."

from Li Sung

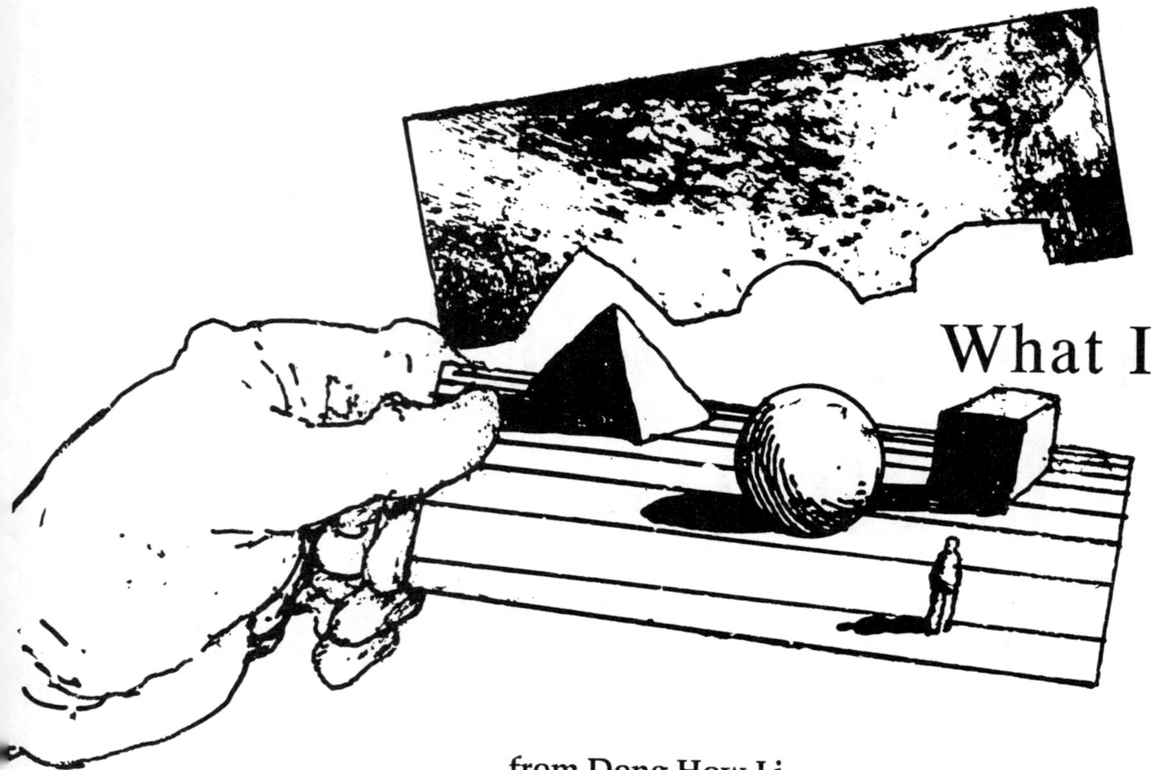

What Is Reality?

from Dong How Li

Often in your culture, reality is thought to be only that which is hard, concrete, and visible. Not so. In other cultures, it is believed that the invisible is more real. That is not so, either. They, together, form what you call *reality*. You would not say *darkness* is more real than *daytime*; so you would also not say *spirit* is more real than *form*. The two together make reality. Or if you wish, the two separately are also real. But in the act of creation (and you can only do that when you call upon your God-Self because God is creator, is initiator, originator), when you go into the act of creation, you cannot come from one place or the other. Or hadn't you noticed in your life? You can't come only from the place of the light or what you can see--you have to come from the place of the wholeness.

In magic, there is a rule called "correspondences" where when you want to make something, you gather all the correspondences together, adding power--amplifying. So if you want to make gold, you do a chant that is appropriate for raising energy; you gather all the other associations in your mind and your life that relate to gold and you use them all together in a ceremony and make gold. And that physical gold is a symbol of a gold of your own transformation.

The physical is always the outer symbol of inner reality.

But in magic, to create, you need them both. When you're going to make outer reality, you have to bring together all the parts of your being: physical, emotional, mental and intellectual, spiritual.

Sometimes people try to make their dreams come true only by working hard in the physical. It's not enough. The psyche is dissenting, so what gets created is not quite what was intended. It is important that intention be clear. Beyond that, it is important that there be consensus within the being on what is desired. So you will want to know, "How can I possibly know what I really desire or what I really want? How can I arrive at such a place of consensus?" Not by will and not by mind . . . by observing, by intending, and by desire.

So a part of the invisible act (or I should say invisible background) of creation is your belief. *Credo* in Latin means "I believe." Your word "creativity" comes from it.

I suggest to you that what you create is an expression of what you believe.

If you are creating something that you are uncomfortable with, you must then look at your beliefs. And they are not going to be in your conscious mind, they're going to be in your subconscious. So that means you'll have to be crafty about how you look at them because they will only sneak out when you don't expect them--you have buried them that well. By the same token, if you want to create something, you not only have to deal with your conscious, but with your unconscious. One way you can engage with your unconscious is by doing a ceremony. People light candles and do movements and do chanting because it reaches deeper than words often do, deeper than the conscious mind often does.

So then you have reality as a combination of many aspects, and in order to create you have to have all of those aspects at your command. Beyond command, you have to have *belief* and *desire*. For once you have desired it (which is an energy and a power in itself) and you then do an action that moves it in that direction, you can release it and allow the universe to bring to you the manifestation. Your manipulation as magicians stops there. If you manipulate any further, what is behind your manipulation (mainly your fear of not getting what you desire) then distorts your manifestation so you don't get quite what you intended. You get something that contains your fear.

What I want to tell you about creation is simply that it is within your power; it is within your *right*. You have all the tools necessary to create what you desire. What it requires to do that is a willingness on your part to look at your beliefs as well as to put energy in the direction of what you're seeking.

How You Create Reality Before Birth

from Soli

My friends, *you decide* on the parents that you will have, on the time and the place, the society, the country--in full knowledge of all probability patterns that you will be faced with throughout your life; *probabilities,* not certainties. *Probabilities,* for you always have free will and choice in every action.

You choose the probability patterns; you choose the genetic pattern of the physical body that you will inhabit. You have (in some circumstances) affected or modified that particular physical body within the womb before incarnating so that it will more closely match your needs upon the planet Earth.

And that, of course, my friends, can be to bring forward those things which society would consider so-called handicaps. No such thing, my friends. There is only experience. There is only growth. There is only evolution and there is always choice.

Every single individual who has incarnated upon this Earth plane has done so from choice. The physical variables that they inhabit are theirs by choice. The parents they have are theirs by choice and, yes, the names that they bear are also by their own choice. For you influence your parents to give you the name that will have the vibration necessary to add to your experiences upon the planet Earth.

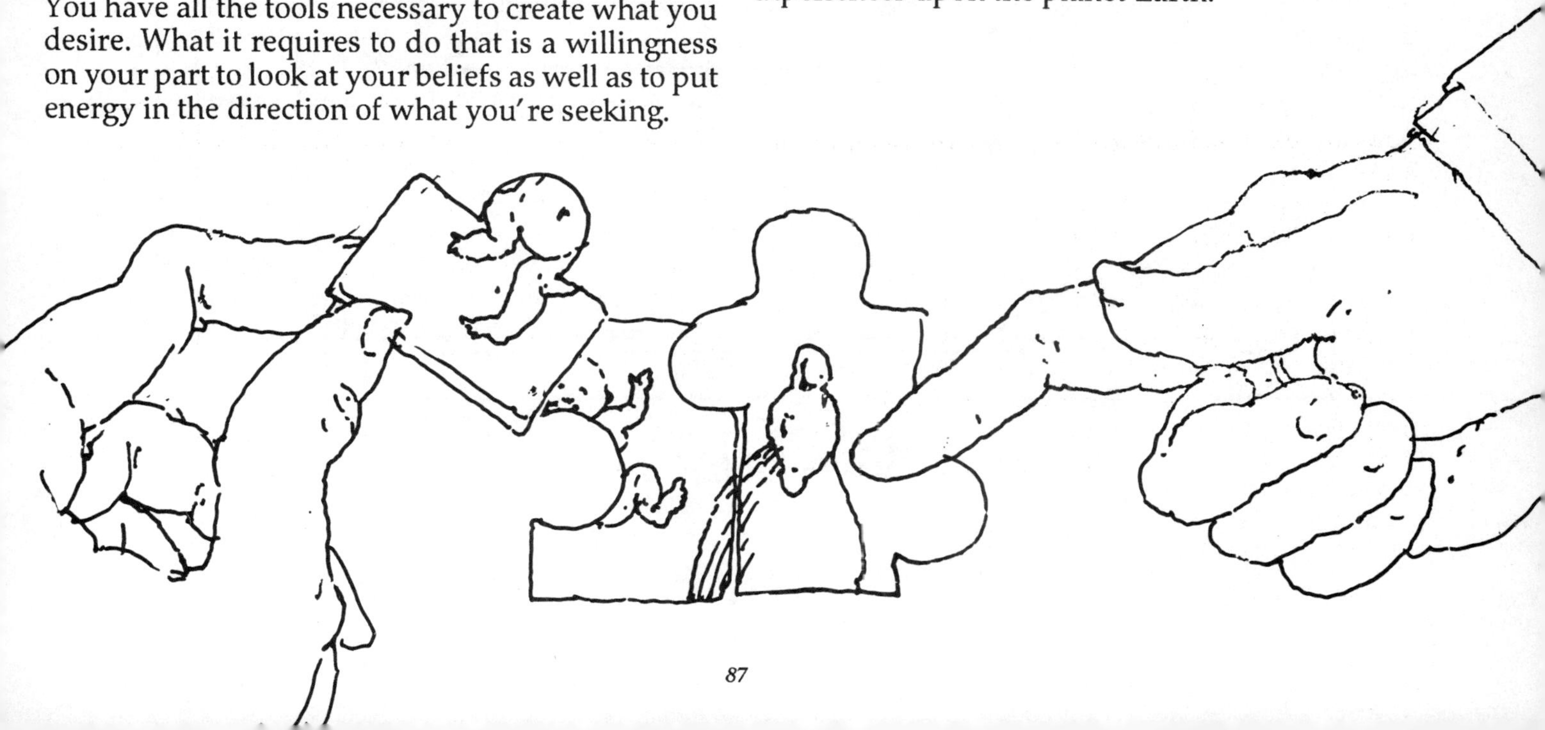

"What you create . . .

. . . is an expression of what you believe." *from Dong How Li*

And so, you incarnate within the physical body any time between conception and some time approximately two months after the physical birth. You choose the time of your incarnation just as you choose the time of your physical birth. And so, they all add up to give you the probability patterns upon the Earth plane that you need for the experiences that you require within your evolution.

You know what type of programming (of teaching) your parents will give you. You know their friends, the society they live in. You know the belief systems that you will grow up with, for those things are programmed within your subconscious mind from the moment you incarnate, even before birth (if you incarnate before birth, that is). For you bring with you a clean slate that some traditions call a "tabula rasa," which some (in more modern terms) liken to a blank recording tape.

Your memory is your recording device. When you bring the subconscious mind into your physical body, it is clear and clean. It has not been used. From the moment you incarnate, that recording device records all signals from the five senses: taste, touch, sight, smell, sound; plus others, also, from the sixth sense--all those things (that you are conscious of) that are recorded within the subconscious mind. You are conscious of them fleetingly and then you forget them, but they are stored there and they continue to act within your life for the rest of your life. You continue to be run by those programs within the subconscious.

All the belief systems (the belief systems of the society that you grew up in; the deep-seated religious beliefs that are part of that society; those things you hear your parents and their friends discussing when they do not think you are listening) become a part of your belief system even if you do not know they are there. You know they are there later in life when you start to find reactions coming forward to actions that you are making, when you begin to feel or discover that you have beliefs, that you have thought forms that you never knew you had.

Where do they come from? They came from the time you incarnated; all those childhood years when you were being indoctrinated ("brainwashed"), some would say. But of course, this has happened by your own choice, for that belief system is what you knew you would have; it is what you required. Those parents, those friends of parents, those teachers, the society was what you required yourself to have to deal with for the rest of your life.

Developing your personality

from Dr. Peebles

Remember, your personalities were born but once. *You* have been born but once and it is this, your current time. Certainly your *souls* have lived many, many times, not only on the planet Earth, not only in human bodies, but in bodies of other life forms as well, for the soul is capable of choosing bodies inanimate as well as animate, according to the needs of its direction, its experience. The soul then chooses that which will give it the opportunity to have certain experiences, certain events that will then determine the balance point for the soul, its relationship to the cycles of birth and death.

The personality is conceived when the body (the physical body) is conceived. It starts developing from the moment of conception. Influenced by the parents, influenced by the environment, influenced by all that it is exposed to, it strengthens even more after the birth process and continues growing stronger and stronger until the age of five to about eight. During that period of time, the personality takes over and determines how it is going to relate to, how it is going to respond to the experiences that come its way. It overshadows, as it were, the soul.

And the soul, having passed through the "Valley of Forgetfulness," retires deep within the innermost recesses of your brain. Certainly it will influence, certainly it will strive to communicate, most often with the superconscious mind. Most often (because of repression) it will communicate on the dream

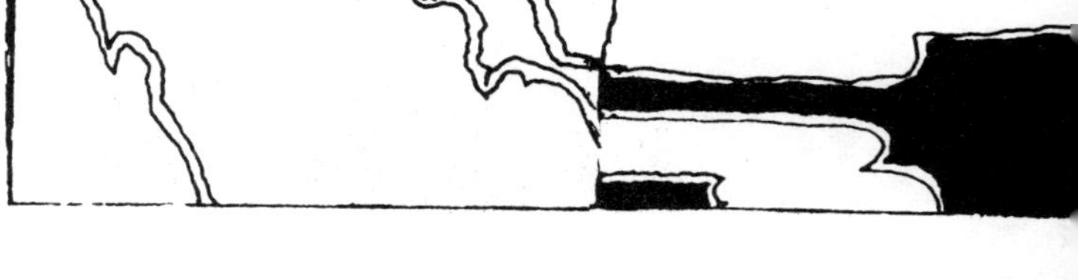

planes (the astral levels). After the age of about eight, the personality has become so intense that it determines what is going to be experienced--when and how--so that it often becomes an interference with the purpose that you came into life to have. It begins determining that *it,* and only *it,* will be the deciding factor as to what fulfillment it's going to allow in this, the current life.

Question: Are there some things about our lives which we cannot change?

from Dong How Li

Absolutely. What you can't change is what you agreed to do and agreed was real before you came into this form. Mostly what you agreed to do was not a specific act. Mostly what you agreed to do on the other side (remember the other side has less to do with form and structure; this side has to do with form and structure) was to complete a certain issue, complete a certain dynamic. When you get here, you set up how you're going to do that. You give it a form, a shape, a person, an act.

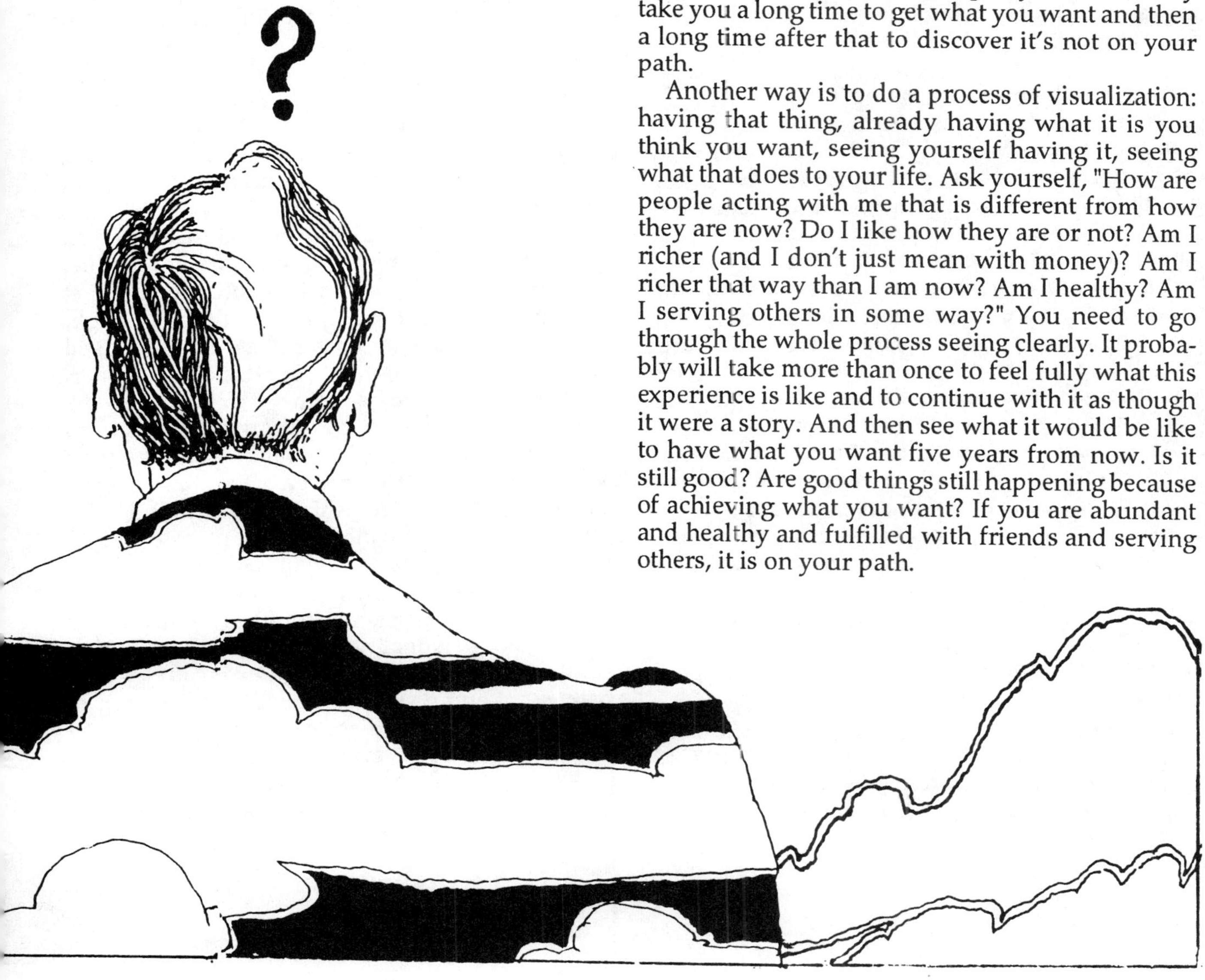

Determining what you really want from life

from Master Adalfo

There are many ways to determine what you really want in life. One way is to go ahead and get what you want and then find out if it's right. That is one way. Sometimes that is the long way because it may take you a long time to get what you want and then a long time after that to discover it's not on your path.

Another way is to do a process of visualization: having that thing, already having what it is you think you want, seeing yourself having it, seeing what that does to your life. Ask yourself, "How are people acting with me that is different from how they are now? Do I like how they are or not? Am I richer (and I don't just mean with money)? Am I richer that way than I am now? Am I healthy? Am I serving others in some way?" You need to go through the whole process seeing clearly. It probably will take more than once to feel fully what this experience is like and to continue with it as though it were a story. And then see what it would be like to have what you want five years from now. Is it still good? Are good things still happening because of achieving what you want? If you are abundant and healthy and fulfilled with friends and serving others, it is on your path.

Create your own personal myth

from Bartholomew

There is written deeply within each of you a wondrous myth that is your own. It is the story of your struggle toward consciousness. It is filled with your own personal journey, encompassing both the successes and failures, the tears and laughter, the expansions and contractions of your life. This myth does not look or sound the way your so-called human life has. It is of a totally different order of consciousness. It has very little to do with the path your physical body has walked. Your life on the physical plane, your actions, and your experiences are really only a small part of what is occurring as your life unfolds.

There are deep, vast, wondrous parts of your being participating in creation on levels of consciousness that cannot be viewed by the human eye or felt by the human hand. These vast sweeps of expansion and understanding are going on simultaneously as you move through your human experience. These other parts of your being encompass such areas as the dream world, fantasy world, intuitive world, and more. You are a multidimensional being, only one small part of which is projected into an Earth body living an Earth life. So when you enter the realm of myth, most especially your own myth, turn within and discover your own story. And as you write or speak it, this story will begin to touch you with its reality, so you will know you are bringing into your consciousness wondrous lessons that different parts of your being have already participated in. This story or myth comes not as an imagining, but as another tool to enliven your awareness.

It is easy to believe you are nothing more than a body with an assortment of emotions, thoughts, and responses, moving in a linear manner through a chaotic world where fear is on every side.

If you allow yourself to write your own myth, you can experience directly the strength and wisdom of your own teaching.

You would be calling on those parts of your own being that have access to those realms in which lie help, encouragement, warning, and also inspiration. You would *know* that the struggles of your mythological hero, heroine, or creature are *your story*. And through this process new ideas, solutions, and possibilities would be presented to you.

There is a part of you constantly creating the next events of your life. By using your own personal myth, you participate more closely in that process. For example, you might find, as you create another chapter of your myth in the morning, that later in the day reenactment of those events might appear in your life. You might find yourself acting in accordance with what you created on your page that morning. You might find yourself facing an old situation that you can now respond to in a totally new way, because your hero or heroine, being faced with a similar one, found an alternative solution you can participate in.

There is a part of you constantly creating the next events of your life.

Let us assume that at this moment each of you has some kind of unresolved difficulty in your life, and you have tried to change this situation but met with no success. For example, the difficulty might be that one of your relationships has become bogged down in repetitious patterns of attack and counterattack. No resolution has come to mind.

May I suggest that, in the quiet of the early morning or in the darkness of the night, you take your pad and pencil and begin to create a story which is not a mirror of the relationship, but with the relationship in your consciousness. Begin to write a myth about a central character, what happens to him or her, and what resolutions and victories are achieved. You can resolve conflicts by using this technique of personal myth creation, as you bring into the limitation of the old a new creativity with vaster sight and deeper understanding. Instead of going through the endless dialogue between you and others, with you trying to win and them trying not to lose, just abandon the field entirely and expand into that realm where the solution lies, and simply bring it through in the form of a myth. These stories do not have to be long. They simply provide you with the opportunity to turn to another part of your consciousness and bring through some practical information.

There is a part of the human consciousness, in its *collective* form, that is available to you. There are only so many dramas that humans can live through, and they are common to all mankind. These dilemmas have been solved countless times by countless people. The knowledge of those victories is available to you because you are a part of the Whole, with access to all the wisdom that the Whole has ever created. The following exercise is one of many techniques that can make part of mankind's wisdom available to you now, in this moment of time-space when you need it.

So, let us begin our myth creation. The suggestions are simple. Sit quietly, eyes closed, feeling the rising and falling of your breath within the body. Allow your thoughts to drain away into the ground below you. Simply sit and feel the breath rising and falling, and the rest of you in a state of quietness. Then, without thought, without planning, pick up your pen and begin with, "The hero's (or the heroine's) name was . . . ," and then fill it in. It doesn't need to be your name. Then you go on. "He awoke (she awoke) to find that he (she) was seated in . . . (a room, a valley, a castle, a car, a spaceship, on a bird, riding an elephant, whatever)." And then when he (she) opened his (her) eyes, he (she) saw before him (her) . . . " (whatever comes to your consciousness). Just move through these occurrences without thought. Some obvious things to consider including are: physical location; people present, if any; what the terrain looks like; animals; any sounds present; and, most important, what the hero or heroine is feeling. "He (she) found himself (herself) in a state of pain. The pain was because . . . " Associate yourself with the feelings he or she is experiencing and simply allow the myth to write itself.

Please do not start by saying you cannot do this exercise. Know that:

These writings are
not for publication,
they are for emancipation.

All of you speak, therefore all of you can write. Writing is nothing more than speech on paper. Travel as the hero or heroine from one event to another, spontaneously allowing all kinds of unexpected experiences, people, and manifestations to occur. This is the realm of imagination, magic and power, miraculous events, miraculous flashes of understanding, miraculous openings of mind and heart. Be willing to create a magical myth. It is through avenues like myth-making that you allow your human consciousness to remember there are always miracles, and life itself is the biggest miracle.

Play with the ideas of what you want

from Master Adalfo

Set aside some time each day to sit quietly and visualize the things which you believe you want. That will help you to get in contact with your soul's need. If, as the story unfolds, you have what you want but you are not healthy and fulfilled, then what you think you want is not meeting a soul need.

Some of you do this type of visualization, but do it on a limited basis. For example, you say, "I will see myself next month with as many clients as I can fit in a day, three days a week, all paying--and teaching every so often. Now, how is it? Ah, it is wonderful. That settles it. That is how I will do it." That is what most of you do. You do not even really visualize--you only think you visualize. You do not go in and experience yourself on Monday with six clients, visualizing the whole process: working with each client; stopping for lunch; working with the rest of the clients; seeing them pay; seeing how other healers around you are affected by that; seeing whether you are happy in the space in which you are working.

You do not really see the whole process, seeing yourself going home at night: are you too tired to prepare dinner? Do you fall into bed? Do you see yourself sick? You do not ever let yourself see all of the possibilities--you only say, "That would be nice," nodding like a great fool. "That would be nice. That is what I want. That is my soul's need."

What your soul's need might be is a long vacation somewhere. And I know, of course, that does not pay the rent, but you need to fully visualize. Play with things in your head; make it fun. It is not a great ordeal; make it fun. Create all sorts of things to see if any of them is even what you want. How do you know what you want, let alone whether it satisfies your soul's need, if you do not play with ideas of what you *think* you might want?

The action of right action

from Dr. Peebles

Inactivity is inexcusable. How'd you like that one, friends? Inactivity is inexcusable for all living beings--even the rock. You may say, "Well that's been there 25,000 years. It's never moved." That is not true. The rock is never inactive. The tree is never inactive. Inactivity, waiting without choice, is inexcusable to your consciousness.

My friends, you ask, in right action, for experience. No matter what experience comes your way, you must do something with it. If you say, "Well, all I have is the opportunity of inactivity," your personality is interfering. If there is nothing in your life--no job, no loved one, no friends, the telephone never rings--then you dial until someone talks to you. Then you go out until someone acknowledges you. If you say, "But there is no job for

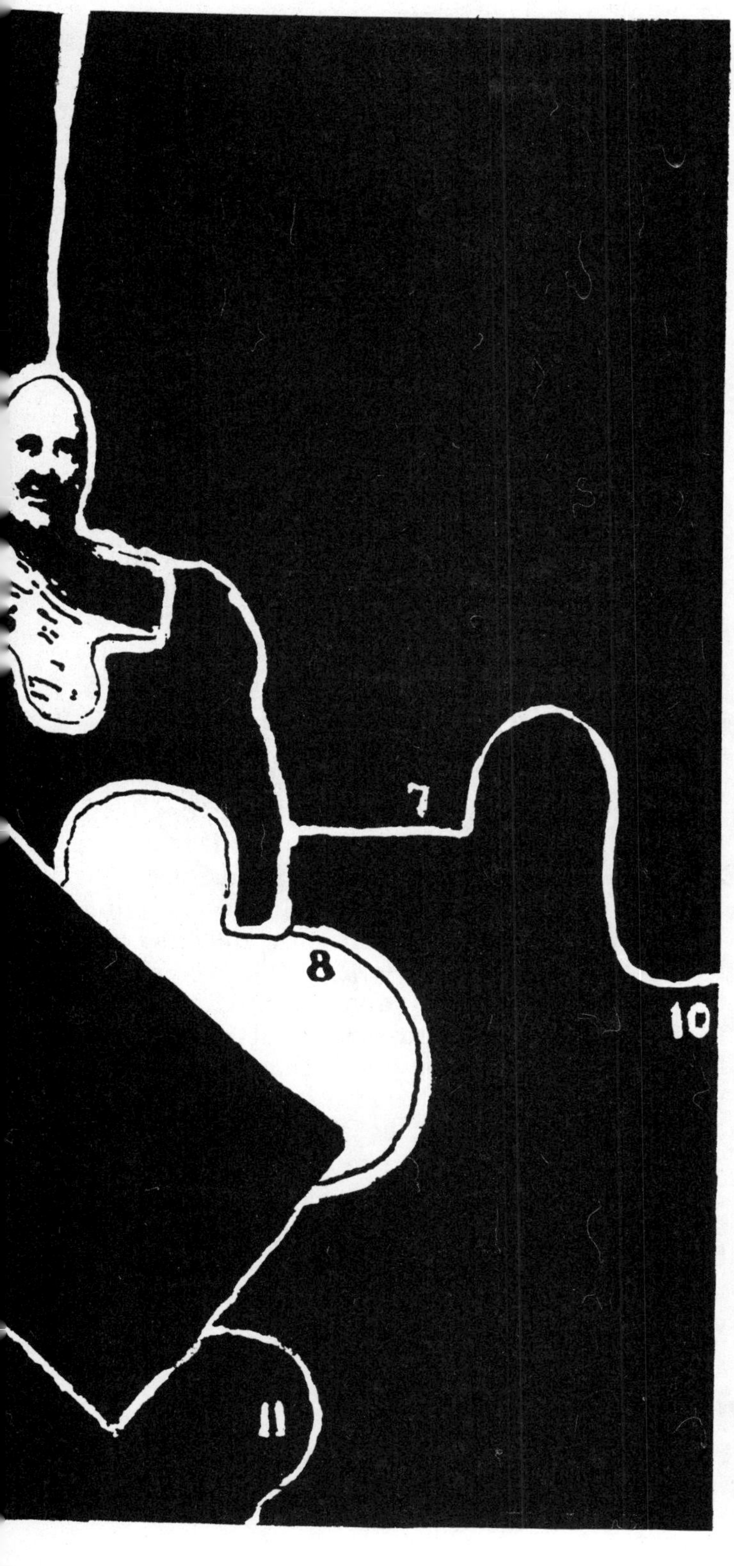

me," then knock on every single door in the city until there is a job for you. That is free will.

You say, "But I should wait for right action." No, you should *do*, so that right action is able to materialize. I am asking that you all walk hand in hand with your guides, hand and hand with God. Do not just say, "I am willing to accept abundance. I want abundance. I sent out my resume. I sent out my request." You must then go in person. God did not design telephones. God did design the strength for them to be invented (over and over again, by the way; they've been invented countless times over many generations).

You must make choices

from Kunda

Like it or not, agreement shapes your reality. For all things happen by *choice.* You are not here by accident, nor are you a victim of fate. You are here, quite simply and emphatically, because you *want* to be here. Because you are an integral extension of the cosmic soul, know that on some level you consciously chose to evolve spiritually within the physical environment as a part of your divine constitution. And before you reentered the physical realm, you made certain agreements which supported not only the continuance of your spiritual lessons here, but the advancement of other entities who are also evolving in clusters with you.

You helped to create the working blueprint which outlines your entire life program and also parallels your chosen destiny.

Now, every life, every personality, every situation and every experience is carefully chosen--right down to the details of your so-called death experience. This is true for all on the physical plane. With the exception of karmic intervention (the Divine Hand which evens the scale of cosmic justice and also assures your spiritual best-good), the life that you live is the very life that you chose. There simply are no exceptions. And the living of it all brings the necessary experiences and lessons to bear, all of which contribute to the ultimate growth and understanding of every soul-fragment.

The life you live is the life you chose.

The agreements which you made with your soul are the operating plans for the unfoldment of that blueprint. They shape the reality of your life environment. And a life in which every agreement is refused, avoided, or even broken will only serve to teach you what such avoidance brings. Regardless of whether the physical life was completed or not, that life will still remain valid to some degree, and whatever was learned will contribute to the evolution of the soul as it moves into the greater essence of its soul community.

The greatest illusion of all

from Kunda

You simply cannot *not* choose. The choice to *not choose* is still a choice in and of itself. Many people erroneously think that if they don't do anything about the circumstances in their lives, they are refraining from choosing and are not held accountable for their life situations. On the contrary, they are allowing things to happen and subsequently shaping their realities by making the choice not to do anything.

The belief that you are powerless over your destiny is the game of limitation and deception that you play with yourself throughout many lifetimes of hardship and frustration. Even though the memory of your divine purpose often escapes you, for now the important thing to remember is that, if you hold the desire to grow in greater understanding, all you need do is *agree to learn.* The cosmic wheels will immediately begin to turn in your favor, and knowledge will be forthcoming. For your life lessons are the most important. All else is secondary and comes quite naturally as a part of the evolutionary process. After all, the underlying purpose of your being here, as it is for all souls, is to learn about yourself. It is impossible not to learn on some level, for that is why you are here. Therefore, at the end of each life cycle the spirit-entity will, whether he consciously realizes this or not, come to understand the basic nature of his life experiences while incarnate on the physical plane.

Again, your life is carefully selected and organized prior to your advent into the physical body in order for you, as a part of your ongoing expansion, to strive towards greater spiritual understanding through your adventures in the physical world. You accomplish this through the application of power through principle, which manifests according to your unique thought patterns within a world of substance. You learn through your earthly experiences, which are monitored by your cosmic soul, whose only desire is to ever expand itself.

Bless each day

from Dr. Peebles

My friends, you should, each and every day, bless the opportunities of living the day as if it were a new lifetime. When each day is over and done, bless it and think of it as equal to a previous incarnation. Take each and every decision of the new day as if it is new, totally new, even when it is based on something you put into motion yesterday. Remember, every decision you have to make exists in the reality of other people, and they have changed just since yesterday. You have altered just since yesterday. No matter what was perfect and right in your appearances yesterday, you must now reevaluate. Your decisions must be based not on what they should have been yesterday, not on what they might become tomorrow, but on what is best for the moment. For whatever decision you make now will change by tomorrow.

There is no greater illusion in the world than to believe you are not responsible for yourself.

If you are then to embrace your oversoul totally, make your decisions according to living in the current moment, the current time, and the current space. And allow a feeling of completeness at the end of each day. You will find greater peace tomorrow, greater ability; you will find an objectivity that you all claim you're working toward. You will find a clearer understanding of unconditional love. And might I say to those reading these words:

Unconditional love is another term that is terribly misunderstood in your current era and is worthy of as much research as the concept of creating individual reality.

Unconditional love will only manifest, my friends, when you live in the current moment with your husbands, your wives, your co-workers, your projects. Love them not according to what might be, what could have been. Love them not according to what era they started in nor what era they will complete themselves in.

The journal of awakening

from Dr. Peebles

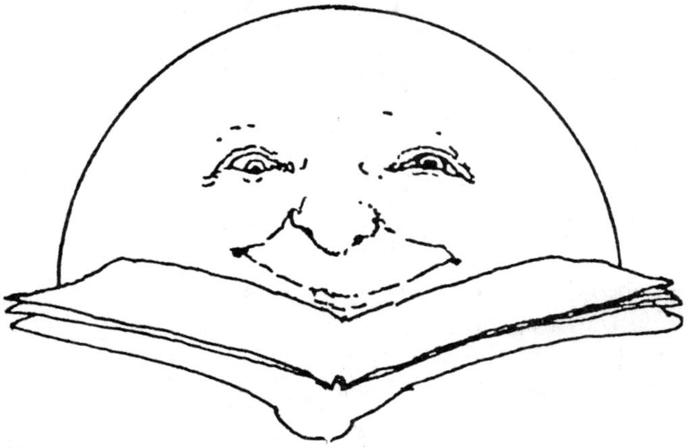

I suggest you keep a journal every day, a journal of awareness. The journal should include notes of how you feel physically and mentally when you awaken every morning: notes of your dreams and astral projections. You might say, "Well, I do not dream." But you do have bodily responses when you awaken. They are often stimulated by your dreams. So write down your reactions: the dry throat, the pressure behind the eyes. Write down the stiffness in your muscles.

Along with the journal of awakening, of meditations, include your sudden awarenesses of the day. I am not saying you must carry your journal with you, but certainly carry pieces of paper. Many of you do that already. You fill up your pockets, your purses, with paper and then you never do anything with it. Take the papers at the end of each day and say, "Oh, I remember, this is the note of the cloud I saw when I was stopped at the traffic light. Oh, here's a note of that interesting man I saw washing the windows of the 37th floor. Many saw, but did not perceive him."

Become the Master of Your Life

from Bartholomew

Often I am asked, "If life is a learning process, why does it have to be so painful?" There is a very poignant point to this question. If it is true that you came to this Earth plane to learn, then why does it appear to be so difficult? If it is supposed to be a life of moving spontaneity, wonder, and beauty, then why does it so often appear other than that?

In the end, my friends, we have to come to one basic reality. There come moments in your life when you realize that you have only one thing, and that is yourself. All of the props that you use during a lifetime to make yourself feel at ease in the world will eventually fail. If you have been in relationships with others who have fed meaning into your life, someday you will awaken and find yourself alone. If you have children, they grow up; if you have an important position in life, you retire or it is taken from you; if you have beauty, you become old; if you are powerful, you become weak and perhaps infirm.

Many come to me and say, "I want, more than anything, to know God." And what they want to know is how they can get rid of all the things that they *know* God does not love about them. They want to know how to get rid of "negative" emotions such as anger or jealousy. But how do you get rid of something that is a part of you?

The first way usually attempted is to withdraw from all the situations and people that can cause anger and never enter into relationships which can cause jealousy. And since those emotions make you feel less than you want to be, you constrict your life to rid yourself of them. In extreme cases, constriction leads to "renunciation," and whether you sit in a cave or your house, the desire is to cut off all stimulation that might provoke those reactions you are trying not to feel. But there comes a day when you leave the house or come down off the mountain and go to your neighborhood store. Someone pushes into the line in front of you and your peaceful interior explodes into anger.

When you finally realize that renunciation is not working, the next attempt is to *will* yourself not to be angry. Then your face becomes a mask. A smile is fixed there and the jaw is rigid. You have to keep

smiling, because if you start to relax you might cry, you might scream, or you might do something else "inappropriate." You try, by your will, to override the emotions that are moving through you. And this works for a while, until one day an unsettling event occurs, and before your jaw can clench you respond with the same feelings and the same fears that you are trying to overcome. Therefore, what have you accomplished?

Concurrent with *all* these maneuvers, you are playing the wonderful game of manipulation. You manipulate the people in your universe so they will not bother you, for if they are behaving, you will not have to misbehave. If your lover is very clear about not making you jealous, you will not feel jealousy; if you pick a boss who never gets angry, you don't have to deal with anger. So, you manipulate your environment. You leave behind the things that are too hard for you to deal with, because you don't want to face that part of yourself. You move from one relationship to another trying to find someone who will be a passive mirror for you, so that you do not have to see those "negative" aspects of yourself.

But in the end, it all fails. You are left, one day, sitting with the understanding that you cannot, on your own, rid yourself of the little "demons" that run around in you. And so comes another brilliant idea--you'll let God do it! You can't do it, so you will let God do it for you. Now, you have to find Him first and then ask Him to take all these unpleasantnesses away for you. Haven't you all tried asking Him to do this at one time or other? Has anything changed? So now comes the wonderful game of *spiritual awakening,* and you begin a long process toward *enlightenment.* You go to the teacher and read all the *right* books, do all the *right* things, chant all the *right* mantras, are very intense, and are *so* good. And at the end of this process you hope to find God and you hope to be free from your negative side.

Please remember that *you are who you are,* the end product of billions of experiences. So you begin by acknowledging that. When you have made this statement deep within your being, and are presented with a feeling of jealousy, for example, you can look around and see again that you are trapped. You are trapped because you cannot get away from the feeling of jealousy. You are not going to get away because *you don't have to.*

Your life has been based on the supposition that there is something wrong with you that you've got to fix. I would like to suggest that there is nothing wrong with you, and you certainly don't need to be fixed. Your inner tension comes from *not loving* certain parts of yourself. And you don't love them because you have been told not to by people who are ignoring those parts of themselves that they do not love. Your freedom comes from going within and saying with all the power of your being, "I love myself in the midst of jealousy. I love myself in the act of anger. I love myself when I feel self-pity." Whatever it may be, in the midst of that feeling, in the midst of that thought, in the midst of that action, your freedom lies in saying, "I love myself in this moment, just as it is."

Your inner tension comes from not loving certain parts of yourself.

You came to the Earth plane to experience the full range of emotions and to become master of those emotions. Mastery comes by realizing that you can *choose* your responses, which thoughts you pull in and what actions you bring about in your life. Most of the thoughts that you pull in are based on the belief that there is something wrong with you, that you are not lovable, and that you have to do something in order to be loved.

I can see the fear, in some of your minds, that if you love that part of yourself, you will be stuck with it for the rest of your life. I would like at this point to give you a cosmological view of what really happens in and around you, and how these emotions arise and why acceptance is your way out.

The reality is this. Thoughts are in motion around you at all times. Between you and these thoughts, there is something you call your "aura." Because of your individual tendencies, you choose certain thoughts as they go by, and draw them to you. You tend to pull in the same ones all the time, so you go down the same roads over and over again. Thoughts of unworthiness, of fear, of depression; depreciating, negative thoughts, again and again.

When the thought comes in, it translates itself inside your physical body as a feeling. The feeling comes into you and records itself inside what you would call your soul. At that moment, a future action is formed. Do you understand the process? The thought is out there. It comes through your auric field. It hits you. It's recorded as a feeling. Out of that feeling within yourself, you formulate a future action. For example, a thought goes by: "That person doesn't like me." Anger is the feeling, and the future action is revenge.

I would like to reverse that process by asking you to begin a serious, ongoing commitment to the repetition of a mantra that has never occurred to you: *"I love myself!"* In an instant you can thereby go from despondency to happiness. Try it. Think of a happy thought and you will be blissful. Think of a depressing thought and you will move to unhappiness. And here you are, just sitting in a chair! Has anything happened to you? Has anybody hit you? Has anybody loved you? No! You're simply sitting, and you find that you have the capacity to move from "high" to "low." And all you do is change your thought. You already know how to do this and you do it all the time.

If it is true that you can sit quietly and change your mood in a moment, then perhaps it is also true that you can sit quietly and say with understanding, "I love myself," and begin to feel something happen inside your being. You will begin to feel a warmth. It is true that there is a flame, a fire, within. There is a chakra that lights up through love. It is all true. By rising in that feeling of love for yourself, you begin to generate a warmth. I would ask you to try, for the next month, to give yourself some time every day to simply sit and feel this.

And what happens when a so-called "negative" emotion arises? You are sitting there feeling warmth, feeling power, feeling wonderful, and the telephone rings. You pick it up and someone says, "You are a jerk." Now a feeling enters that was not there a moment ago. The process is in motion, the thought goes by, you pull it in, and you feel it. Maybe it feels like a large, heavy, sharp rock. So you want to get rid of it. Your mind then starts the process of negating whatever statement came through, but in the end it doesn't work. You've tried it before, and it hasn't helped.

What will work is this. The moment you sense that painful feeling within you, say to yourself, "I love this feeling. I welcome it. It doesn't have to go anywhere or change. It is a part of me. I accept this feeling." And the warmth which is always there moves over to this sharp rock and begins to smooth it, surround it, and make it porous. So out of the power of your love for this rock, it takes on the power of your love. It becomes filled with your love! Love pours through this "un-lovely" feeling-mass, surrounds it, uplifts it, and it becomes "lovely."

You find you are capable of holding two things: *your love and that agony.* Your love is so vast that there is nothing that it will not hold, and using that vastness is what you've got to learn. No grief is so great that you cannot hold it within you and also hold the vast power of love at the same time. You do not have to choose. You can have all the grief, you can have all the illness, you can have all the sorrow, all the regrets, all the guilt, and there is no need to worry because the love in your heart is so vast it will hold anything.

Emotions are your children.
All they want is your love.

You have created them, and then you treat them like bastards. But you created them! When you warm these emotions through your love of them, through your acceptance of them, then the words "transmutation" and "transformation" become real. Once you decide that you are so vast that you can hold anything, you will be fearless--fearless because you have learned there is nothing that can come to you from this world that you cannot hold. There is no grief so great, no event so horrible that you cannot hold it in you, smooth it, warm it, open to it, and love it. Those of you who have had traumatic beginnings, don't run. Love them. Don't try to love the people. Love the feelings.

Organized religion (or even disorganized religion) would have you say that your job is to love your neighbor, but there's a little line that comes after that--*as yourself.* There is not one of you reading these words who is not basically an entity who wants very much to love. And so when you're presented with the dilemma of having been hurt by someone and you want to love them but cannot because of the ache, you go through a lot of "trying to love." And that is honorable.

The problem is that it doesn't work. And the reason it does not work is because you are asking yourself to do the hardest thing, which is to give something to someone that you want for yourself. *You* want love. And you are asking yourself to give it to someone whom your feelings tell you doesn't love you. I would like to suggest another position. Love yourself for not loving them. *Love yourself for not even liking them!*

I'm not talking about a mental process, I am talking about an experiential *feeling,* and there is not one of you that cannot feel that warmth in the heart that I am talking about, if you would give yourself the chance. When you start to love yourself for *not* loving, or even for disliking someone, this wonderful alchemy begins, and the entire situation takes on a warmth, and you are no longer in a position of feeling bad because you can't love.

When you finally understand that *you can generate* that which you have been desperately looking for outside of yourself, you become the master of your life. You have been looking for love, security, and peace outside yourself, and the minute you find it inside yourself, you are the master. Not in the arrogant sense, but with a sense of wonder. Then you are in a position to love somebody else, and not before. Because until *that* moment, you are all asking each other for something, no matter how subtle you make it. And if they won't give it to you, then you' re hurt, you' re sad, you' re lost, you' re unloved, you' re despondent.

When mastery comes into your being, and you know that you love yourself, it isn't an *act* of love, it is love in motion. And you feel it, no matter who is before you, because then the love is not personalized. The dog goes by, the child goes by, the neighbor goes by, the enemy goes by, and *it is all the same.*

It is frightening to think of loving the enemy as much as your own child, but when you become love in motion--*you are free!* When you have done for yourself what you have begged, pleaded, bartered, and manipulated the world to do for you, the game is over. No game remains because now you are love in action, and everything you do comes from that state of abundance. It does not mean that you don't want to be with people, but it does mean you do not *need* to be with people. There is the difference. Out of the centered wonder of your own being you can be with others in a totally committed way. Not out of need--out of joy! Out of choice, not desperation.

As you sit with yourself and begin to say, "I love myself," there is going to arise a *long list* of things that you have judged as unlovable about yourself. "I would love myself if I wasn't a drug addict, or if I wasn't jealous, or if I didn't have a bad temper, or if I wasn't so fat, or so skinny." You have a long list that you may not even have thought about, and I suggest that you physically write out your list. Get it out there and then, no matter how long it takes, reverse it. "I love myself *while* being a drug addict." I am talking about the willingness to love all the "bastard" parts of yourself which you have not allowed yourself to love before. Many of you think you were "conceived in sin," and that from the very beginning there has been something wrong with you that you've got to figure out before you die. There is nothing wrong with you. What's "wrong" are your thoughts, and that's all that has *ever* been wrong. You will *never be free of these "children,"* and who wants to be? You do not want them living in your house when they' re 45; you want them to be free, creative, dynamic, alive, and going about their business. But you don't want to be free of them. And these emotions are your "children." They make up the wonderful substance of you, of your creations, of who you are, of who you have been--they are a part of you!

Religion would tell you that there are sins in the world that have to be overcome; but it is my experience that when you love your "children" (emotions), you love *all* those parts of yourself that have been labeled sinful, that keep showing themselves year after year. You are going to be at this process until you die. And why not? Every day something new is born. You are a creative, dynamic, exploding wonder and you are going to change every day. Parts of your being are going to come forward daily and every new experience will show you a new face. You are going to find out things about yourself that you never dreamt possible. Some fears, some courageous powers, some humor, some laughter, some tears, some anger--it's all there in a beautiful, ever-changing pattern, and that is the wonder of it!

If you will stop trying to freeze the pattern
into a perfect form, then you can
enjoy the movement of the parts.

You are trying to freeze yourself into a "perfect form" based on an unreal idea of who Jesus Christ was, or who Buddha was, or who you think God wants you to be. You have even tried to freeze God into some form, and I tell you that He is smarter than that, and means to be ever moving, ever changing, ever evolving, ever extending, ever wondrously different. Otherwise, why bother? Do you really think God wants to sit around bored with Himself *ad infinitum*? What kind of a God would create all this, to have it always the same? This power that spawned you in the beginning was brilliant! You didn't create yourself, but you are a part of it.

Because you have believed that unless you are perfect you cannot have God's love in you, you believe you are not capable of love. That is a lie! Some of your parents have even said, "If you have sexual relations before you are married, God will not love you." And you believed it, but not well enough not to do it, just well enough to feel guilty about it. Your nature is such that it wants to experience, and parents want you *not* to experience! So you are in a paradoxical position from the beginning. The drama is set from the moment life begins, and the basic difficulty is in your believing that lie. I have told you that you did not create yourselves, but that out of the Source of all things, you came; and just as every child is a part of the parent, so are you a part of the Source, and there's no way to escape it. That Source is within you! When you say "I love myself" you can feel a response, because within your physical body there is an essence, a power, a substance, a light, that is there waiting to be kindled. Meditation, for many of you, has not kindled it because you have not loved yourselves.

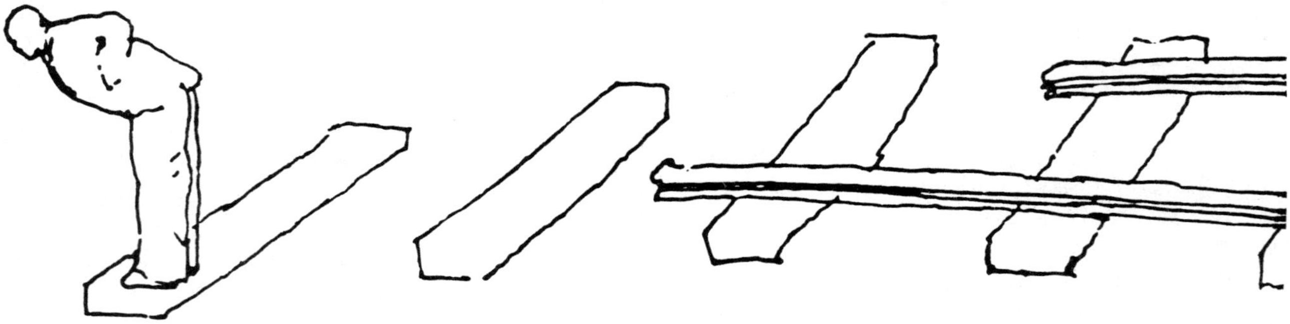

Each time you say "I love myself" and are willing to feel that love, you are turning up the power, fanning the flame, letting the light in. You do not have to go out and find the "substance" of love, because it is inside you. By turning your attention toward self-love, you ignite the *power* of your love. There is no more love in any one of you than there is in another; there is no less love. There is no difference.

Let's talk about this in terms of something simple like soup. You all have a bowl of soup in you. In the Christ's or the Buddha's case, it is an ignited, powerful ambrosia. It has a wonderful aroma, and They can feel it because it is on fire and warms them, and it motivates their lives and gives them a strong sense of aliveness. So, *your* problem is that you have cold soup! And that is not a very large problem. Once you understand that your job is simply to turn up the fire, you will be your own Master--because you know exactly how to turn up your own fire. *You* know the things that make your life alive. *You* know the things that make your life feel worthwhile, the things that make you want to get up in the morning and go about your business. And you also know the things that make you want to stay in bed and pull the covers over your head.

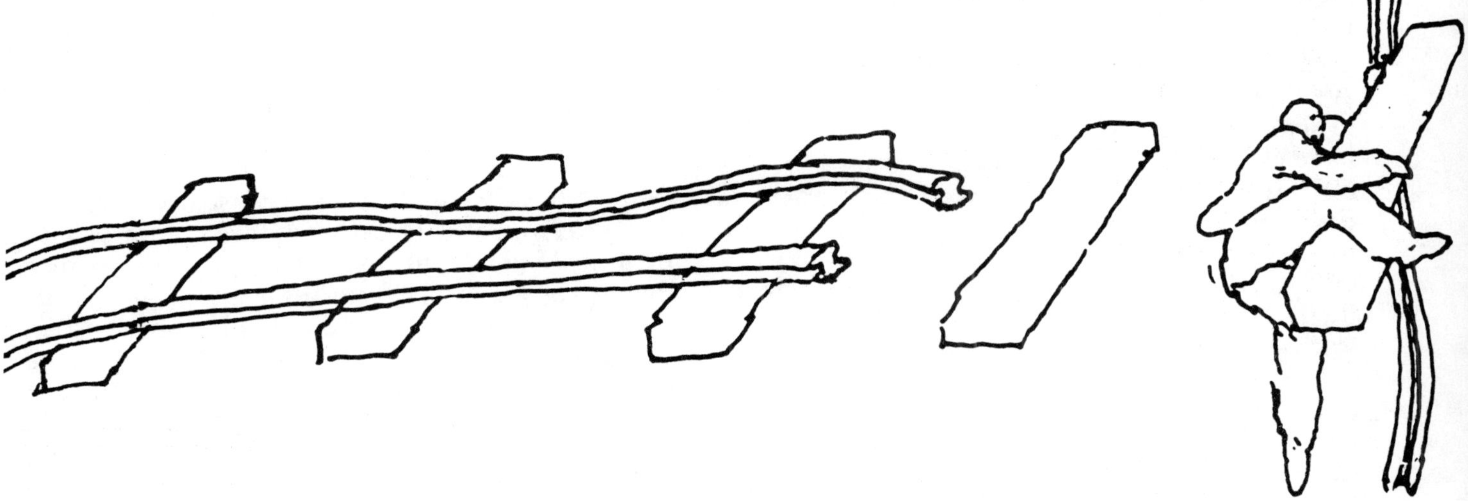

So, for God's sake, and I mean that literally, do the things that you want to do--things that ignite your life, give you power and a feeling of inner warmth. And stop doing the things that deaden you! The power within you that moves at your command to love and embrace your "children" within you is the love of God. Do not forget, you are That. You have always been That; you have never been anything other than a part of God, ever! And that divinity, that everlasting divinity is always there, moving at your command.

You have never been anything other than a part of God, ever!

And when you will your divinity to embrace your agony and your fear, it does. And it will hold them in an embrace of total acceptance, and in that embrace you will not be agonized any more. Do you think Christ never cried? Do you think Buddha never ached? You are not going to be less human; you are going to be wholly human. Because in your wholeness you will know that those emotions are you, but they are not all of you. In the amazing otherness of you, as mother and father to those children, you embrace them, hold them, and love them, and in that love you are one with them. You become one with yourself through your love of yourself and all of the parts of you. There is no other way home, because you *are* home, and the wholeness of you is waiting. You are all of it, so please stop trying to be less.

Laying tracks

from Enid

Think about life as sort of laying tracks in front of you. Just before you step, you put a track out there for yourself to walk on; you continue to put it there. Now once in a while, during our lives, we say, "It's hard putting out my tracks. I'm tired of planning for my life and working on it." So you just sort of take a chance--then you take the chance of falling through the cracks, and the cracks can be really deep, really deep and narrow, and you find yourself looking up and you only see a little piece of the sky, you don't really see what else is up there. So you can stay down in these cracks for a long time. For that reason, it's good to lay your tracks.

It's not good to walk in someone else's tracks, and this happens with husband and wife and mother and child a lot where tracks are laid and you're expected to walk on them because they're laid for you. Well now, you can do that sometimes if what you're both doing is concurrent or parallel to one another. It's fine to do that but there comes a time when the tracks begin to war with each another, so it's good, even though you're agreeing, to say, "We're going to share these tracks, but over here we're going to have other little tracks for the other foot," so you can walk with one foot on the common track and have other interests. That brings fresh experience onto your common track.

If you have an idea that you have to put every little thing that's going to happen out there on your tracks, you're going to stultify yourself. Part of the enjoyment of this universe is enjoying the surprise. You'll learn to enjoy surprise. "My goodness, it's so wonderful. Never believed it would snow this late in the year--how lovely." But if you'd planned that to happen, you'd say, "Oh well, here it comes. I had it all planned, so I'll sit here and wait 'til it's all over." You need to lay just enough tracks so that when these extra things come around, they're fun for you. They excite you, they put new fabric and texture into your thinking and into your life.

Living in the now

from Enid

Being willing to experience *now* is living in the *now*. You can look at *now, then,* and way out into the *future* all at the same time. You have great scope as a being. So if you've laid your tracks and you say, "This is what I want to have: I want this general thing to happen for me and I want somebody out there waiting to be my partner too," you can put that out there too. And you can put it close to you as soon as you want it to happen. If you want it to happen right now--this minute--you put it right there inside.

So as you walk along the tracks, you don't continue to put those things out the same distance as you walk on your tracks--you're literally bringing them to you. You bring things to you that you want. You're not having to do a thing; you're just floating through life and you're bringing life to you. You're not having to go out for it; you just bring it to you. And that makes your power grow more and more, and it makes you more in charge of what's happening instead of saying, "I've gotta run to keep up; I gotta run to keep my tracks put out there."

If you are wondering what to do with your attention, remember that you've got a lot of attention and you don't have to put all of it anywhere. There's no reason why you have to put all of your attention on *now*. "I'm going to put all of my attention on *now.*" You see how boring that is? Because if you're putting all of your attention on *now*, then nothing's happening. *Now* is constantly disappearing because there's not a motion in *now*. It's *now . . . now . . . now.* So if you're just putting your attention on *now*, then you're trying to stop *now*, so the attention is on the motion of *now* and *then*. Coming to me: the *now* is coming to me. This doesn't mean that you have to pay a lot of attention and worry about your future.

You can live life from any kind of viewpoint you want. First of all, the big viewpoint that you want to look at is: just how do you want to live your life? Do you want to live your life from the edge and just take chances? There are many people who do exactly that--mountain climbers, race car drivers, and hoboes--they never know what's going to happen next. They're living in the *now*, but they're also living in the *future*, winning that game they're playing. There's nobody that can live totally in what you call the *now* and have any success or feeling of accomplishment.

The rhythm of life

from Kyros

Life itself is a vibration which moves like waves upon a great sea. Each individual's life is similar to a smaller sea. You know that there can be no valleys without mountain peaks and there can be no golden-peaked waves without something beneath them. It is possible, with increased awareness, to jump from peak to peak and to be in rhythm with the waves in such a way that you are always upon the crest. Let me share with you some positive thoughts which will help you to live your life experience more fully and joyfully:

1) *Begin with love.* Love is light and thus cannot enter valleys or be under the darkness of a wave. It shines on peaks and crests. If you feel darkness in your life, analyze your own vibrations of love. You will discover that you entered this state because of some lack of loving in your own being. Be reassured though that you would not know darkness unless there was light somewhere and, therefore, it still exists. Do all things with love. Love trusts and it believes and it has a knowledge from whence it came. It crowns the crests of the waves and sparkles on the mountain peaks. Love restores balance to your life and renews all things. Love is blind to all things which are negative and dark and yet has perfect vision of the love contained within Creation. It becomes a mirror image of itself. It penetrates through the waves of illusions and the valleys of physical manifestations. It sees the Creator because it is the Creator.

2) *See things for what they are and render unto them only the importance that they deserve.* You have been magnifying situations and are creating thoughts which, when given enough power, can manifest into form and self-created action. Take life as it comes to you without being unduly concerned or without attempting to image the future. Do what you are able to do within a given experience, with love and trust. Be patient and allow life to flow according to Universal Will, rather than trying to direct it according to your will. Trust that the Central Intelligence will work for the ultimate good. Patience is the key to physical life, for if you will wait upon the Cosmic Will, all is to your benefit. Align yourself with the Universal Mind and you will be ever directed in right decision-making within your life. When you make an error in judgment, again be patient and allow the Source to correct the error, for it shall be done. Always the cosmos is striving to create perfect balance and rightness within Creation.

3) *Accept your life and experience and know that you are where you must be to learn and that when it is time to move in a new direction, you will be led to do so.* But, let the spirit lead, for the ego may lead you from the path. Even if you leave your path at the ego's urging, be patient, for the spirit will come and guide you back. Do not envy or begrudge the lives of others or think that their lives are better, for they are where they must be for their learning. Be patient with yourself and with others and wait upon the will of your Creator, knowing that He will act always to your benefit and highest good.

4) *Become one with creation and flow with its rhythm.* See no beginnings and no endings, but rather an eternal flow from dimension to dimension toward oneness and perfection. And lovingly accept the changes as you move through your space-time dimension, and do not allow the changes to become obstacles to your growth, and do not perceive in them the darkness of valleys and undertows. Do not resist, for you will suffer and drown in your own self-created waves. Take your life one moment at a time, shower each moment with vibrations of love, and flow in cosmic rhythm.

5) *Do not worry or fear, for these negative vibrations produced by the ego create negative thoughts and, when powerful enough, create negative illusions and negative manifestations.* Follow your inner guidance with regard to experience. Be concerned if necessary, but not worried. Use caution if inner guidance dictates, but do not fear. Worry and fear create negative manifested illusions and dream forms.

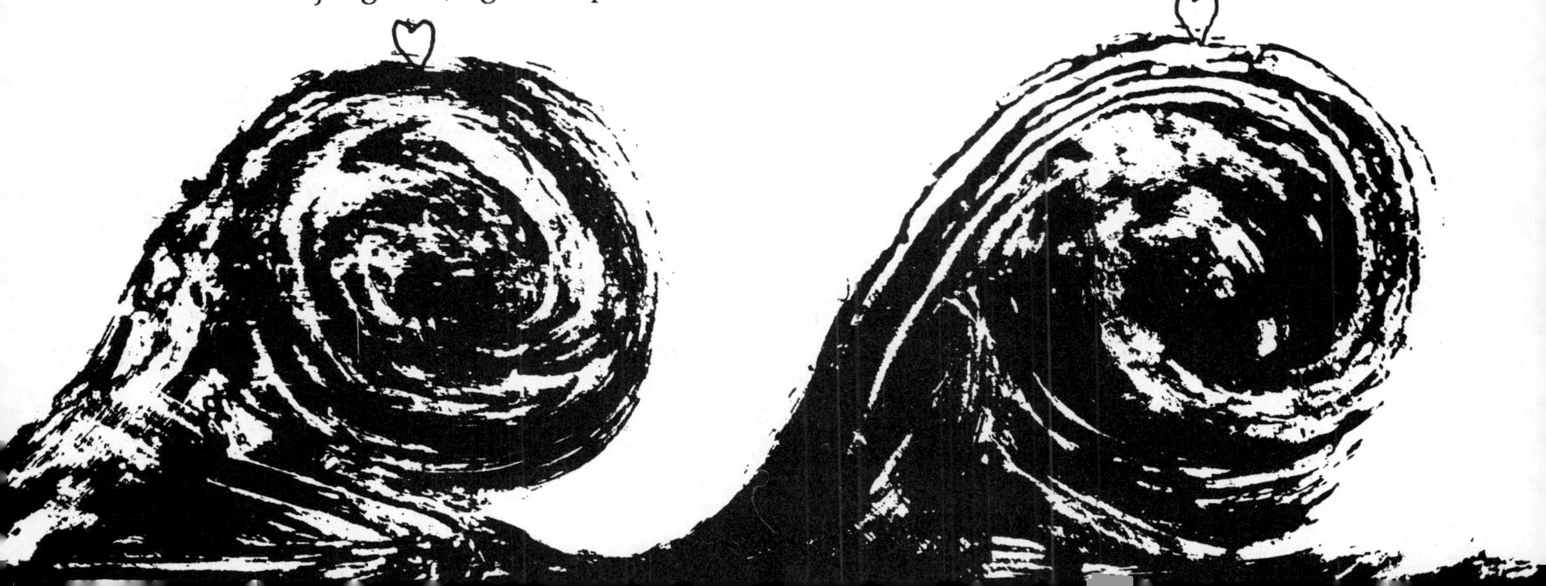

Remember that you have been given all the equipment necessary to ride the waves and stay upon the peaks. You have intelligence; you have seven levels of consciousness to direct you. You have the direct connection to Universal Mind and thus to Universal Wisdom; you have many entities assisting you; and you have the qualities to call upon to keep you in the light and above the darkness. But it is for naught unless you surrender to spiritual control so that you will flow and become one with the rhythm of your own life experience and thus one with the rhythm of Creation. Helpful affirmations include:

I will do all things with love.

I will see love in all things.

I will accept what is and where I am as a garden of my learning and my growth.

I will trust in divine Will and be patient, knowing that all things will be for my own good.

I will not worry or fear and will not give negative thoughts power.

I will become one with Creation and flow in the rhythm of eternal change, knowing it is for my growth and good.

I will see things as they are and will give them no more importance than divine Will dictates they should have.

I will surrender the negative aspects of my ego and will render control of my being to my spirit.

When affirmations don't work

from Ting-Lao

There is a great movement to use affirmations and visualization to create one's own reality. It is good to use affirmations to create one's own reality. And it does work, especially when it is empowered by the person's emotional energy of truly knowing that this is right.

Oftentimes, a person is putting out energy and wanting and wanting and praying and affirming for something or some growth or passage, but then forgets to surrender. When you are constantly putting out, the flow cannot come in.

I want to remind people to surrender. Say, "This is what I need, dear universe, and I thank you for it and know that it will come in its universally just time and space." The universe does not need reminding.

Now sometimes people do many processes that are known to create their own reality and nothing happens. They are still in pain in their body or lonely or in pain emotionally; things are not how they want them to be in a relationship, or materially they still have many challenges and cannot add pleasure to their lives. Oftentimes they are getting older and older and getting disillusioned and getting very disappointed and becoming bitter and angry and disappointed in the Gods. It has often been said that *faithing* is vital to life--to be able to surrender and trust and have faith that the universe is just, even though many times it does not seem to be.

A person must *judge* many times when to surrender and when to take action: that is a great lesson of life.

How Former Realities Affect Your Current One

from Li Sung

There is the concept that the past can be changed by your mind, by your consciousness. Strictly speaking, this is not so. However, there is a possibility that your mind can react differently to the past and experience it at a different emotional level, so that there is an impression of the past having shifted. When you engage in your reveries and memories of bygone days, of childhood, perhaps of sitting on the lap of grandfather or a stroll through the countryside, watching the fish jump from the brook, the sun shines brightly in your eyes as you recall the experience of a 10-year-old. Yet, we--in our dimensions--might have looked upon that scene and experienced it differently. We were witnessing what *we* thought was reality, but you might experience a different sort of reality. It may have been an emotional peak experience for you, but for us, as onlookers, it was merely a lad walking by the brook.

It is the emotional experiences that are most important in creating your reality. You can alter your emotional reaction, and therefore alter your recall of the past.

But the essential progress made by the soul through its journey in time and space has to be measured by the relativity of that soul. Each lifetime you experience adds to the soul bank great emotional varieties, experiences, and challenges, and yet you in this lifetime have only a small ability to recall the other lifetimes.

And so it seems perhaps unfair for you to be burdened with karma from past lives of which you have no memory, or, indeed, to be burdened with karma from future lives.

Although the soul may be able to view other lives as if they were simultaneous, in fact they were lived one before the other. There is a cause-and-effect reaction. So, when a person was in the Roman arena 2,000 years ago and slew another by his prowess, well, he will reach the full cup of that in a later life than the present one. And although they seem to be simultaneously experienced, in fact, the Roman life *did* come first.

When you experience the future life, that has yet a different quality, for there are no firm actions in the past, there are only the soul's trances, the soul's projections. And so there may be, in fact, different lifetimes, some of which come into being and some of which remain fantasies of the mind. In this regard, you must always keep your patience; we believe that you can foresee the life that will bring you great fulfillment, and focus your attention on that life. Bring it to your mental reality with greater vividness and by that very action you help to bring that life into being.

Yes, there are lessons and there are plans; there are challenges of life which are planned out. And we meet those challenges, almost always imperfectly, but still we attempt. So, what we see as our physical world is but an image drawn from the spectrum of consciousness. We do not mean to insist that this is a fantasy or an illusion. It is reality, of course, but it is a reality which is not what it seems.

The nature of reality is drawn not from cause and effect in the physical world, but rather from cause and effect in the soul world.

Do you know that your mind can go through atoms, through space, through electrons, through time and all matter? The mind permeates the whole universe, is part of the universe. Without the minds of men and other ascension creatures, there would not be a universe, for, you see, we are part of it. We have been given the gift of life by the Great One. We partake of the Great One, and we partake of the universe.

You might say that our universe is a dream in the mind of God, but it is also a dream in our own mind, a very real dream that plays out its drama of purposes, many purposes, for you have not come into this world by chance alone.

You have chosen to incarnate, to extricate your soul's journey, to discover your reasons for being, to paint on the canvas of life the variety of love and of attainment of sensibilities. You have within you the remarkable gift of creating the space- time world little bit by little bit.

God created you so that you have responsibilities--otherwise the game is no fun.

We know that many of your scientists would be somewhat disappointed to think that physical reality is not so predictable. They would rather that essentially things fit into an order (the chemistry, the physics of the universe, the astronomical laws) and that these all fit into a cohesive whole which can be part of the predicted. Well, you see, these laws (as they are called) are not laws, but they are merely rules, rules to simplify the universe, which is quite simple. For you see, in the universe there is a place for everything, a reason for everything, and each entity changes the universe. Each changes the reality of others as part of the cohesive whole ("root mind," you call it). We then change our reality when we focus on our own divine aspects; we enlarge our spiritual being and we sometimes join together to create very rapidly a new order. This is not yet glimpsed by the scientists, but it is glimpsed certainly by those who now explore the worlds of metaphysics.

Question: Can you suggest a process to enable someone to get in touch with past-life experiences which might be influencing their current life?

from Li Sung

The first thing to do is to ask the question, "Why on Earth did that happen?" and expect to receive an answer. "Was there something perhaps in a past life that created this condition in my present life? I wish to see a picture, please." There is not necessarily the need to go to hypnosis or deep states. Your mind will flash whatever you need--provided you believe that you can have this. So you will be surprised at the ease with which this understanding comes, but you *have to expect the answer.*

So often people curse God because they do not understand. There is a grievance in their life; they expect God to watch over and protect them. They expect God to have responsibility for their lives and their families.

But you see, God created you so that you have responsibilities--otherwise the game is no fun. It is you who are in charge, and so you can ask your soul-self, "Why has this happened?" Admittedly, we want to ask such a question when things are not to our liking. When great fortune favors us we tend to say, "Oh, I deserve this." Well, perhaps you do, but often there is also a karmic reason in the past; and we should not neglect the karma of the present life, for that is operating at the largest percentage of impact. We estimate that 60 to 80 percent of events in your life are from the present lifetime's karma.

Now, your question "What did I do wrong?" is perhaps wrongly put. It should be, "What is the reason for this?" Do not judge yourself as having made the karma before you know the answer. Perhaps something terrible happened because you did something *right.* And this is a time for balance. Expectations do not always bring the correct answer. But the right questions bring the right answers.

Dealing With Your Subconscious Mind

from Soli

If the subconscious is controlling your lives (as in the majority of cases it is), it comes forward in the reaction to circumstances around you. It brings forward fears, doubts, misunderstandings, and guilt because you are taking action against deep-seated

beliefs that you do not know you have. How can you get beyond that subconscious mind? First of all, recognize its power. Recognize that you have those beliefs. Recognize that you do not fight the subconscious mind, for the subconscious mind is also controlling, creating your physical body.

Your subconscious mind is creating your reality around you.

What you see around you is your own projection, the projection of your subconscious mind. The things that you deal with daily (your interactions with friends, acquaintances) are all stemming from subconscious projections and beliefs that you have.

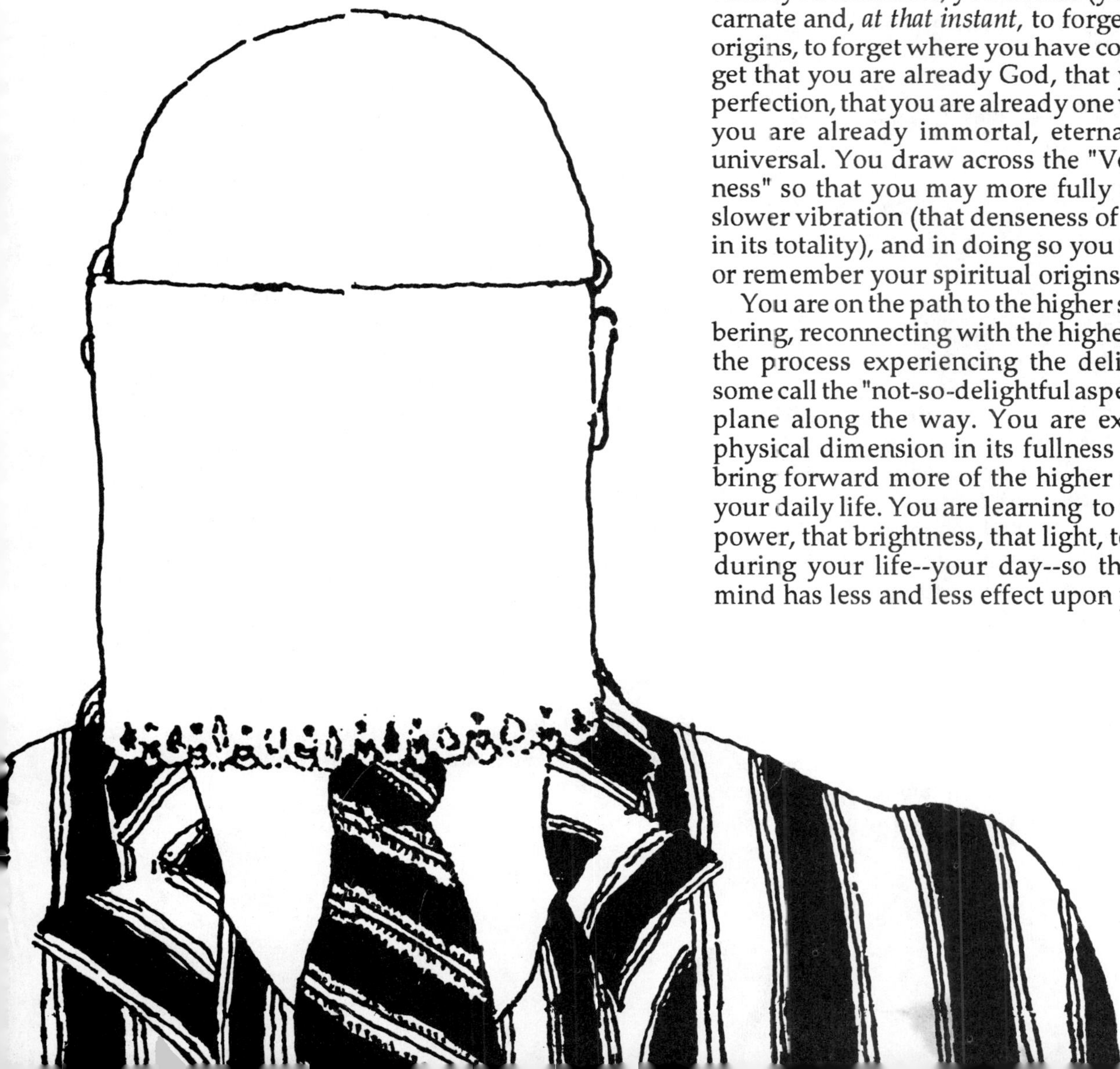

Raising your level of consciousness: what does this mean? It means to become conscious of the Earth's subconscious; to become conscious of those belief systems which are controlling your life; to become conscious of the thought forms that you repeat daily and that create your reality--create what you might see as *negativity* around you. Yes, you create that yourselves. Then become conscious of those thought forms and change them, not only in meditation and specific affirmations (which is important) but also throughout your day. Catch those negative thoughts that come forward which create your reality. Turn them around. Tell yourself that you have no need to deal with them any longer.

My friends, why are you here? What are you doing upon this Earth plane? First and foremost, when you incarnate, you decide (you choose) to incarnate and, *at that instant*, to forget your spiritual origins, to forget where you have come from, to forget that you are already God, that you are already perfection, that you are already one with all life, that you are already immortal, eternal, infinite, and universal. You draw across the "Veil of Forgetfulness" so that you may more fully experience that slower vibration (that denseness of the Earth plane in its totality), and in doing so you then rediscover or remember your spiritual origins.

You are on the path to the higher source--remembering, reconnecting with the higher source, and in the process experiencing the delights and what some call the "not-so-delightful aspects" of the Earth plane along the way. You are experiencing the physical dimension in its fullness as you learn to bring forward more of the higher self throughout your daily life. You are learning to allow that inner power, that brightness, that light, to shine forward during your life--your day--so the subconscious mind has less and less effect upon your life.

It is not to fight the subconscious mind--you do not fight yourself. The subconscious mind is your storehouse, your memory, your ego of this lifetime. It is necessary. You are here to walk with it. Once you have gone totally beyond the subconscious (once you have no more subconscious reaction within your life) then there's no longer any point in being upon the Earth plane, and so you move on to the next dimension of experience. You are here to walk with your subconscious mind.

My friends, you create your reality daily. What you think, what comes forward within your subconscious mind, is constantly what you'll see around you. If you think you are poor, then you'll be poor. If you think you're unloved and unlovely, then you will have no one around you. It is your doing--your belief. You receive back exactly what you put out. Whatever you believe, you will have, regardless of what it is. Why then not turn that thought around?

Give love; believe you are loved and you will be.

Believe and know that you are one with the universe and abundance is yours and it will be.

There is no limit, my friends; you can do anything. You can walk on water; you can swim in the earth. You can do it.

It is your belief that says you *cannot* or you *can;* that is all it is. Literally, without limitation, whatever you believe totally is your reality. Absolutely. It is why we say there is no *one* truth. As you change your beliefs, then your truth changes. If you look around you within society and judge others, what you are saying is, "That person's life does not match my belief system. That person is wrong." What do you do when you do that? You draw yourself into conflict with that vibration.

If you feel that you are a victim of crime, it is because you have drawn an energy to you either through fear that it would happen or because you have some need in your life that you are not addressing and the only way that the higher self can get you to address it is to create within your life a situation that will *force* you to address it. And so the individual who seems to be making you a victim is not. That individual is in service to you, creating for you the reality that you require--that you have created through your thought form.

You are always creators of your lives, my friends. You are never victims. Remember the Loving Law of Allowance for all things to be in their own time and place. Nonjudgment, my friends, is a key to greater understanding, to a higher vibration, to allowing everyone to live their lives as they believe it (not as you believe it), to allowing you to live your life as you are (as you see it--as you believe it), to loving self, to accepting totally all that you are, where you are and why you are. For you are *who* you are because that was your need--that was your choice before incarnating. That does not mean that you must remain in that projection for the rest of your life. It *does* mean that, until you learn to love yourself and accept who and what you are, you will not move forward. You will not move forward until you have learned the lesson that you came to learn in that particular circumstance.

You are, my friends, on a quest for the higher self, to return to that knowing of that spiritual nature that you truly are.

You are on a quest to remember that you are truly one with all life, that you are not separate, that the physical body gives an illusion of separateness which is not reality.

My friends, there are no problems in life; there are only events and circumstances. It is the subconscious projection, the intellect--the mind--that creates the problems out of those events. This is not to say that intellect is wrong; it has its place within your life--otherwise you would not choose to have such a vibration to deal with. There are the physical, the emotional, and the mental within the physical dimension. And you're here to work with them all and to balance them, not to allow one to overdominate the other, to balance them and move beyond into the philosophical (your own beliefs) and beyond that into the spiritual until you are connected again with the higher source.

from Enid

So don't be afraid of changing your realities. Try them on as you would a coat to see if they fit or don't fit. And if you don't find one that suits your needs exactly, take another and say, "I'll wear this one for now until I find something that suits me better."

Channeling Your Higher Self:

Finding theGod Within.

"The greatest of all the prophets sought not to teach you to believe in them, but to teach you to believe in you. For the power of the Holy Spirit works through you, not you through it."

from John

"Your higher self is the doorknob that opens the doorway to enlightenment, to wisdom, and to perceptions of things that are most meaningful."

from Li Sung

You Are More Than Your Physical Body

from Soli

You are not who you think you are. You are not your physical bodies. You are not your emotions. You are not your intellects, your egos. You are spirit. You are God. Literally, *you are God.* You are a part of the spark of the infinite All There Is. You are infinite, immortal, eternal, and universal.

You are the creator and the creation both. There is no separation between the creator and the creation.

You are the higher self, the Christ consciousness, the God force, whichever term you wish to use. We use the phrase "the higher self." You are the higher self; by this we mean that part of you that is spirit, that is not only infinite but is also all-knowing, all-powerful. You are experiencing your own powers of creation by experiencing through a physical vehicle within this dimension. You are experiencing the power of your own creativity so that you may experience what you have created.

You don't know yourselves, my friends. You have been brought up in a society that tells you that everything is outside of you. God is outside of you, your savior is outside of you, your doctor is outside of you, your entertainment is outside of you, your lover is outside of you. You don't look within. Consequently, you don't know *who you are.* The only way that you can know who you are is to see how you are reflected from what is around you. And in order to know more of who you are, you create for yourselves circumstances and relationships that reflect to you who you are, to give yourself the opportunity to examine who you truly are.

from John

You are not what you appear to be. We know that you have heard it before, and we know that, in your lives, you have made efforts to understand these principles. But, you see, you haven't learned yet that it is not through *understanding* that you learn who you are, it is through *being.* It is not through words. It is not through word expressions and phrases, but more through the *process of being.*

The process of being involves allowing that being that you are, which is selfless, which is judge-less, to participate in your life. You have accepted the role of judge. You have accepted the role of executioner, simultaneously. When you judge, you are judged.

The being that is you is beyond judgment. But it loves you *so much* that it will allow you to experience judgment, because All That Is wishes you to have that capability to play in the grand game of life. Whether that reflects success or not is up to you. And yet, neither is that important. What this is all about is not failing or succeeding, it's not about being right or wrong. It is about allowing your life to change. It is about *accepting* the being within.

Aspects of yourself

from Enid

The personality is an *aspect* of an infinite beingness. When we talk about infinite, we're talking about no barriers at all. And understand there's not just one infinity that we all share, but each of us is our own infinity. You are your own infinity and so is everyone else, and your infinity *is shared* with all other infinities. And that's what makes up the whole. When all these infinities come together, they are greater than the sum of their parts. So, your higher self is greater than the sum of all of the aspects of you. It's greater than the sum of all experiences that have been experienced throughout eternity.

Let's take a look at the fact that you have this eternal self which is unending, which is totally majestic and totally "nonmaterial," because in a material world we think in terms of barriers and boundaries. We want to put everything in perspective. It's like saying, "Let's put little sides around this and draw a picture of it." So we've got to put barriers on it so that we can understand it better. That's what happens in the material world: you want to put up boundaries.

For just a moment, allow yourself to think of the idea of there not being boundaries at all. Allow yourself to think that there are no boundaries of mind, no boundaries of heart or love, no boundaries of any kind of existence vibration; there are no limits whatever.

Then you can see that when we have experience in a material sense, we experience those limits as an idea, as a thought of, "I wonder what it would be like to experience limits, to experience not knowing everything, to experience not having, to experience the feeling of being buffeted about, or the feeling of being enamored with something that I can't let go of." You begin to wonder whether something will have a bad feeling or a good feeling or be a bad thing or a good thing. Sometimes you become enamored of things that you really should leave alone.

Your personality is a part of that infinitude. For the sake of argument, imagine that your higher self is like your body, and you are one of the toes. Now you can put your big toe in the water and your whole body experiences the temperature, the joy, and the delight of that feeling of the water; it shares in that experience. And yet the toe doesn't share in the experience of the rest of the body except only minimally. You see how that works? Not that I want to tell you that you're reduced to big toe status, because you're not.

But, just for the sake of argument (to show you how much an integral part of your higher beingness you are), imagine that when you return again to your higher self you are no longer a big toe, but rather you are that infinitude. And yet that personality is always remembered and always regarded as a wonderful experience. And you always know that part of yourself--the part of yourself that you feel deep inside you right now as being *you*. That part never disappears. That part, that identity, is never a part you lose in a big "glob" of beingness. All of your identities are integral. And they are a part of the whole.

Every person who knows you knows a different person in regard to yourself. You are someone different to everyone you know because they seem to draw out different parts of you.

You know, sometimes you're with someone and you find yourself getting very angry and "bitchy." When you're with this person you're just griping and agreeing with all these things you dislike together. And you're just gossiping, and it's so

much fun. And yet you'll be with someone else, and you'll not have a feeling of wanting to do that at all. All of a sudden the conversation is elevated to a different level. You're talking in a different way so that another aspect of yourself is coming into play.

Making decisions to experience life in a specific manner

from Enid

So let's take a look now at the personality that decides to come down to Earth. There's a great mathematical thing that goes on as you decide exactly the time and the place, the parents, and everything. And when you've got all this decided and the higher self says, "Yes, let's do it that way," the higher self is experiencing those aspects through you. And thusly, you are responding to the world because of when you were born. You said, "I want this kind of personality this time. I want to view this life through this kind of lens." So then you have a lifetime that responds to life in a certain way. And aspects of that lifetime's personality will respond in different ways to different parts of the world.

You send out certain aspects of yourself when you write a letter. You will surely communicate in a different way when you write a letter than when you talk on the telephone or when you talk in person. It's a whole different thing.

You are always your higher self. You are not someone else. But your personality is responding to life differently than the rest of the sum of your parts, in a very specialized way. And it's different from each lifetime that you've ever led. You may say, "Okay, we've done that, and we're going to do something else." So perhaps you'll be a fisherman. And you'll view life through the smell of the ocean and the smell of fish and all those things. And then the next time, you may be viewing life as a baker, in with the smell of the yeast and the sugar and, oh, all the wonderful bread you create. And everything that you experience--all of the smells, the colors, the places, all the textures of everything that's available to each personality--bring about a whole new panoply of experience.

Life is experienced differently so that different things are gathered to oneself. When you communicate then to your higher self, you say, "All right, I'm awakening now, darling, and I realize that this isn't all of me. I'm looking at my body, and I'm looking at my personality, and I'm looking at how people are viewing me, and I'm experiencing their response to me and my response to them. And now that I've experienced my response to life, I see that there's more to me. And I want to communicate with whatever that is. There's more to me than I view here in the mirror. There's more to me than others view of me."

And what is that more? That more, then, is the higher self. And it's as though the big toe is looking up and saying, "Oh, my goodness, look at the rest of me. There's the rest of me . . . this wonderful, beautiful creation." And you are a creation. And when you look up into yourself, into your higher beingness, you can see yourself as a creation. Aren't

you feeling it now as you're reading about it? You're beginning to feel yourself as this wonderful creation that's been viewing life this way and that way. And now that you're awakening, you say, "Wait a minute, hold it. Stop the car. I'm going to get off now because I'm not just this person sitting in this railroad car. I'm something else. There's more to me." And this is why in ages past they would say, "I'm going to find myself." That is totally valid because that's what you've been doing. You've been finding yourself.

Once you find your inner beingness, life changes for you and it's never, never the same.

Finite/infinite

from Enid

The only way your higher self can experience physical life is by sending forth an aspect of itself. The physical world is what we call "finite existence." And because infinity cannot exist in a finite world, sending an aspect and telling that aspect that you are now finite allows you to relate to the idea that you are finite, that your body will be finite, and that you have only so many years in which to have this experience. So, in order for an infinitude of beingness to experience any kind of finiteness or even the idea of finiteness, only an aspect of oneself can actually be materialized.

Now, you are *not* an emissary for your higher self, *you literally are your higher self.* You are always your higher self. But at this moment, you are not totally aware of the entirety of yourself, and you cannot be while in body. You can take the concept as far as you can go, and you can reach great outer limits of understanding of this part. But if you really get right down to it, each higher self is All There Is. And beyond each and every other "All There Is" you are always All There Is. Although you're an infinitude and you are an individual, you are still a part of every other infinitude.

In a finite world, we cannot totally understand infinity because we came here to experience finiteness.

Outside of this world and outside of all physical worlds there is nothing but infinity to experience. In all the other worlds, infinity is a part of the fabric of what you experience. But in this world you said, "I'm going to put myself in a state of consciousness in which I pretend that I cannot see, I cannot hear, I cannot know, and I will grow and discover these things all over again. I will discover reality all over again."

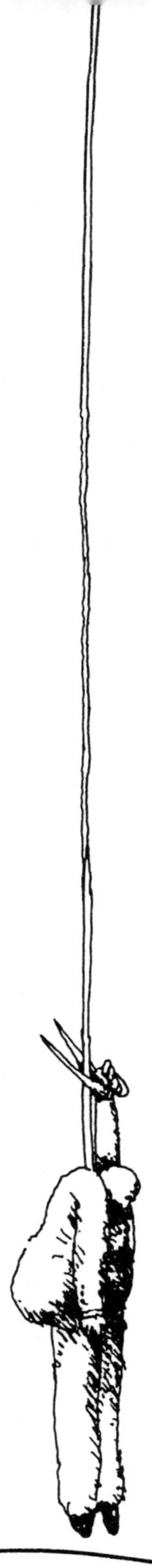

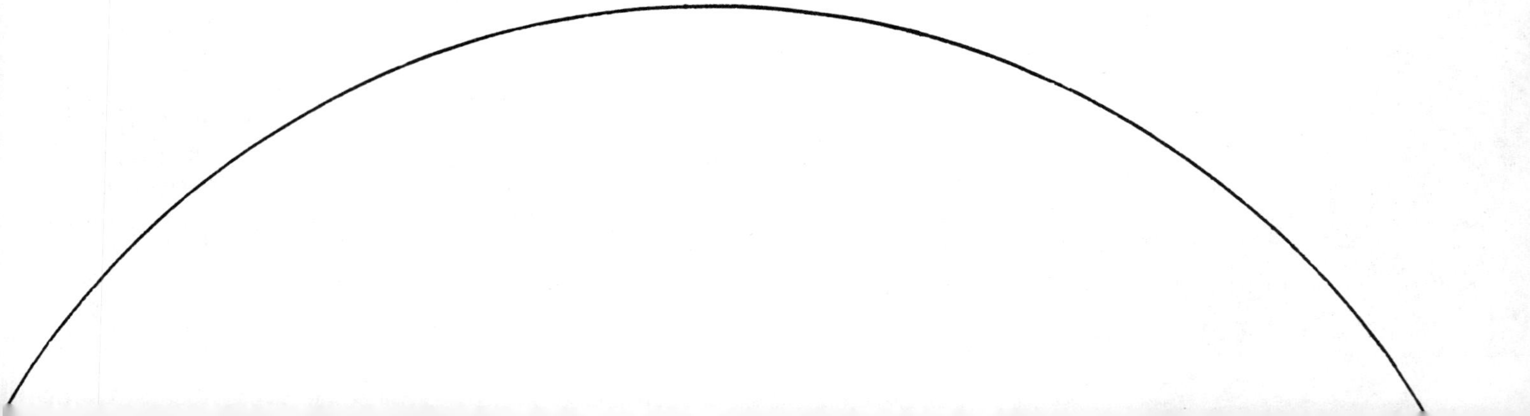

THE STORY CORNER

The Girl and the Mirror

from The Eternals

There was a young girl who often looked into the mirror and talked to the image which she beheld, but the image which she beheld was unable to answer. Still the girl would speak and speak and speak while the image remained helpless to reply.

As time passed the family began to worry that the girl spoke to herself so often in the mirror. The mother said, "Worry not, it is only a passing phase."

But it did not pass and the villagers began to speak of the girl who spoke to herself in the mirror. The villagers laughed and mocked the poor girl, yet she continued to talk to herself in the mirror.

Then one day, while combing her hair, she remained silent and the mirror began to speak! The girl started back and screamed, "Mirror, why have you not spoken before this time if you can speak?"

The mirror answered, "Child, you never were silent long enough that I could speak."

From that time forward the girl knew the truth of the mirror. The villagers never knew and they continued to laugh. The family could accept the girl, yet they were not sure of the mirror and they could not completely believe, so they never spoke to the mirror and the mirror never spoke to them.

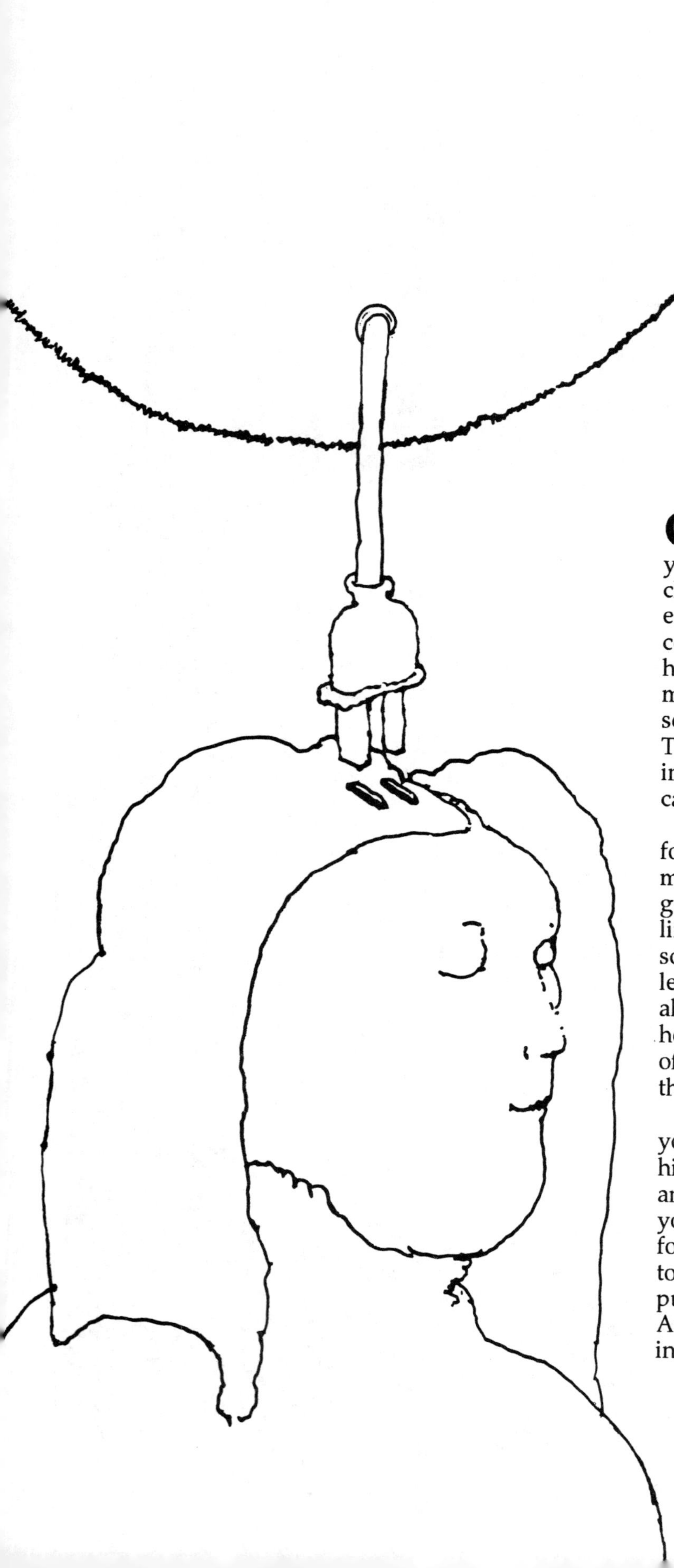

Illumination Comes From Your Higher Self

from Li Sung

Channeling your higher self is the very best thing you can do. Some persons, without realizing it, channel their lower selves. Their lower selves, their emotions, and their physical desires completely control their lives without any direction of the higher self. The higher self has been around for many incarnations throughout time and space. And so the higher self has great wisdom, great knowing. The higher self knows the reasons that you came into this life in the first place. You came into life because of the *choice* of your higher self.

When you come into physical incarnation, you forget this, for you have to discover it moment by moment in this life. But the higher self's plan is geared not only to equalize karma from past lifetimes, but more importantly to promote the lessons in life that are most necessary for the soul. These lessons very often revolve around relationships, but also around certain types of accomplishments and honors that a person wants to work for, the types of debts that they need to pay, or the realizations they have to consider.

And so when you channel your higher self, when your consciousness becomes higher, it vibrates at higher rates. Then you merge with your higher self and begin automatically to follow this plan toward your manifest destiny. Now the higher self is no fool. It realizes that you have many earthly things to accomplish; yet there must be a higher spiritual purpose behind it all for life to have any meaning. And so it is truly from the higher self that the meaning of life comes.

When you grasp the wisdom and the knowingness from the higher self, you see the track of your life lit up, proceeding into the future like stars into the night. They form a beautiful pattern.

We are very hopeful that you, as readers, will give more and more thought to this channeling of the higher self, for in this way your lives will become more bountiful, more meaningful, and certainly more fulfilling. For those who tune in to the higher self come closest to manifesting their plan to perfection.

Illumination comes through the higher self. The connection with God comes through the higher self, and so does the connection with other entities in our dimensions. It is, of course, a connection with a great consciousness, with a God consciousness that partakes of all knowledge, all wisdom, and also all of eternity.

The higher self is the doorknob that opens the doorway to enlightenment, to wisdom, and to perceptions of things that are most meaningful.

We believe that in your age there is greater awareness of this higher self. We see a new spiritual awakening. More and more persons are reaching up, raising their vibration level, and are attempting to channel the wisdom of the universe, the laws of karma, the laws of love. And as they do this, they create a vibration that enhances the whole planet, that brings about a raising of the consciousness of the whole planet.

This can be very important for persons in this New Age, for they are now taking a great step in spiritual evolution. We hope that you will see the day when it is very common for persons to channel the higher self. Just as children go to see cartoon movies, the very next day they will be channeling their own higher self. And so it is this way that the Earth and its peoples will quickly reach a higher understanding and then be able to put these principles to work, to construct a truly spiritual society, a society that brings love and wisdom to the side of law and justice.

Question: Is there a difference between our spirit guides and teachers and our higher selves?

from Li Sung

The difference between your spirit guides and teachers and your higher self is like the difference between your mother and your aunt. The higher self has primary responsibility, where the others are merely friends who have a good interest in you and sometimes a relationship to you. There is a matter of responsibility here, for the higher self has, in fact, produced your physical organism and brought you into life. So it is the primary one responsible for how close you come to carrying out your life plan. The others are like teachers, aides, helpers, those who would inspire you, and those who will sometimes prompt you when you need it. But it is the higher self that is always with you when you need it.

Experience is the name of the game

from Soli

You are the higher self, my friends, and the higher self does not care how you experience this reality. All it cares about is *experiencing*. It is your subconscious mind that tells you whether this is a good experience or a bad experience. From a spiritual perspective, there is no such thing as good or bad. There is only experience.

You are as a boat traveling down a river. The higher self decides it wants to travel and explore this particular river which it has never explored before. And in order to explore this river, it must have a physical boat or vehicle, and so it creates one, and even helps in its process of creation. The higher self may even change the genetic structure of the fetus within the mother's body before it is born.

The physical vehicle has a belief in its own reality. You begin to believe in your own beliefs. You believe in your isolated individualness. You believe that your physical body is all that there is, that it is the only expression of your being within this dimension. And the physical body has (as you would say) a mind of its own. It becomes very obstinate. Your subconscious will take you in directions that your higher self does not wish you to go in. And when your subconscious mind takes you in directions opposite to that which the higher self wishes, you create for yourselves physical, emotional, and mental disease. You create the disease within your own minds by the resistance to change that comes forward, the resistance to doing those things that you are being guided to do by your own higher self.

The higher self does not care *how* you experience the river. If you want to experience the river in pain and suffering, so be it. If you want to experience the river in disease, so be it, as long as you go down that river. Alternatively, if you wish to experience the river in joy, feeling the excitement and the challenge, also so be it, as long as you go down the river. The higher self will do everything to get you to go down that river.

If it cannot, if your subconscious mind takes you too far off course so that there is no way of getting back onto that river, then the higher self will terminate this life and say, "Okay, we'll come back and have another experience, another expression, in a different physical vehicle, in a different time and space."

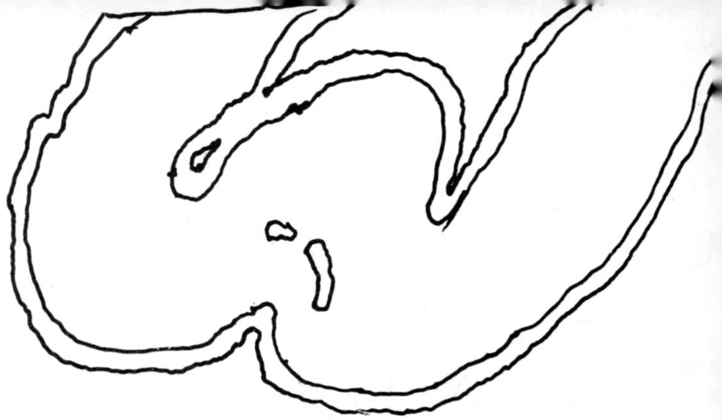

You see, my friends, there is no time. You are infinite. You have an infinity of time to do whatever you need to do or want to do. You don't have to do it this lifetime if you don't want to. You can do it the next or the next or the next. There is no such thing as failure. But on the other hand, you are here to experience.

If you want the highest evolution and fastest evolution then become in tune with your higher self.

Go within, be centered, contact that inner core of your own being. Listen to your internal guidance. Listen to that part of you that is telling you, all the time, the things that are "best" for you within this dimension, this lifetime. In the sense of "best," understand that that is a term that your subconscious mind would use, for you judge everything to be

good or bad. The higher self is simply wanting experiences, and if they don't happen now, they will happen later. But if they can happen now, so much the better.

The second coming is you

from Soli

You are, my friends, the second coming. The Nazarene taught how it is possible to transcend the subconscious mind, to go beyond the belief systems, and to become a clear channel of the energy of the higher self. That is what you call the "Christ consciousness."

As you become that clear channel, you become the second coming the Nazarene spoke of.

You and your brothers and sisters of like mind are working now to be channels of that energy, to allow that energy through, to radiate within this dimension and to change this dimension. You do this not because there's anything wrong with this dimension as it is, but simply because you as creators have decided it is *time for change.*

You have played this game long enough. You want to change the rules of the game, and you have decided to do so. You have infinite power and absolute power to change the rules to however you wish to have them. For the laws of this dimension (or any dimension) are not imposed upon you. You have created them and continue to create them. Every law of nature (so-called), every law that science ever discovers, is a creation of your own thoughts--you and large numbers of other entities working with you.

You have forgotten that you are God, that you are infinite Spirit, infinitely powerful. You have forgotten because your mind, your belief systems have clouded that memory. You chose to have that clouding occur before you came here. It is as though you are children playing the game of make-believe. And you can't play make-believe if no one believes. And so you have created circumstances for yourselves where you come within this dimension and totally believe in the dimension.

But now you are getting tired of that game. You are realizing it is time for a different game. You want to change the rules and you are beginning to do so. The New Age will come about *only* when enough of you think that you want to change the rules. And there are growing numbers of you wishing to change the rules. And as you begin to think that way, so you will begin to create that so-called reality around you.

Nothing comes into being until
you think it into being.

Nothing can occur around you unless you first think it. And the more individuals who think the same thought, the more probable it is that that thought will become what you will see as reality around you. You are channels, mediums for the energy of the higher self. You are here to learn that.

You are beginning to discover your own powers of creativity, how your every single fleeting thought changes your probability pattern, creates your reality around you. And as you become more aware of that, you begin to control your thoughts and to be aware of your thoughts day in and day out, recognizing those that you want to use and those that you don't want to use. Then you become in control of your environment, especially when you are listening to the intuition, that inner guidance.

from Enid

It was planned that eventually there would be one cycle and that at the end of the cycle there would be the millennium and everybody would awaken, and those who hadn't awakened earlier would come and project themselves into a body and really experience the awakening and being alive again and doing this whole thing. And that was supposed to be the end of it.

But, oh no, you beings became so enamored and said, "This is wonderful stuff, and I'm coming back. I love liquor and I love drugs and I love coffee and I love tea. And I want to come back, and I want to experience. Oh, I love sex. It's so unique! That isn't anywhere else except in physical life. I've got to come back. I've got to do this again." And so many beings just kept going on and on until finally we're looking down at you and we're saying, "Wait a minute. We've rung the bell. It's over now." And many people reply, "No it isn't. I don't want it to be over. I'm having so much fun." And these are the people who aren't awakening now. Oh, they're so enamored. So we're just shaking the tree.

Those of you who
are awakening
are prized beyond
the greatest
of prizes.

This is very exciting to us because we're finally getting through. We're finally getting you to hear us. The alarm has gone off and it's time to awaken. Every single being who is here right now, is here for that awakening.

Opening Communication With Your Higher Self

Claiming the divine within

from Kunda

The first step towards awakening is to *acknowledge* your godliness and divine counterpart. For until you are able to do so, you disconnect yourself from your greatest strength--the power to realize you are divine--and the force behind that power. So long as you alienate yourself from the creative force, your education here will be awkward, misguided, and most painful, to be sure. For whenever you perceive the self as divided and existing apart from the force of creation, you place yourself beyond God's reach and will only continue to recreate realities of dissatisfaction, fear, and helplessness. Placing yourself within the God-force aligns your mortal understanding with soul-consciousness and thereby enables you to reestablish your link with the Creator.

How do you acknowledge your divinity? Merely by accepting that you are a part of God's will, and for your life, a part of His intelligence and purpose, a part of the cosmic plan of unfoldment. This requires that you be willing to abandon all thoughts which separate you from that idea. Remember, you are in pursuit of self, and in order to know the God-self you must be willing to shed any and all identities. Like peeling an onion to its core, you will be casting off many layers and identities in order to look at the divine within, the immortal soul of all souls.

Identify with the greater perspective of your true soul mate and, if need be, play-act for a while until you gain confidence that you are loved, guided, and cared for every inch of the way. Your life will take on more meaning and your role will soon be better defined as you look for the cosmic direction and higher wisdom which is all the security and proof you will ever need.

Indeed, your evolvement into divinity begins by being knowledgeable that it exists for you, and that it is only a thought away!

For upon the energy of your thoughts is how you traveled here, and through uplifted thoughts shall you return as one with the Light of all-thought.

Trust, trust, trust

from John

Trusting yourself is one of the most rewarding experiences that an individual can have with self. What it does is to allow for the inner portion of yourself to take a more active role in your life. But you see, when you can't do that it's because you don't know *how* to trust yourself. Trusting yourself begins with one word, *acceptance*. Do not confuse the word acceptance with agreement; they are two entirely different principles.

You can accept your life without agreeing with it. It is easy to be confused about our use of the word acceptance, thinking that what we mean is that you agree with your life the way it is. Your agreement is not necessary, nor is it sought. What is sought here is your responsibility toward acceptance so that you can realize that you can transform the quality of your life in an instant. And through that instance of acceptance you can accept your life for what it is. Notice we are not saying that you need to like it for what it is or to dislike it for what it is. *Accept* that you are able to be with your life, that you are able to be with yourself, so that in this process of being with yourself you can begin to free yourself from yourself. Why? Because you are your own worst enemy.

from Master Adalfo

The first thing that is required in contacting your higher self is trust. The second thing is trust. And the last thing that is required is trust. People who want to get in touch with themselves, through processes like meditation or whatever, get insights they do not believe in. They're often waiting to have someone else tell them so then they will know they are right. So first, it is so important just to trust that you are getting in touch with your own divinity. And you must trust in the divine in order to do that.

All the tools which you will read of, meditation, astrology, runes, etc., all of those are just tools. They are only as good as the trust you put into them. Once again the issue is trust. It is of primary importance. You cannot go around always testing your own inner wisdom and all the wisdom of these tools that you have chosen to use. You cannot test them all the time because they will reject being tested. And so will spirit guidance. This is not a test.

I think one thing that we can do on my side of life, perhaps most of all, is to encourage people to trust themselves. For the answers are all within each one of you. If you've got an answer, why do you not trust it? Try it out. If it does not work out, then you can go for another answer and trust that. But you cannot develop the trust if you do not use it. And you cannot develop your own inner knowing if you don't trust it at all. Why should it develop? If no one pays any attention to it, what is the point?

Channeling your higher self is like letting your body be a TV antenna. And thus, it is important that your body be nice and straight and tall. Then you can turn it as you turn the TV antenna, to face the direction from which you get the best signal and the best reception. But it has to be straight and tall first. And then you shall receive guidance, perhaps from your own higher self, perhaps from a spirit teacher, perhaps from a physical teacher, perhaps on the news on television. And when you pick up what is good for you with the best reception you can, and then take it into you, into the television set of yourself, you can then look at it, resonate with it, and decide what action to take.

Disconnection

from Ting-Lao

You have heard people say, "It is not possible to be off your path because whatever you are doing is on your path." This is true. But again we get into a paradox because it is also true that you may be walking on a path and *not* progressing as a soul. You are not connected with your higher self when you are not growing, and many people do this their entire lifetimes.

There are some specific things that get you disconnected from your higher self on the various planes (the physical, emotional, mental, and spiritual).

On the physical plane, many times your higher self cannot be active in a body that is very confused with substances such as drugs or alcohol. Even chemicals and sugar can set up a vibration in the physical self that the higher self cannot be in touch with or plug into. That can cause the higher self to disconnect.

One way that emotional disconnection can be caused is by trauma. Oftentimes people become "mentally disordered" after a trauma, such as the death of a loved one, or perhaps after being raped. Another way an emotional disconnection can occur is through constant abuse, such as when a child or an adult is a member of a society or a minority group that is constantly abused.

A mental way to disconnect is to succumb to the entropy and apathy that is so prevalent in the mental state of this society. Often your way of life is so narrow that you focus on one thing only. Work, money, one relationship, or any area of obsession creates a more narrow viewpoint of *all* the essences of life.

A spiritual way to disconnect is not to pay the price for connection. The price for connection with your higher self is paying attention. You have to *spend time in spiritual endeavors.* That may be simply giving time to your higher self or thinking about your purpose in life or caring for others. But you have to be doing something spiritual, for some part of the conscious day. For if you do not pay any attention to spiritual ways, then when your higher self checks in and hovers around the body of your personality, it will say, "Oh, that person is not paying any attention to me this month. I will check in again next month."

To prevent disconnecting from your higher self, it is not so much that you have to do anything, but rather to not do certain things.

Take care of your body. Do not pollute it so that it can disconnect from your higher self. Take care of your emotions by listening to them, feeling them in your body. Think for yourself and work through your own programming. And be aware of the race consciousness of your society and do not succumb to it.

Just like there are sins of commission and sins of omission, it is not so much that you need to *do-do-do* certain things as it is that you need to be careful not to slip into lazy ways so that you detach from your spiritual energies.

from Li Sung

Many persons are not sure that their higher self exists. Or they fear that if they open to the higher self, there are other entities who may wish to take over; someone else might creep in the door. They must find, by experience, how to control this. It is often through ignorance that persons do not realize that the higher self, the God-Self, is there to be tuned into. To them it is all one great unknown sea of danger.

They just have to go through that sea. It is like children learning to swim. They first have to wade out a bit and get used to it, proceeding slowly so that they feel confidence and they feel, in their contacts with higher self or perhaps other positive entities, that it is harmonious for them. It brings their life greater meaning and greater exhilaration, for they will often feel the heightening of the spiritual emotion or what you may call mystical experience as they open the channel and join not only with their higher self but with the God force.

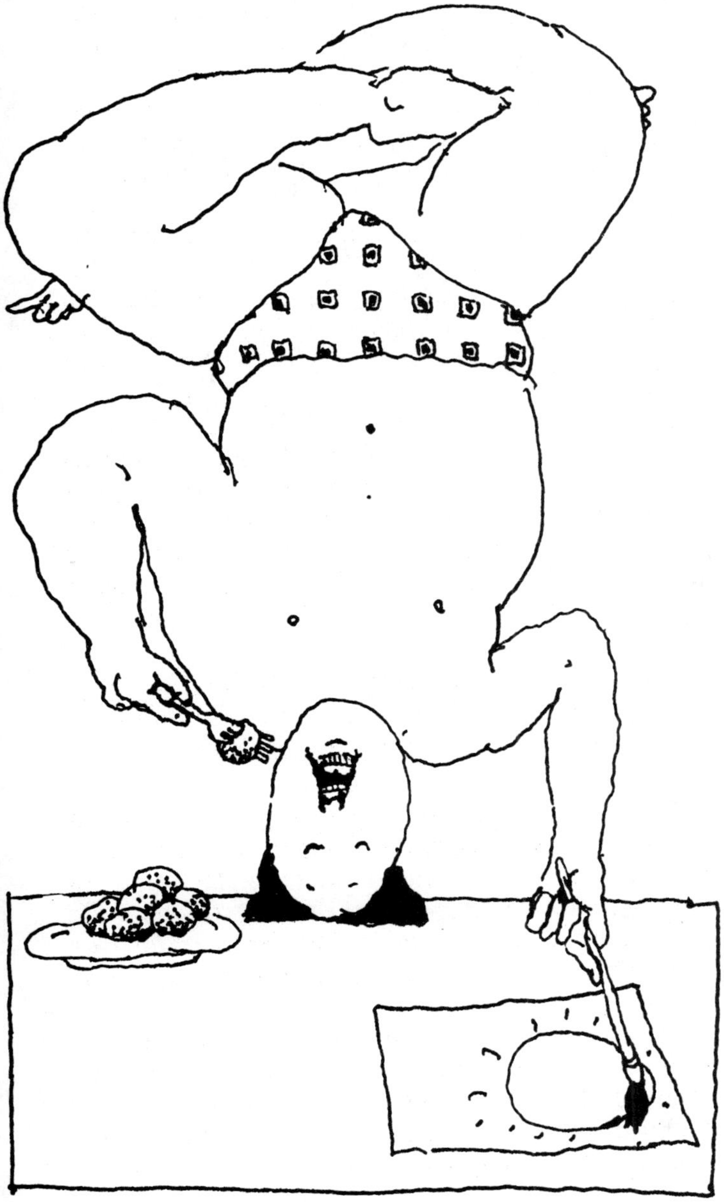

from Master Adalfo

There are many different ways for people to get in contact with their higher selves. Some of the ways in which you people do that are quite funny. You have one person who says, "I will get in touch with my soul's purpose by eating only vegetables. I will get in touch with my soul's purpose by doing yoga postures for three hours every day. I will get in touch with my soul's purpose by meditating or doing art every day." Those can be helpful.

It is only by living that you get in touch with your soul's purpose.

It is only by doing those things that you need to do today and examining closely how you are *feeling*. Ask yourself, "Do I feel I'm on my path? Or, in some things I have to do, how can I make that a part of my path?" It is a matter of attitude, and really being conscious. There are many ways to have clues. The first way is to trust yourself and to listen to yourself. People who are wanting clues frequently are not paying any attention to them when they have them! *Your body gives you clues.* Is your body not feeling good? That is a clue. You've got to pay attention, see what is going on, and what you can change. Are you feeling angry? Why? Don't just ignore it, and blame it all on someone else, because that is not why you are angry. You are angry because something has happened that has made you move off your path. And now, you have to get back on it.

The Power of Meditation

Your brain, the computer

from Kyros

A great portion of your so-called unused brain is used to receive higher-dimensional information in the form of universal symbols. These are then transformed into something comprehensible on a level of your awareness, whereby you can interpret it into something understandable. The used portion of your brain is primarily for your survival in your three-dimensional world. You are using all of your brain without realizing it. If you could bring all of the information flowing in and out of your total brain computer into your conscious experience, you would be able to read and understand the thoughts of others; you would be able to see beyond future time warps; you would be able to molecularly break up your own vehicle and anything around you; you would be able to translate at will; you would be able to heal any affliction; you would no longer see illusions, but rather essence; you would know and comprehend the Absolute.

When you channel your higher self, you have consciously opened up the *passage* between the so-called "usable" and "unused" portions of the brain computer. But that which you call individual mind (composed of seven levels of consciousness) is not physical, so because you are living in a three-dimensional physical world, the brain computer is utilized to bring the information contained within your mind to your conscious life experience. The brain computer is organic and will be transformed into new energy at your transition. The individual mind will continue--it cannot die. Individual spirit is composed of individual mind which contains all that you are, all that you have been, and all that you will be, in terms of time. It is the mind which holds all of the data you have accumulated during your journey from the point of origination of spirit.

And, as below, so above: universal mind is contained within universal spirit; individual mind is contained within universal mind; and creation is contained within the Creator. Essentially, all is God. Many human entities do not realize how linked they are to universal mind and to the Creator. They may block communication between themselves and the Creator, but the linkage is ever present because it can be no other way. The more that you allow the passages to be open without blocking them with doubts, fear, human logic, and so forth, the greater your ability to channel will be and the purer your answers will be.

Centering and retraining the subconscious mind

from Soli

How then to listen more closely to the higher self? Of course, my friends: meditation.

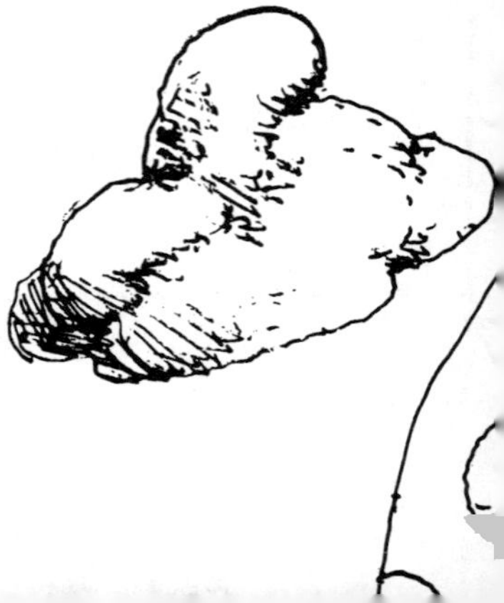

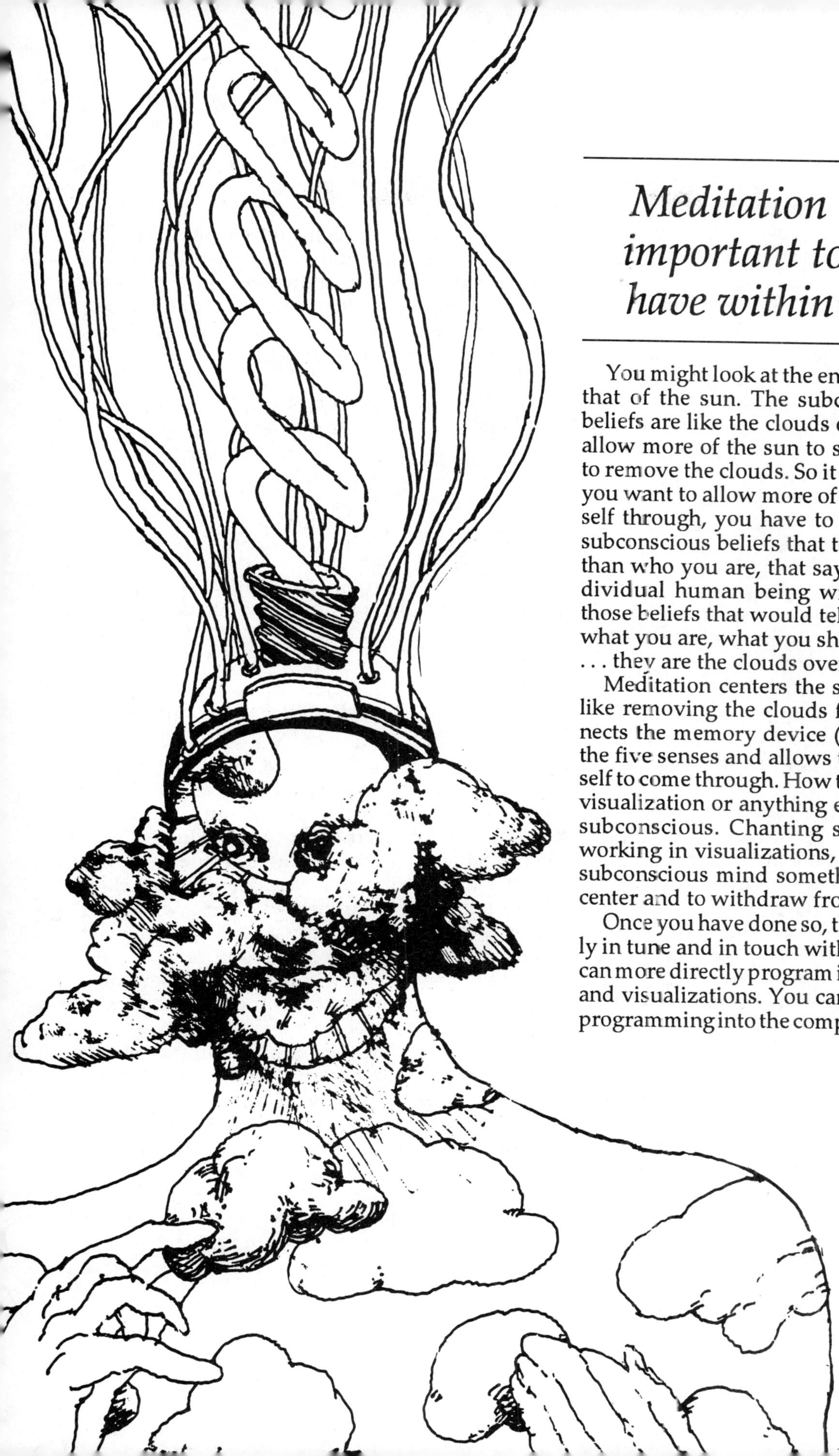

Meditation is the most important tool that you have within your lives.

You might look at the energy of the higher self as that of the sun. The subconscious mind and its beliefs are like the clouds over the sun. In order to allow more of the sun to shine through, you have to remove the clouds. So it is with the higher self. If you want to allow more of the energy of the higher self through, you have to remove the filter of the subconscious beliefs that tell you that you are less than who you are, that say you are an isolated individual human being with limited powers. All those beliefs that would tell you what you are like, what you are, what you should expect around you . . . they are the clouds over the sun.

Meditation centers the subconscious mind. It is like removing the clouds from the sun. It disconnects the memory device (the subconscious) from the five senses and allows the energy of the higher self to come through. How to do this? Well, through visualization or anything else that disciplines that subconscious. Chanting sounds, seeing images, working in visualizations, anything that gives the subconscious mind something to do helps you to center and to withdraw from the external world.

Once you have done so, then you are more directly in tune and in touch with the subconscious. You can more directly program it with your affirmations and visualizations. You can more directly put that programming into the computer. And in the process you can communicate with the higher self. The higher self, my friends, communicates in many ways. Ultimately it communicates in *feeling.* You simply *know* within your heart of hearts what to do, how to do it, and when to do it.

But you are all intellectual beings and you love so much to have reasons for everything--you want to know that this is why you are doing that. The higher self will play that game with you. You can ask intellectual questions and you can receive answers of the intellect that say, "This is why you are doing it." Ultimately it has no meaning, but since your subconscious (your intellect) plays such a powerful part within your lives, especially in your society of logic, the higher self will play that game with you, giving your subconscious, your intellect, something to do so it thinks it's very important, so it keeps itself busy while the true communication is going on at a very, very different level.

And so, within your meditations you can ask questions of the higher self; and each of you will receive answers in a different way. Some of you will receive answers clairvoyantly (seeing pictures and images), some of you will hear direct communications and words, and some of you will feel the answers. Some of you will have all three different aspects of this.

An excellent method is to use writing. In writing you are helping to center the subconscious mind. You are disciplining the mind. Ask a question and write down the very, very, very *first* thing that comes into your mind. As you take each word and write it down, the subconscious mind can't race ahead with its "stream of consciousness" quite so fast. And in the very process of writing, you are disciplining the subconscious mind, for the subconscious must control the muscles. You might also speak into a tape recorder. The same thing happens. It slows down the thought process as you take each word and speak it.

Be aware that your communication can come at *any time.* You might ask yourself or your higher self a question in the morning and in the afternoon be walking down the street and there in the gutter is a piece of newspaper that's been there for six weeks. There is a headline on that piece of paper and it leaps out at you and you recognize that as the answer to the question you asked that morning. You, my friends, have to be open to the communication when it comes.

You might be idly walking down the street in the afternoon, smelling the flowers, when suddenly a thought will come into your mind, and that is the answer to your question. You have to be aware, open to the communication when it comes. Work with the higher self, my friends.

Be in tune with the higher self, and you will then have always the highest and fastest evolution you could possibly have within this particular lifetime.

You talk yourselves out of possible experiences all the time because you don't believe in miracles. You don't believe in the possibilities. You do not believe in your own unlimited beingness.

Question: How can we retrain the subconscious mind?

from Soli

Suppose you have a need that is financial in nature and you express that need to the universe. If you know that you are God, if you are open to the universe, and you can receive abundantly in all areas of your life, you do not limit yourself as to where that abundance is going to come from. For example, suppose that you have deep-seated beliefs in your mind about working 40 hours a week, and you believe that there's only a limited amount of money, and that the only other recourse is to steal it, or to borrow it, or to win a lottery or some such thing. If that is your reality, you do not believe in the unlimited power of your own being.

You have forgotten that you are the universe. You are in tune. You are infinite. You are one with the universe. You are God. You are unlimited beings of light. And thusly, you do not allow yourselves your own inner power.

And so when these thoughts come up, stop for a moment and ask yourself, "Is this a thought that I need any longer? No. Well, then thank you, thought. You have done what you need to do for me up to now. You have brought me to where I am. I chose to have these beliefs in my subconscious mind, but now that I recognize that I have used them, they have served their purpose and I don't need them any longer. Now I choose to replace them with a different belief. I now choose to believe that I am worthy of abundance. I choose to believe that I have what I need."

Make the affirmation that "All my needs are met every day," and recognize that to be true. It is when you see or say, "All my needs are met," and then you look around and say, "Oh, I need this that I don't have, and I need the other that I don't have, and I really want this, but I don't have it," that you are negating your affirmations. Learn to turn your thoughts around. When you see what you *think of* as lack in your life, don't see it as lack. See it as something that you don't need right now. If it isn't there, you obviously don't need it.

It's a matter of pulling yourself up by your own bootstraps, my friends, of turning your thoughts around, seeing *what is* and accepting *what is.* It is when the mind does not allow you to see what is and says, "This is the way it really should be, and there's a vast gap between what is and what should be," that you are constantly seeing the gap.

When you see lack in your life, you are constantly saying, "I don't have this. I don't have that. I need this. I want this and it isn't there." Even very often when you make affirmations, you affirm, "I am rich. I have what I need right now," but you don't mean it because you constantly, day in and day out, look for the return from this affirmation. You are saying, "Oh, I am affirming that I am rich, but where's the money? I don't have it." In this manner, you negate your affirmation.

You can learn to creep up on the subconscious mind, to simply tiptoe up to it with new information. If you have ten cents in your pocket, and you say to the subconscious mind, "I am rich," the subconscious mind says, "Fine, being rich means having ten cents in your pocket. No problem. We can create that for the rest of your life. That's easy."

Alternatively your subconscious mind is going to say, "Don't be ridiculous. Who are you trying to fool? You have got ten cents in your pocket. Throw that one out." But if you creep up on the subconscious mind and say, "Every day, I am becoming more and more abundant in all areas in my life. My needs are met each and every day. I experience that my needs are met each and every day," then the subconscious says, "Fine, I'm becoming richer every day. I can accept that. It doesn't mean we are now. But, yeah, tomorrow a little bit more and the day after a bit more and a bit more and a bit more." You creep up on it.

In this way, your subconscious will allow that affirmation to begin to work for you. But not if you look day in and day out for the results. Suppose you look the next day and say, "Where is the money in the purse? Where is the money that is coming to me?" If you look for it, you will not find it, for the expectation will kill the affirmation that you were trying to bring forward. *It is a matter of trusting and knowing.* And if you search, if you have expectations, if you are looking for it, then you are not trusting. You are doubting. You are saying literally to yourself, "I doubt that this is working. I have to see the results." Simply make the affirmation and then trust in the results.

You can learn to creep up on the subconscious mind, to simply tiptoe up to it with new information.

from Spirit

Many beginning students of meditation are taught to meditate upon such things as the flame of a candle or even upon a rose. Then, if one would reach into the higher consciousness to communicate with the higher essence of self, with the higher self, one should first seek the protection of the white light of the Christ. Visually surround the body with the white radiant light of the Christ.

Second, you would ask for the presence and the guidance of the Holy Spirit, that the Holy Spirit's presence may assure you that only that which is the highest and the best, only that which is from the true source, from God, would thus flow in such a way that the communion can be made between the physical self and the higher self. These are basic to every seeking, to every communion, to every communication.

And when this has been then done, one sits in reflection and concentrates the mind upon the name of the being that the one who is doing the seeking is known by. Thereby, one calls upon the name of the Lord. If you are the one who is asking the query, and you are the one to whom we would bring the answer, then all that has been said here would apply to you.

The next step is for you to sit silently and open yourself and be receptive while you concentrate your mind upon the single tone of the word that describes the nature of your character and the beingness of your soul, and that is your name. Thus, you concentrate upon your name and call upon the higher forces of yourself, by name. Thus, in this way,

the higher self will acknowledge that it is being called and the spirit will then come into focus and you will be able to be more perceptive. Your receiving apparatus will be attuned.

We are speaking here of attuning the mental channels, or that which we would call the "mental faculties." Thus you would attune the intuition, inspiration, imagination, the instinct of the self and

all that which brings forth from the higher self. You do this through one or the other of these channels within the mind or through that which we have just indicated are the psychic senses, the senses of the soul or the faculty of the soul.

How does one attune, then, to the higher consciousness of the self? One must be in regular attendance, being persistent every day in one's seeking to have communion with the self.

Broken periods of meditation will accomplish little; thus it is the requirement of the path, dear ones, that there shall be regular attendance to the feeding of the soul and the distributing of the food to the mind, thus stimulating the creative centers.

Thus, sit receptively, regularly and as much as is humanly possible, in the same location each day for 10 to 20 minutes, concentrating upon the name of the individual that is seeking and calling upon the Higher Forces of that soul. This is calling upon the universal spirit and calling upon the universal mind to manifest through the higher faculties, as one trains the mental faculties to be perceptive to these finer or more subtle frequencies.

When this has been done properly, then one simply waits. One does nothing after one attunes oneself. After one radiates properly by transmitting the energy, then one simply quiets the self. One quiets the mind and one sits in contemplation. The request has been made. And now, as the scripture says, you will wait upon the Lord.

And then, in this waiting-ness, you may have occasion to be entertained, outwardly in the physical world. When you visit in another's home or place of business, they will offer you a cup of tea, will they not? And they will offer you, perhaps, a wee tad of food, perhaps a shortbread or a sweet? This they bring to you while you are waiting for that for which you went to that place, a bit of comfort. In that same way, you must be relaxed, and in relaxing the mind, release the tensions of the physical expression. Thus, in a relaxed fashion, sitting regularly, concentrating upon the name, you wait in patience. Did you hear that, dear ones? You patiently wait upon the Lord.

Now while you are waiting, it is possible you may experience various colors, or you may experience various geometrical designs or various other astral functions. You are to acknowledge these. You are

not to deny them. You will acknowledge them. You will note their beauty and you will observe that this is not what you are going after. And having observed this is not what you are seeking, you will then allow it to pass from the mind and bring your attention back to concentrating upon the name that you are and that which describes you. Thus, whenever the mind would wander, you will train it and discipline it by simply and gently, but persistently, returning the mind to its point of concentration, to its point of focus.

However, you must not expect results. To expect results is to tell God what to do. You may properly *anticipate* an appropriate response in due time, in God's own time. Beyond that, release it. Thus, it is seldom that while you are sitting in contemplation you will receive anything. And indeed, if you did, Spirit suggests you might want to consider it suspect and question if indeed this is reliable. For while you are sitting in the quiet you should receive nothing at that point but the preparation of self to receive. Do you understand?

Thus, after the meditation has concluded and you have gone on about the day's activity, at some point throughout that day or another day or another day, you will, through the mental faculties we have discussed, receive an insight, you will receive an inspiration, you will receive intuition, you will find some response coming from your request through these mental faculties. Be alert to this, for often it will come very quietly and very subtly, and if you are not alert to it you might easily miss it.

Begin each day

from Master Adalfo

I suggest that you begin each day by finding your center. Many people do that by meditating, but you can do it briefly sitting on the bed! Call in your guidance for the day, feeling your own power, your own center, knowing your connection to the earth, to the sky, to the world around you. For just two minutes, briefly. This is not difficult. And then, during the day, remind yourself, "Let me find my center." Then be open to sharing that feeling with others, allowing them to share in it.

This also means you must be willing to share in their version of center, which sometimes will be off center. How do you know that if you do not experience it? How can you guide them back to center if you do not know where they are? It is like someone lost in the desert. If you have no idea from where they are lost, how can you get them home? So you must be willing to take others in and share this centering energy with them. It encompasses everything that you do, every person you are with.

When you read about someone having the Christ consciousness, that is what it is. It is that awareness, that consciousness, that they are a part of Source, that they are a part of the Divine Spirit.

The Divine Spirit does not work well if it is hidden. The Christ consciousness is not a hidden thing. It is everywhere, it is light. So it goes that you cannot hide your light under a bushel. You cannot hide the Christ consciousness. So some people are a little afraid of getting there because it puts them out where they can be seen.

This can be a little uncomfortable at times, especially when you are around people who don't like the light because they are not wanting to see where they are for fear that they may be off their path. But you can lighten them up too by simply sharing your light.

The power of prayer

from Bartholomew

The goal of prayer is to pray without ceasing. It is to pray constantly in whatever way appeals to you, so that prayer becomes a part of your life.

Very simply, prayer is turning your consciousness within and starting up a higher vibration. The more you do it, the stronger the vibration. This is why I don't care *what* you pray for or *how* you pray. With the action of prayer, you build a vibration which increases, until there will come a time when you feel bad because an hour has gone by and you haven't in some way prayed. And soon you find that you need, more than anything, a way to live every moment so that some part of you is *always* turning its face toward the Divine--no matter what else may be happening. That's when you move into the realm of praying without ceasing.

Eventually, before the path ends, each one of you has to find a way to keep your face to the Divine, and prayer is certainly one way. The only difference between "good" prayer and "bad" prayer is whether you're doing it in your heart or in your head. If you are doing it in your heart, you can feel the vibration being set up. If it's an automatic mental process, nothing very much happens. But there are no rules.

You want to do something you can *feel* inside. That means getting *inside* of yourself and praying from there. You want a dialogue with the Divine that your whole being responds to. And where you feel that is in the chest area--what you call the heart. Why do you think there are pictures of Jesus with His heart open and surrounded by light? Because that is where the feeling was. Why are there pictures of the saints with their hearts aglow? Because that is where the feeling was. So, if you are going to expedite your prayer-learning, get into your heart and move from there. Prayer is not a mentalization or mindless repetition of someone else's words. If you *feel* your prayers, you *will* become alive to them.

My friend, you know clearly from your own experiences what ignites your heart and what doesn't. So I beg you to do those things. Without anybody's permission. I don't see any reason why you can't begin to feel that power getting stronger and stronger--until it floods your being and gives you a desire beyond all others, the desire to feel God all the time.

Simply yearn for whatever you hold the Divine to be. Yearn for Its beauty, Its wholeness, Its power, Its wonder. *Yearn for it!* See these things in your mind and feel them in your heart as real and alive and filled with light.

Regardless of how you pray, in the end the results are the same. Prayer is done to increase vibrational frequency. When you are increasing vibrational frequency in other ways, you are doing the same thing as praying. You are feeling vaster, acknowledging it, being grateful for it, and living in an expanded state. Then, with the discipline, you move into experiencing the *wonder* of that state. You move into the doing of it, just living life, feeling life live you. Feeling life live you *is* a form of prayer.

For you, it is appropriate just to trust the wonderful spontaneity of living. The test is whether or not

Before your path ends, each one of you has to find a way to keep your face to the Divine, and prayer is certainly one way.

you feel more love. If you feel more love, then whatever you are doing is right. Prayer, in whatever form, increases frequency. What was regimented and disciplined in order to get that frequency going, you did. Then one naturally moves to other parts of one's being. And that's what you now do. So the next step is to blend both the discipline and the spontaneity.

The thing I ask you to remember is how necessary it is to find a way to be aware of the energy-in-motion all the time. If it's through prayer, do it. Whatever the method, allow yourself to feel it and be grateful. Please be grateful. You are all part of an experiment. There is something going on here, isn't there? The question is: What is it? What's happening? Pay attention to what is going on inside yourself. Whether it's through prayer or observation, whatever it is, just *be* there! Don't go on automatic. Live your life from a point of empowered awareness. It is delightful, and why not?

Live your life from a point of empowered awareness.

Life is never the same. You change all the time. You go from one room of your psyche to another and it's beautiful. I do not think you need to worry. I think the more you enjoy your life, the more wonderful it is. Because the more you love, the more love will be around you. Less humbug and more wonder. And it's beautiful!

Do not get stuck on rules. Praying without ceasing means finding the Divine in your life, watching yourself, and moving through life with gratitude and power. Be the "observer" of your own process. There is an ongoing, central "I" that moves through your life. That is what you pay attention to. Sometimes it moves through prayer, sometimes through breathing, sometimes through sex, sometimes through walking. It moves through everything! Get in touch with the central "knowing" that you are the "I" of yourself. Stay with it. There are no rules. And above all, enjoy it.

Recognizing and Using Your Truths

from Dr. Peebles

Dear friends, I suggest that in your prayers and affirmations you think in terms of accepting and acknowledging the guidance of the higher self. If you say, "I request it, I want it, I am going to have it," at that point you are still caught in an attitude of self-awareness. Instead, just accept it. Say, "I will *accept* my experiences as guidances from my higher self and I will acknowledge that the experiences that come my way are guidances from my higher self. And I acknowledge that when an experience presents itself, I will have the opportunity to determine if I will participate or if I will observe from an objective point of view." Do you see the difference?

In dire times

from Enid

When you are truly disturbed or agitated, get yourself into that quiet space until your heart has quieted, and allow it to quiet more and more and more. Talk to your body and say, "Quiet, my dear, quiet. I want my body to be quiet. We have questions to ask here." You can't channel yourself from an angry place or from a totally devastated place or a place from which you're caved in. You can't say, "Please help me," and get a booming answer. What you need to do, if you're not enjoying that state too much, is bring yourself out of that state. The only reason you continue in that state is because you feel there's some value there. But you do always have the option of moving out of it.

You have this tiny little split second in which you decide how to respond to anything that happens. Suppose you decide, "Boy, this is really big. I just know I'm really going to get upset here. I'm not even going to be able to speak to my guides, I'm going to be so upset." That's when your guides are standing out there laughing their heads off and saying, "Isn't that cute?"

Now, jesting aside, sometimes you're in a really dire situation. It is so dire that you find that you can't bring yourself out of it. What I suggest you do at that point is pray to yourself. You say, "Dear one, I am in so much trouble now. I am in such terrible trouble and I've done all I can to come out of this state and I can't come out of this state enough to channel you, so I'm going to trust that you're going to help lead me in another way. So please help lead me in another way. And please, guides, stay around me and help sustain me until I get through this experience. And help me bring this experience to a higher level so that it can be of use to me in my growth." And you certainly can do that. And you will be inspired. Believe me, you will. And it doesn't matter whether you've ever channeled your higher self before or not.

You've always been a part of your total self. And you've always talked to it. You talked to it so much when you were tiny. It's no different now. So talk to that beautiful part of yourself--the mature, wonderful, totally developed part of you that has grown spiritually mature.

Divisions of self

from Abrham

The first thing you physical beings can recognize is that during each and every moment of time you are functioning totally. You are never without any portion of your being. You are never *minus* any portion of your being. You are always total in your beingness and you are always functioning within your own totality.

Too many times you physical beings try to analyze consciousness. And as you try to analyze consciousness, your conclusion is confusion. Within your process of analyzing, you lose sight of your feeling. Your feeling is how you are existing at any given moment in time. What you feel is most definitely real. And if you take a moment's time and look about in your life, you will realize that all things in your life are physical manifestations of how you feel about yourself. What type of automobile are you driving? What type of home do you have? Look at your furniture. Look at your friends, your family, your children, your parents, your pets, your plants. How do you like what you are seeing? If there are some areas of your life that don't quite seem to be what you want, realize one thing: those areas are what you have always wanted in your life.

Now, maybe some of you physical beings are going through hard times, and you may be thinking, "Well, this is not of my choosing." Hogwash!

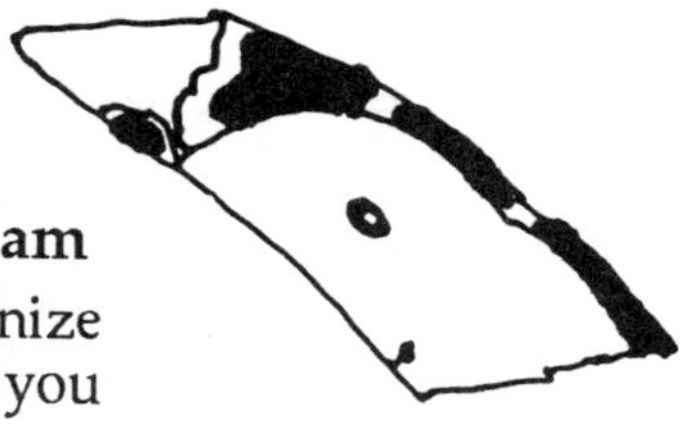

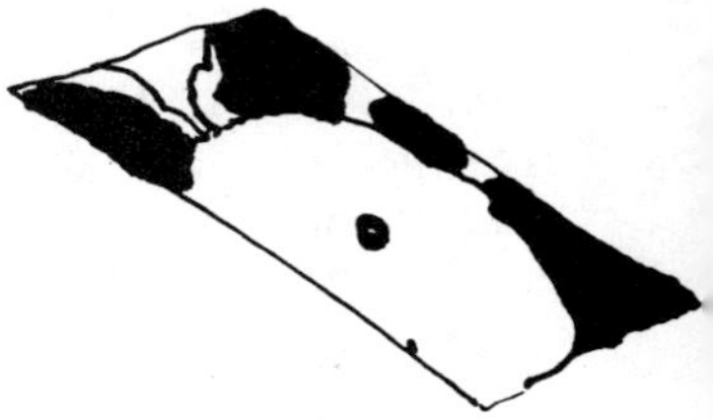

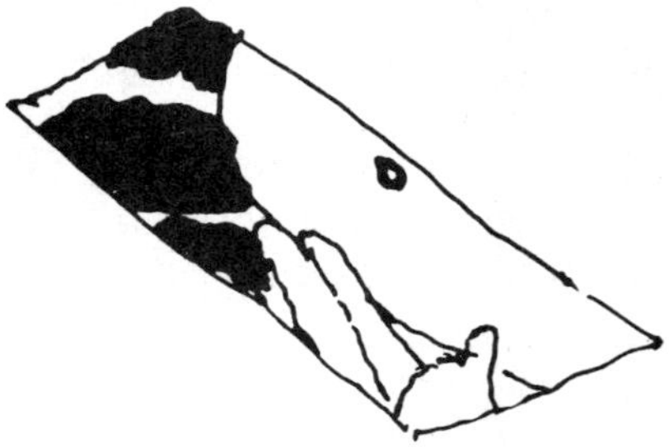

Yes it is! You choose everything. You create everything in your life. You create with emotion. You are emotion. You are emotional energy. All that you think and feel, you will express in one way or another. And when you express what you are feeling, you then begin the process of physical creation.

Now, how many times do you awaken in the morning, *feeling very good* about yourself, and your day is brilliant? And how many times do you awaken in the morning, feeling not so good about yourself, and your day is less than brilliant? How many times, as you are feeling good about yourself, do you look in your mirror and enjoy what you are seeing? And how many times when you are feeling not so good about yourself do you look in the mirror and not quite *enjoy* what you are seeing?

All things in your life are your
emotions
being shown back to you in a
physical form
that you can relate to.

Look at any object in your home and you will find that the moment you look at the object, you will have a feeling. Why? Because that object is a creation of your emotional energy. Desire is your energy set into motion within your psychic self. And the psychic self is that magical aspect of your beingness that seems to be free, *totally* free, and, at times, quite elusive. And that psychic aspect of you is what creates your reality.

If you examine the issue of reality you will arrive at one startling conclusion. That is that reality is the illusion. Why? Because all things change. The only constant in the universe is *change.* And as each moment changes, you, yourself, within yourself, are changing. Your body changes in size, shape, and mass. Your thoughts change, your moods change, your desires change with each moment of time. You measure your reality by and you base your reality upon your achievements.

Many times you do things to make yourself feel good about yourself. When you function in that way, you begin creating beliefs that the only time you can feel good about yourself is when you are functional. In thinking and believing that way, you are overlooking the fact that you are always totally functional, and you then begin placing limitations upon your own functionality. You begin then to judge yourself, to ridicule yourself, to criticize yourself. And you fall into a pattern of insecurity. You function then with and within what you term "negative emotions."

Once again, drop the judgment of positive and negative and function with and within allowance and equality, and realize there is never a moment's time when you are not functioning. You are always total in your own functionality.

Quit dividing yourself into
a higher self,
a middle self,
a lower self,
and just begin
accepting yourself
as the self.
You are only of one self.

Again, it is your own analysis of consciousness that brings you to believe in a higher self, a middle self, a lower self. You are all looking for your higher self and usually avoiding your lower self, and you place yourself within your own middle self. Now if you have selves, if you have a higher self, a lower self, a middle self, how does it feel to be of a middle self? How does it feel to be of a lower self? And how does it feel to be of a higher self? If you ask yourself those three questions, I think your answers will be, "I don't know."

As you divide your life into positives and negatives, you also divide your life into highs and lows and mid-grounds, and, once again, as you function in that way, you lose sight of your commandment. You function then within certain patterns of certain emotions and you lose sight of being total emotional energy. And then you play victim to the idea of higher self and to the idea of lower self.

All the journeys that you will take in your life are journeys within your own self. If you wish to find something in your life, the best place to look is within, within your own self, your one self, your total self.

You are what you are *right now.* And what you are *right now* is what you will always be. Rather than trying to find a higher self, why not just allow yourself to be more of what you are right now? And that means, why not just try yourself out? Quit hiding away in your own safety zone. Quit placing limitations upon what you can do. Quit functioning in a structure of what you must do, must not do, should do, should not do.

Those separations began when you were a child, when you were told what to do, what not to do, how to act, how not to act, and so on and so on. You began to structure your life upon, and within, positives and negatives. And as you were growing up and maturing, you had structured the framework of your reality to be of a division, and all of your actions and reactions had and have their positives and negatives. And as you go throughout your life, viewing your reality in a divided way, you come to accept yourself as being divided within your own beingness.

So a very convenient way to deal with all the positives, all the negatives, all the ups and all the downs in your life is to believe in selves within yourself. All of those selves will deal with all of those positives, those negatives, those ups, downs, highs, lows, and you will assign your focus of attention to cover all of those areas in your life. You will realize yourself as a divided being rather than a total being as you assign portions of your focus of attention to various aspects or areas of your life.

And you will then create personalities that will deal with positives, with negatives, with highs and lows and ups and downs. And in time you will begin searching for a way out or a way into freedom, and you will think that when you reach your own higher consciousness or higher mind, you will find that freedom.

Question: Is there a way to help little people (children) understand their totality?

from Abrham

You can, by eliminating positives and negatives, rights and wrongs, goods and bads, and by teaching experience. All things are experiences, and *nothing* has a fixed consequence.

Now, when you are dealing with a child's creative force, always show the child that everything that he or she will do is a *creation.* Erase the judgments and direct the child's creative force in such ways that the child understands that life is a self-created experience.

For example, walking out into a street as an automobile is approaching: what does that mean to you? What would that mean to a child? You adults attribute very different meanings to life than children. Children do things because they are always expressing their creative force. Too many times you adults do things because you have fear. The child has no fear until you, the adults, teach fear.

So, if the child is taught that everything in life is an experience, the child then will function free of limitation. And when the child functions free of limitation, the child will mature into an adult who will be totally fnctional.

Now, in considering cause and effect, realize that a cause will always cause a consequence. That effect is what is taking place in the now moment in time in one's life. Now, by working with the effect, the child then can realize his or her own potential, his or her own ability. And then, when the child views life with his or her own imagination, the cause has no value. What takes place then is simply that the effect becomes an idea that is subject to change. And the child then understands that life is change. Nothing will stay the same. Change is found within the imagination. Now, as the child views his or her life within the imagination, the child then is opened up to freedoms and not limitations.

In your world which has been raised on cause and effect, too many times you people base your life on cause, and when you *cause* things in your life, you also cause a consequence.

But when you *allow* things, you change the effect. And when you change the effect of your life or in your life, you realize creative freedom. Having then a sense of creative freedom, you will also understand more of how you function as a total being. And with that knowledge, you will realize there is no real reason to strive to reach your higher mind, because you are existing right now in your higher mind. You are also existing right now in your lower mind, if you wish. But, again, if you consider higher mind and lower mind then you are judging yourself as if you are a divided being.

As you were growing up, how many times were you told you were brilliant? How many times were you told, "Watch out! Don't do that! You do not deserve everything! You'll never have everything, so why try?" Do you understand me? Change your life's training. Trade in your life's training and create a brand-new training that allows you freedom--freedom to function.

The little gods

from Ramtha

(Speaking to a small child or to the small child within us all.)

Once there was greatness in the sky--thunder in the sky, and lightning in the sky, and a wind that blew a warm rain over a land that was as beautiful as you. And when the gentle wind blew the warm rain over the land called Terra, it nourished all the little things therein, and all the elements rejoiced.

That which created the thunder, and the lightning and the gentle wind, and the warm rain, were gods littler than you. And the wondrous thing about what they created is that they loved it all! They did not know what is termed evil, or wrong, or ugly, or fear. They knew only love.

When many of the gods came to Terra, and they each became a little child, just like you are, someone told them they were not perfect. And they became scared, and confused, and frightened. That made them grow very tall. It made them grow tall to protect themselves. And they became giants.

When they became giants, each tried to be stronger than the others, more esteemed than the others, more knowing than the others.

The little gods who did not come to Terra looked out the window, so to speak, and watched with great curiosity as their brothers, who had grown very tall, became very hateful, and spiteful, and angry. And they watched them, and they could not understand. And they began to weep.

Soon the Father of these little gods came, and he asked them, "Why weep you?"

And they said, "We know not why they feel the way they feel, why they cannot feel the way *we* feel."

And the great god, the Father, pondered for a moment, and said unto them, "Do you still love your brothers who are tall, who are expressing those things you know not of?"

And the little gods said, "Indeed, we still love them. What else is there?"

The great god said, "Indeed! What else is there." So he took the little gods, and he put them in a great force around Terra, and he called them the Overlords of the Universe. And the great god said unto them, "You will keep balance in this universe. And you will be a constant reminder to your brothers, who have grown so tall and have become so limited, of what purity really is."

Beloved child, there are cities of gods who protect the entire universe, and those gods are smaller than you. Yet they can hold the sun in their hands and the stars upon their fingertips, and their laughter brings harmony to the world.

I find you most beautiful because you are like the little gods who are more powerful, more loving, than the bigger gods.

Look at your little hand. I have made it magical. When you feel bad, put your hand upon your being, and it will be well. When someone else feels bad, put your hand upon them, and they will be well. When you forget that you are wonderful, and beautiful, and perfect, look into your hand: it will remind you of it. And when you think you are small, and helpless, and powerless, look into your hand. It will remind you of the little gods who protect all the others, and how small but powerful they are.

Never be in a hurry to grow up. Continue to be the magnificent god that you are, just as you are. Be happy with who you are, and be a little child for a long, long time. For all those who have grown up and have become weary in their lives are needing to become just like you.

All of them were born knowing about the gods, just like you, yet they were brought up to have it reasoned out of them. I will teach them to be like little children again.

Dealing With Your Hidden Fears

from Ting-Lao

For some people, becoming connected with their higher selves brings a fear of success, and a fear of feeling the God within, of feeling self as an aspect of God. You fear that you will then feel separated from the rest of the people. You do need people, but you also need God.

from Enid

For many beings, the idea of communicating with something not totally physical is very frightening. The reason behind this is that writers and movie-makers who make movies for dramatic effect like to really overdo the possibilities of the "evil being" coming through and tearing up the house and kill-ing. They do this for dramatic effect, but some people take it to be the truth.

The fearfulness comes from people who are afraid they are going to run into an evil being who is going to do terrible things, and that they're then going to vomit pea soup. Now, that isn't going to happen. No matter what you are afraid of, your spirit guides are going to make sure it doesn't happen. They love you so much that they're going to do all they can to make channeling easy for you.

I can give you a little tip so you'll never worry about running into what you might call an "evil being." I like to think of them as being a little mischievous and loving to play jokes. They get a great big kick out of making people fearful.

There are beings who are wafting around, who haven't made their transition yet. But you can avoid communicating with them or bringing them into your space if you go into a state of consciousness that is actually "coming out" of the state of consciousness. Instead of reaching for a deep state, one that is deeper into the physical universe (which is where they are), you want to reach a *light* state of consciousness to bring you out of the physical universe state.

You know when you are in that state because you feel brighter, you can hear sounds further away, and you are more aware of what's going on around you. Everything seems more available to you. You may feel that your body is less available to you, because you may feel a wonderful, soft floating sensation. If your ears and all your other senses are sharp, you know you are on the right track. And then when you reach out you are reaching out "beyond" this universe. When you do this, you reach for the God-like beings.

When you reach outside this universe,
you don't find a poltergeist or the being
who is going to play a trick on you.

And if you miss the mark, the way you can tell right away is if they say negative things, or they say something terrible about you, or they give you dire warnings. Then you know that it's someone playing tricks on you because your spirit guides won't give you these dire warnings and make you feel bad.

Ridding yourself of unbiddens

from Spirit

If a spirit does attach itself to you, either as a thought form or as a desire form or as a passion or as one of the vices, the way to stop it and detach it is by first acknowledging its presence! You can never deal effectively with an enemy that you run away from.

You can never deal effectively with an
enemy that you fear so much that you hide.

Thus, you will not exhibit fear, but instead, you will do as David of old: you will prepare a table in the presence of your enemy. Acknowledge its presence and you will give direction to it, just as you would to a mouse or to some other vociferous form that would enter your physical house. Shame on you if you would kill it, for it is not yours to take its life. You may pick it up by the tail and put it out in the field. If you will not do that, you will bless it with the light and give direction that it will go of its own accord and leave you alone.

Anytime you are afraid, or experience fear of an animal, it will immediately gain the advantage. Even a bear is ordinarily, in its own natural habitat, afraid of humans, and will not approach one unless the human stinks with fear. That's an open and direct invitation. Naturally, the bear, because of its own nature, will follow that instinct.

Dear ones, what we are saying is, acknowledge the spirit's presence, and do not avoid it through fear because that brings stench and stink to your body and mind. And next, bless it. Now what does a blessing do? It effects a change. The *intent* of any blessing is to change something, to change the form of it. You change it from a form of a spirit or of evil or of negativity by neutralizing its form, and then, when you are thus learned, you change its form into a positive form and you bid it go with your blessing. Go where? Out into the universe? No, you bid it go back to whence it came. You send it back to its own source.

In the same way that you deal with that unwelcome and unbidden spirit, such is the way you learn to meditate. First, sit in the quiet to meditate. You will then find yourself amazed at how many thoughts will sudenly begin to rush into your mind. Some of those thoughts dare to tread where an angel would fear to tread. How do you rid your mind of that complete clutter?

First, acknowledge the presence of all these unbidden and unwelcome travelers. And then, gently but firmly, take each single thought one at a time and neutralize it by blessing and releasing it so you change its form. And then give it direction and send it back to whence it came.

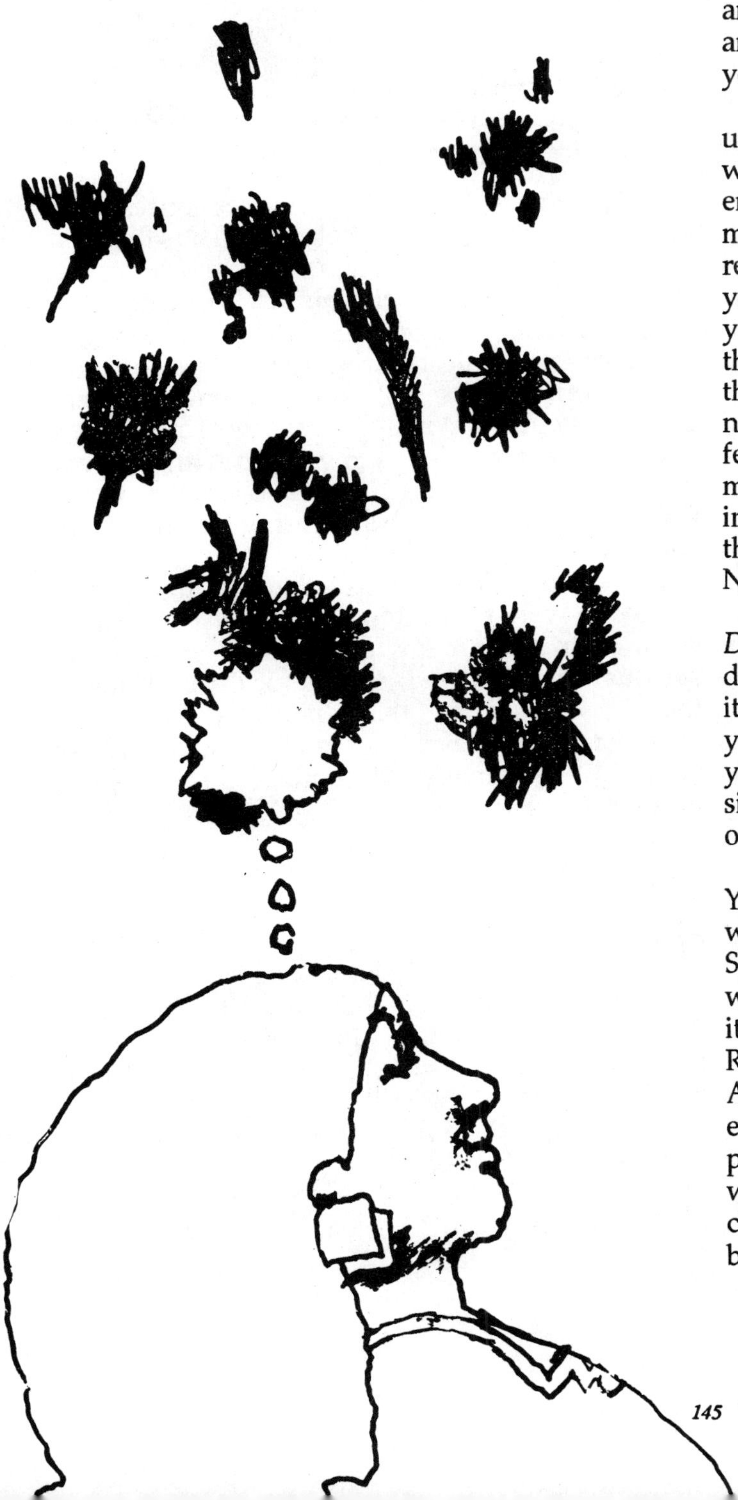

And once you do that often enough, regularly enough, your mind will soon get the point that you are no longer going to tolerate its wanton mischief and that it's now going to have to knuckle down and get to the business of thinking the thoughts that you want it to think.

And that applies just as well to the cleansing of unwanted spirits. Acknowledge the presence of that which is unwelcome, face to face. Your greatest enemy is fear. Be it from the bill collector or the mother-in-law, it is immaterial. You will always remain in charge when you stand face to face with your enemy and say, "How dare you! How dare you!" And you will say to this unwelcome spirit, to this unbidden thought, "I bless you in the name of the Father and the Son and the Holy Spirit. I change now the form of your being from that which will affect me negatively into that form which, if it affects me at all, will affect me in a positive way. And now, in the name of the Christ, I bid you to go. Return this moment to that source from which you came. Now, go in the name of the Christ."

And then you put it aside because it's finished. *Da capo al fine*, leave it alone. Don't worry about it, don't gloat over it, and don't pester it to death. Leave it alone. Don't hang on to it with one hand while you bid it go with the other. That's what many of you do. You enjoy the titillation, so you are responsive to the law while you hold it back. Let it go, dear ones, while you do your Father's work.

And once it's departed, you must cleanse the area. You will shine a radiant blue light upon it, from within your mind's eye, that is the light of the Holy Spirit, the shimmering, radiant blue of the spirit, which will cleanse the area and effectively sterilize it. And you will cleanse the area with cold water. Running cold water over it is all that's necessary. And if that's not practical, walk upon fresh grass, even in the snow, even in the rain. And if that's not practical or possible, stomp your feet. Even in that way you effectively neutralize the charge and discharge it. When you have finished, go on about your business and carry on.

Optional Tools of Communication

Dreams

from Li Sung

Dreams provide opportunities for the contents of the unconscious mind to come through to the conscious mind. Both the lower and higher selves take this route, but we would make note that spiritual dreams come from the higher self. Dreams which would provide inspiration and motivation, dreams which promise love and help a person to achieve a goal, these come from the higher self. Dreams of lost loves, of accidents, of painful experiences, of agonies, these come from the lower self. So we wish for you to pay attention to the dreams from the higher self, the spiritual dreams, for they are truly guiding principles to help you map out your life.

Tarot cards

from Spirit

These are indeed an acceptable form, when they are properly understood and when they are properly applied. When they were first developed, they were not meant to be a method of divination. These are keys that help unlock the mysteries that are concealed within the Qabbalah, and the Qabbalah is the

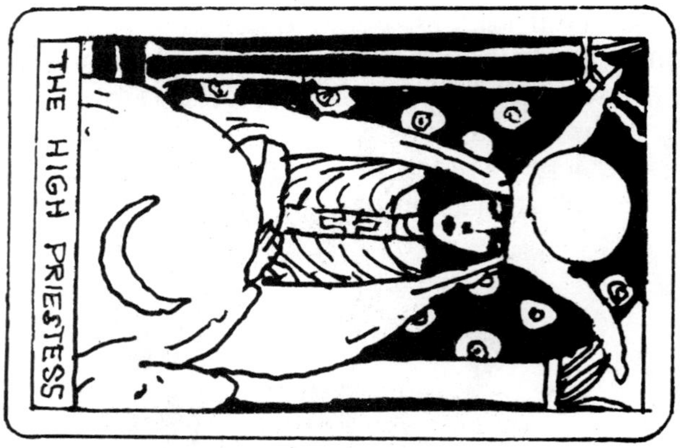

key that helps to unlock the mysteries concealed in the sacred writings, in the holy writ. Thus the tarot is a symbolic language and, as we have often stated, there is no language where spirit is. We do not have language here. We function at this level by thought. Thus, we communicate through symbols. And tarot is a pictorial representation of the universal language of symbols. When these symbols are properly understood, studied, and worked with, they are that key which reveals the arcane wisdom in the Qabbalah and thus they help to bring enlightenment and lead one from darkness.

But a warning again is issued: these ought not be used--nor were they intended to be used--for personal divination or for fortune-telling. These are spiritual keys that are intended for the uplifting of the consciousness and the expansion of the awareness and for the development of the soul, and are not meant to be maligned or misused for personal prophecies or predictions.

The I Ching

from Spirit

The *I Ching* is actually a book of wisdom and it comes to the human family through the Chinese influence. It is a record of wisdom that was trumpeted and scribed and put in that form for ease of transmission. It goes along with the books of Li and of Confucius, and the five great books in Cathay or in Sheena. These five books together are the sacred writings of those places, just like you have two parts to the *Bible* called the Ancient Testament and the New Gospels Testament. In China there are five

major books, each of which contains smaller books. The *I Ching* is one of the major writings. And they are used in the way which reveals the higher self through the application of the mind.

Runes

from Spirit

This is another symbolic language that comes from ancient and arcane experiences in Nigeria and along the Nile and in the Egyptian influences. And these go back thousands and thousands of earth years, prior to that which was known as the land of Is Ra El. Thus, these go back to the Chaldean influence and they go back to the influence of Ur. And you will find these are that which, again, when

properly charged and when appropriately dedicated by sincere seekers, can be a guide and a key that will lead to the deeper understanding. Again, these are not meant as a play toy for children.

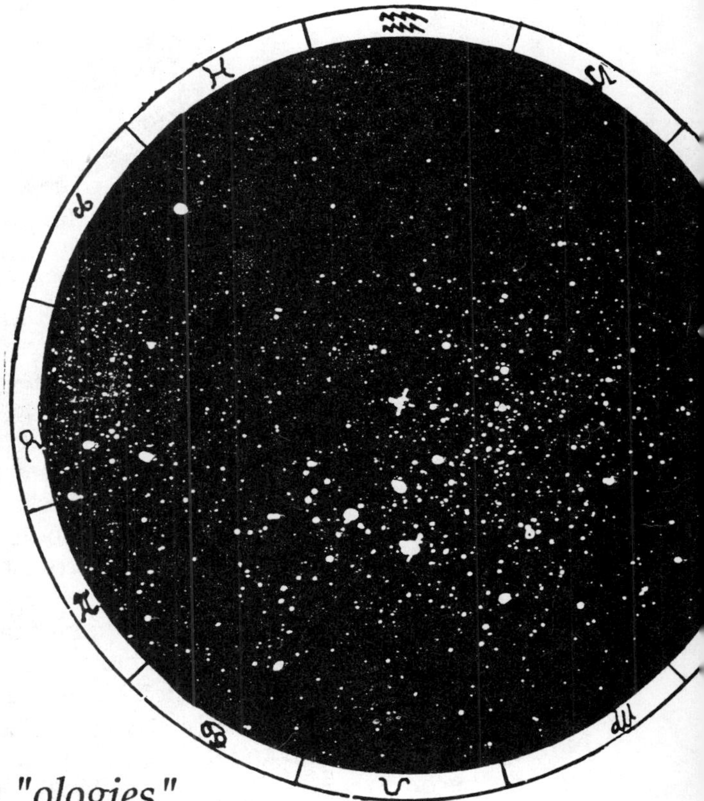

The "ologies"

from Master Adalfo

Astrology, numerology, and such are very useful tools. And they often encourage people. But *how* you use them is critical. It is not a game, you see. If they are used only as a game, you will have play time, surely, but you will not get much insight. It is how you go about it. If you work with astrology, who is your astrologer? Is your astrologer on his or her path? Because it may be difficult for astrologers to help you find things on your path if they are not knowing what their own paths are. If you are using something like the runes, they are very good indicators if you use them in a holy way. It's like a sacred ceremony. And if you do it in that way, it can be very enlightening. But it is *how* you do it; it is not just the doing.

Preparation and charging

from Spirit

Dear ones, suppose you will take the tarot, or you will take the little sticks or you will take the runes. There are many, many different versions of these, are there not? When the seeker accepts that these can be a valid method of inquiring, of seeking, of learning, and of experiencing, then these tools must be charged. So it is that after you have presented yourself as worthy, these tools must be charged by each individual, just as a crystal would be charged by the one who would use the crystal.

They must be charged in much the same way as you would charge a battery. Thus, you must apply the electrical current to it and let it sit and be charged before it becomes useful; is this not so? In the same way, the individual who will make use of these particular forms must charge them with the electrical apparatus of that individual. Thus, the individual must give of his or her own essence before that activity will be anything more than just a mere set of cards that have pretty symbols; do you understand? It is when they are charged with the atomic force of the individual and then properly used after that, that they will be capable of releasing their secrets. Thus, they then function in such a way that they conceal their secrets from the profane who would misuse them, for the profane will not be able to charge them. But they will reveal themselves to the sacred and to the true seeker. According to the degree they are charged, they will release their secret.

You are your own guru

from Soli

Your higher self is your highest being, my friends. There is *no one* higher than you. There is no teacher, no spirit guide, no guru of any shape, kind, form, in any dimension anywhere in all of creation that is higher than your own higher self. Your own higher self knows what's best for you above and beyond anyone else, above and beyond any other teacher or entity of any kind. When you are listening to your own higher self, you have no need of Soli. You have no need of a psychic, guru, teacher, or anyone else. Our job is done, my friends, when no one wishes to speak to us any longer, for then you will have truly gone within and discovered the God that you are.

Our job is done when no one wishes to speak to us any longer, for then you will have truly gone within and discovered the Gods that you are.

Going Home:
Life in the Spirit World

from Robbyn and His Merrye Bande

Life after life! What does this mean?

You, on this planet, look at life as if it were its cycles. When something is living and breathing and capable of growth and change within its cells, you say it is "alive." When its cells are no longer capable of any change except decay, you say it is dead. And that is natural given what life is really like on this planet. You *compress* your consciousness into a limited body and you can only see what those limits will allow. You see things as *life and death* rather than as just one cycle of a constantly ongoing odyssey. When someone you love "dies," you grieve because you have lost something dear to you.

When a baby is born, you rejoice: a new life has begun (even if the soul of that new little body has been around the universe for millennia!). And that is pretty much how you see things on this planet, and that's fine. Of course, some of you have a different perspective, you believe in an afterlife and so on, but we're just talking here about the normal, natural human response.

One of the lessons of this planet is to learn to care very, very much . . . not a detached, universal love (although it's good to practice that, too) but an intense, personalized, focused attachment to one or more other human beings. Those of you who have a hard time with this personalized love have a hard time on the planet, indeed. And that love is one of the most fulfilling opportunities on the planet when it is a clear expression (and a pretty frustrating one when it is not!), and it is the most important lesson you will learn here, including loving yourself.

So what does love have to do with life after life?

Well, it is the very universal type of love that caused you to manifest and express in form in the first place. That form first existed as the energy of what you don't have an English word for, but what we might call "pre-soul." The pre-soul came from what you might call idle thoughts and fantasies of the Creator, or different aspects of the Creator. Now the Creator desired to express itself in the form we call "soul," and, in most cases, soul went on to have a physical body. And this whole chain of events had a very specific purpose.

As we and several others have said before, that very specific purpose was to allow for greater and greater expression through form (an expanding universe), so that all that each soul expressed as form was also put in service for other souls to use, learn from, and grow from, and so that more and more souls could express as form. (More ideas and thoughts of the Creator could come to life.) And so that the thoughts and ideas of the souls could come to life, too.

Well, folks, that's it . . . life after life after life; life, the universe,and everything in a nutshell. Of course, that doesn't say much as far as astrophysics goes, but it really is just that simple. The rest of it, all the explanations, the theories, religious beliefs, and so on are just a process for the form. That *process*, we suspect, is what you, dear people, are *really* interested in.

It's not as if there aren't tons of satisfactory explanations already. Many of you believe that when you snap that silver cord (die, physically) you go to your eternal rest and reward, and if you believe that strongly enough, you will. Some of you believe that when you snap that silver cord you pop into another body and come right back, and if you believe that strongly enough, you probably will. Some of you believe that unless you've been somebody else's version of good, you might go to purgatory or hell, and if you believe that strongly enough, you probably will. And there are those of you who are so confused and attached to your concept of life that when you do snap the silver cord, you just hang out on Earth and sulk because people don't pay any attention. (Until someone exorcises you and brings it to your attention that you died.) And the rest of you are sitting there thinking, "Yeah, and so what *really* happens?" (Oh boy, you really give us a lot of power, don't you?)

Well, as we said, your beliefs will have an influence on what happens. Some of you will go to your eternal rest and reward, but after 60 billion years or so of floating around on metaphysical clouds singing and playing harps, you do tend to get a little bored. Those of you in purgatory and hell tire of it almost instantly. And some of you even get tired of reincarnating. So then what?

Well, the Creator and universe are always happy to have help, so most of us (and you) go looking for something nice and fun to do. That may be helping to design new planets with new lessons, or it may be helping to sort out events that seemed a little disastrous on a planet somewhere (like the Dark Ages). Or it may be taking a special assignment to reincarnate somewhere to help a planet that needs the influence of your specialization.

Or some may decide to tend to and record in the Akashic Records (like any good library, they always need help). Or maybe you'll decide to be an angel, guide, or teacher to someone reincarnating somewhere. Not everybody needs this help, so in general you have to be fairly advanced to have a chance to do this. (But you never know when someone reincarnating might need your areas of expertise.)

Or, and this is a really fun and challenging job that everybody loves to do, maybe you will decide to help with creating reality. It's a great job, because you get to work with everybody else . . . the specific angels, guides, and teachers, the spirits who study specific occurrences, and the recorders at the Akasha. (The eternal rest and reward devotees and the purgatory and hell devotees tend to ignore the rest of us until they're good and ready to give up their prevailing beliefs. You have to step over them once in a while, but that's really no problem.)

So what advice can we give you to live on the planet? (If we were inclined to give advice, which we aren't, but which we will, since what we're talking about is paradox--and you thought *Alice in Wonderland* was a children's story!) Well, plan and dream, but don't plot and scheme. Be concerned with the future, but live actively, creatively, and lovingly in the present, in the light. That and that alone will provide you with the tools and building blocks for the future. And that's what life and life after life is all about. And, really, they're one and the same.

Practicing for the Change Called "Death"

from Dr. Peebles

Dear friends, it is then for each of you to practice for the experience known, to the human mind, as "death." In your affirmations, on a daily basis, have the acceptance of the fact that you are willing, ready, and able to take on the responsibility of the change called death at any time, in any way, when it comes to rest upon your doorstep. Affirm that when you make the transition you will be stepping into light, you will be stepping into your higher self, you will be giving up your personality of this, the most recent lifetime. And you will be willingly moving toward the rediscovery of all that ever you have been and all that ever you shall become.

Those who practice on a daily basis (preparing for the change called death) are the ones who will step from the physical density into the light. They

Being born into life is little more than the forgetting of a familiar place, and so it is death.

will not sleep on the spirit side. They will not withdraw on the spirit side. They will give up the physical and take on the nonphysical in the blink of an eye. Even if they make the transition called death from illness, through plague, through flood, through war, they will say, "Experience, thank you for being here." And they will step onward and upward from that moment.

And so it is that you should also be adding to your affirmations that you will accept the change called death for all around and about you. You affirm that you will accept the change called death for your friend as joyfully as you would accept the change called death for the stranger that you have never met. Say to yourself, "I will grieve no more for the death of my mother than I do for the death of the child in Afghanistan." Am I asking you to be cold, calculating? No, dear friends. I am asking you to manifest the unconditional, objective love that allows each and every one to be fulfilled in their own time, space, and way.

Recognize that you chose your lives. Well, so did everyone else. They *chose* to be born in a life of starvation. They *chose* to be born in a life of abundance. They chose to spend many, many years without abundance, then to awaken one morning and find that they have tremendous wealth. Know that each and every one came into life knowing that they would *leave* that life behind. Give them the right to live up to their choices as you have demanded the right to live up to yours, as you have demanded the right to do things your own way. Let everyone else have the same privilege. Let them do it their own way. You do not approve of how they do it? That is acceptable. Then you have the right to choose not to be around those people. No matter how good, no matter how less than good you perceive them to be, if you cannot accept totally, joyfully, the way and the direction of another, rather than confronting them, confront yourself and recognize you are immature, you are spiritually limited, and then you will grow again.

Death in the physicality is little more than a birth into remembrance of that which was once comfortable. The anxieties of birth and death are little more than the psychological, earthbound limitations, not accepting the unfamiliar. But still and all you are human.

Your forms of meditation come in differing densities. Your deepest realm of meditation is equal to stepping out of the body, equal to moving from conscious intellect into conscious higher self. And it is stepping from one plane to another. And so it is both death and birth simultaneously. Re-embrace the familiarity of your higher self. Meditation could easily bring a remembrance of the relationship to birth and death into the subconscious elements of this, your current incarnation.

Your meditations are to focus upon conscious interaction with the purposes of the higher self. But remember, all meditations, even those that are earthbinding, are equal to both birth and death simultaneously.

The dream state is a wonderful area of exploration. When you dream, both during your hours of sleep and your hours of alertness, you are projecting into other brain-wave consciousnesses in physical form. You are projecting into other dimensions, other realms. Often, either the dreams during sleep or the dreams during conscious alertness are steps into what you know and define as the astral. Each time you enter these spaces you are making the change called birth and the change called death. You will want to work toward building conscious recall of all of your dreams. Even though you do not remember *everything* that transpires in that dream state, remember that you did dream so that you will be consciously remembering the familiarity of being outside of the physical body, removed from the current sociological structure.

Your dream state is a state of guidance, reminders, inspiration, discipline. Your dream state is available for you, each of you, to complete oh-so-many experiences with a coworker, a friend, a business associate. The dream state is yours to use to complete your growth. Program yourselves so that your dream process will prepare you for the change called death through getting you back into the conscious *understanding* that there is no time, there is no space.

Dealing with grief

from Dr. Peebles

All of you have lovers, parents, children, friends. You build relationships with them. Now when you say, "Oh, my goodness, one day they too are going to make the change called death," you become apprehensive and irritated. You might not willingly call it irritation, but when you become upset that one that you are close to has died, you are irritated because this person went on to something and couldn't take you along. They went on to remembering what you have forgotten. And so when you have that experience called grief (and it's rightfully yours), you are grieving to a large degree for the fact that you have not remembered that which was once familiar and someone else has. Someone else has completed that which you are still working to complete.

When someone makes the transition known as death, no matter how you are grieving emotionally, psychologically, give them the ceremony of release. Send them into the light visually. Separate from them. Objectively say, "I loved you and I love you but go your way in peace." And as you release them to grow as they are able, accept that you must, from that moment on, with all of your grief, all of your fear, *grow* for your own experiences.

The grief experience during the time of the change called death will not suddenly be gone. Years will not take it away. It will always be with you. It is one of your experiences. But you will be able to *adjust* to it. You will become familiar with it. No one, nothing, will ever replace the ones who moved to the next place; don't *try* to replace them.

And when you think of them, and you have the momentary tear of grief, say, "Thank you. Thank you for remembering another on a similar vibration who grew. Thank you for the reminder that I must go onward and upward myself in physical density." And so when you have grief, take a few moments and demonstrate it. If it means a tear, cry. If it means anger, be angry. But in the privacy of your own time and space, in the privacy with other dear friends.

Do not carry your grief as a banner upon the streets. Do not carry your grief and impose it upon everyone else. It has nothing to do with them. Your grief is yours. Celebrate it.

And when you must stand up in public--going to your job, going to your office, going to your business meeting, your social event--immediately after you have had the experience of grief, do not deny your grief, but do not wear it as a symbol to impose your fears, your irritations, upon others. This helps them develop even greater inability to live in light when they must die or when they must face one close to them making the transition called death.

If you cannot find that kind of strength in your own consciousness, find an individual from history who has demonstrated great strength of character during times of grief and emulate that person.

Be a way-shower and say to the world through the demonstration of your higher self, "Yes, I have grief. But I go onward to success." Those for whom you grieve, their higher selves would want you to go on with your productivity.

But here is an interesting point. As you grieve for the ones who make the change called death, they grieve for you. Yes, your father, who has made the transition, grieves for you for a period of time. He looks back and says, "Oh, I wish they could have come into this kind of life. Oh, wouldn't it have been wonderful had I been able to take them with me." Some will hold on to that grief for the human beings for a long, long, long time, lifetimes even, because you continue to feed their grief with your own grief. You must release them so they are capable of releasing you.

Grief is your right. But remember, your grief is little more than another delightful opportunity to manifest your spiritual faith and light and love. And in this time of great change that you are all living in, these words will be most important. For none of you reading these words will be free of grief in the next few years. None of you will miss the experience of someone dear to you making the transition. None of you will totally circumvent illness, accident, and problem.

Learn how to use grief rather than being used by it. Learn how to be in grief and celebration simultaneously. Take the moments of the good, the days of clarity, and use them with affirmations and treatments to prepare yourselves for the conflicts and the challenges that are awaiting you. And remember, dear friends, you have chosen to be born in a time when you would have these confrontations.

Birth is little more than death from one density to another.

Death is little more than birth from one plane to another.

Grief is little more than the anxiety of not returning to that which was once understood.

Making the transition through suicide

from Dr. Peebles

The subject of suicide always opens up a can of worms. No soul is born other than by choice. Each and every one of you made your choices long before you entered this life. Your death, as you know death, is not always chosen exactly. It could come in various ways according to your growth, according to how soon, how quickly, how willingly you have chosen it.

Many have *chosen* the option of that which you call suicide. But only for their own growth. They chose parents, society, and environment according to the others' growth also. The parent of a being who commits suicide has the need for that experience. The mate, the lover, the friend of one who commits suicide chose, long before they were born, to be associated with one who had the tendency to commit suicide. The committing of suicide is little more than another choice. Many of those suicides become earthbound, not out of a spiritual law, but out of the programming of lifetimes and social standards. Many who commit suicide are capable of moving clearly into the light just as if they had made the transition through old age or through a heart attack.

Suicide does not carry an earthbinding connotation, although many, many in your Christian world will say it does. That is acceptable. But that is only guaranteeing that oh-so-many who commit suicide will bind themselves to the earth plane unnecessarily. And that is only guaranteeing that many--the parents, the friends, the neighbors--will bind themselves to more fear within themselves, of their own growth, their own change, their own lack of willingness to accept the right action of the higher self.

I would go so far as to say that suicide might be in some cases a far more positive choice than choosing to remain in bed for fifteen years of moaning and groaning. If you lie fifteen years and moan and groan and make yourself and everyone else miserable, you are quite probably creating far more karmic interaction than if you were to make the change called death and the choice called suicide.

How Beliefs Affect Passage to the Spirit Plane

from Soli

There are those who maintain their belief systems so strongly on Earth that they have them still when they are in the spirit plane. They are so strongly held that they do not change them even when they have another incarnation; and so they maintain, as it were, the personality that they had in a previous lifetime up and until their new incarnation.

Such beliefs create your reality. There are those who make their transition who have a strong belief system in their continuity of self.

When you make your transition you are still the same individual. It is simply that you do not have the physical body that you had before; you no longer have that around you. So you feel a certain lightness and freeness, but you still are the same individual. You take your soul, your subconscious

mind, with you. You have that continuity of belief. And so what you believe is instantly your reality, it instantly occurs.

There are those who, in making their transition, do not even realize that they have done so. Their belief in self is so strong (their physical environment is so strong) that they do not realize that it has happened. And so they continue to drive down that road within their automobile, within their thought form, and it is reality, totally. There are those who remain upon the Earth plane thinking that they are still alive. They have their physical bodies, created from thought, just as, my friends, you create your physical body within this physical dimension--by thought. They maintain their living place, the same space within the Earth plane, the same way of projecting self, only there is one difference. Now others around them can't see them, do not react to them. It oftentimes causes great frustration and anger. It is those "earthbound" spirits who remain in the house that they've always lived in. And others are there and will not relate to them, which causes difficulty for those on both sides.

This is what you might call the lower level of the spiritual plane, the lower astral. It is a continuous transition from the denseness of the physical to the highest spiritual planes. "High" we speak of in terms of frequency of vibration. We do not wish to imply judgment, for every plane has its purpose--every dimension has its purpose. You will choose lives and experiences in all dimensions for the growth that there is within. The number of lives that you have had and the strength with which you have held opinions and beliefs within a physical lifetime create what you meet within the spiritual plane.

You, my friends, with your knowledge of self, knowledge of the spiritual aspect, do not have such strongly held beliefs that you will create reality so strongly that you cannot see beyond them, which is what many do on passing. You will be met by your spirit teachers and guides. You will work with them, reviewing the lifetime that you have had: reviewing, learning to see that you have nothing to be emotional about, nothing to be angry about, nothing to be guilty about, nothing to be frustrated about, that your life was exactly as it needed to be. It was right and proper. And you will work with your guides

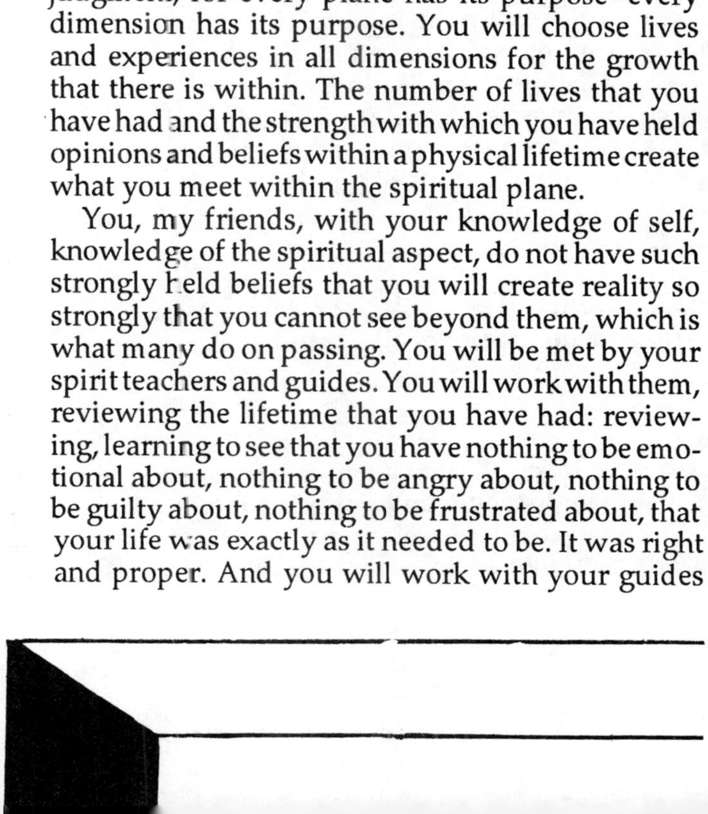

and teachers to understand that, and then to begin to integrate this one lifetime with the other lives that you have had.

To live in the light

from Dr. Peebles

Be in light; live in light until the transition. You are all familiar, hopefully, with the term "hospice." The hospice concept is only the rekindling of a concept used over and over again in societies on the planet earth. The hospice is an environment which acknowledges that your physical life is just about complete, where you attract light, where all around you live in light, acknowledging the pain, acknowledging the anxieties, the fears, but calling upon the guides, calling upon the higher self.

If you cannot go to a hospice to die, you should *live* your job, your home, not according to what worked *yesterday*. You must tell everyone, "We know that I am about to make the transition. I am frightened." Or you must say, "I'm not frightened; and if *you* are, go for a ride for the next ten years because I will not have anything except joy and light around me no matter how difficult this is."

My friends, when you know you are about to make the transition, don't say, "Well, I wonder if it will happen tomorrow or in ten years?" Just surround yourself with light. Call upon the light. And if you say, "But I have to keep working my daily job," do so, but tell everyone, "I'm doing this because I wish to. I am ill physically. I am about to make the transition. And if you can't deal with it, and smile and have a good time, any of you who get caught up in the earthbound way of it, go your way." Do not allow less than light around you in the transition.

Question: Is it possible to explain crossing over to those who are not of like mind?

from Master Adalfo

You can talk until you are blue in the face, and if they are not listening and not believing, it will not help them. They are still going to have their own reality, their own belief, which they will create after they cross. For those who believe there is nothing, they will experience nothing. Reincarnation will have its effect anyway, but they will spend a long time (perhaps) in nothing. After a given time, their spirit helpers will make contact with them and will work with them to help them see how it really is, so to speak.

Many people speak of "near-death experiences" and recall having seen loved ones who are no longer physical. This frequently occurs. After passing, the person is greeted by relatives whom they know. There are also spirit teachers, helpers; and again, people experience what they need to experience. Many people who have had these near-death experiences (as you call them) have seen the one we call "Master Jesus" because that is who they expect to see. He is important to them; He will be there.

from Dr. Peebles

The daily preparations and affirmations that you do for yourself, you may also do with your friends, your companions, your loved ones. You can greatly assist those with illness, physical or mental; those in coma, in deep withdrawal; those unconscious. You can read them materials of the light, the spirit (these do not need to be religious; they need not and should not focus on one specific dogma or creed), and speak to them of moving into the tunnel of light, of embracing as much light as they see. Tell them silently and verbally of your love and the love of all the universe for them. Send them musical notes surrounding them with color.

You could read to one from the *Tibetan Book of the Dead*. You could read to one from the writings of a great poet. You could read from the *Bible*, yes, the Christian *Bible*. Read anything that reaches that inner core of the light of that human being, that tells them they are all right exactly as they are, that they are safe exactly as they are, that they are loved by an eternal vibration, that it is acceptable to go on a new adventure.

The majority of you are not prepared for travel, prepared for adventure. You pride yourselves on being able to pick up your bag and go at the drop of a hat to any place upon the planet earth, but you are not prepared to pick up your invisible bag and make the transition.

So, dear ones, read to people. Project to people sound and color and words that say to them they are loved by the spirit, they are loved by the visible and invisible, they are one with each other's consciousness, they are one with the universal mind. Many are doing this. More will do this. This form must eventually be reinstituted, particularly in this, the approaching of the Aquarian era.

You are all moving into the collective consciousness, the density of freedom while still in the cycles of birth and death. And read to the one, sing to the one who is in a coma whether that one be a stranger, your friend, your child, or your parent. Sing to the one injured in the accident that you pass on the freeway. Though you are not with the one in a coma in the hospital that you drive by, as you drive by send your higher self to read the works of light to those in the coma, those in preparation for the change called death.

The same is true for those who are confined to what you call "nursing homes." Help them to make contact with their higher selves. You can go to these nursing homes physically. You can also go to these nursing homes, retirement centers, vibrationally. When you are gathered in your classes, with your friends, in your centers, you can do such things. You can project to those rooms, project to those places. Do not only send to those who know. Send to all who are hoping, willing, and able to perceive.

Question: Do beings (after crossing) visit their Earth-side families?

from Master Adalfo

There is no one rule. Generally speaking, after crossing, people may visit very often for a period of time. This, of course, depends on the belief system of the person who has crossed. If someone is prepared for life on the other side, they will visit very often at first after crossing, perhaps every day or several times a day. They may even stay around in hopes to make it clear to their family that they have not gone anywhere, that there has been shift, a change, but they are not gone forever.

Gradually after that, the visits will slow down and not be as frequent. But it is important also to know that if you have a need to talk with a member of your family who has passed, you can invite them to come and they will come if they are able. You can ask questions to which they could provide answers, sometimes more to give you peace of mind than anything else.

If someone on this planet has been very ill before crossing, they do spend time in what I will call a "hospital" because that is what you understand it to be--a resting place. They will not always be able to make contact with their family right away.

There is no hard and fast rule to this question. The possibility is there for you to contact those on the other side. Those who have been on the other side for a long time may not be *as* available, but they would be available if you were to ask. They would already have been embarking on other studies and things like that, forming lives of their own now, just as a child does when leaving home. When a child grows up, he makes a life of his own and is *less* available, but *not* unavailable.

Question: Is it possible, using astral travel, to visit loved ones after they have gone to the spirit world?

from Li Sung

Well, it is somewhat safer to wait for them to visit you. For those who are accomplished in astral travel and projection, there is a likelihood that they may join you, in the astral, for a moment. But realize that the choice belongs to the person that has made the transition.

You may open up your light so that they may see it and will be attracted to it and can seek to join it. But if you set out in search for them, you may get lost.

Shine like a beacon and they will be attracted to you when the time is right for this communication.

There is often a period of days (and sometimes longer) in which the soul, having crossed over, is very intent on learning about its new surroundings and finding out what must be done for progression in the next world. That soul may not immediately think of going back to say "Hello" to this world. If you consider that you, one day, may go to a new planet, how long would it be before you came back to visit Earth to say "Hello"? It is a vigorous journey for some.

from Enid

When a being leaves the body, they sometimes like to stay around during the funeral to make sure everybody cries enough. And after that, they stay to comfort the family mostly because they feel such joy and they say, "Mother, don't cry for me. I'm so happy now."

Compressing/decompressing

from Enid

After leaving the body, there are degrees of what I like to call "decompression." You decompress because you had to compress yourself to feel smaller than you are in order to play this game here.

It is exquisite to be compressed, and then you begin to decompress and your feathers begin to lighten and you begin to throw your wings back.

What you feel most in this world is pressure, and you really *become fully aware of this* once you leave the body, because all pressure goes and there is an enormous feeling of lightness and relief.

This is why people who die and are brought back are almost angry sometimes. They don't really want to come back but their guides will push and shove them back to the body because they know it's a mistake and it's not time yet. And they wake up the next day and say, "Well, an angel came to me and the angel told me I still had work to do." And this is how they convince themselves to come back into the body.

Sometimes people are ejected from the body quite unexpectedly, for instance in a sudden accident of some sort--just ejected. Sometimes they go into a confusion and then they don't feel light (they still feel the pressure because they don't know they're out of the body), so the attention is still on that. And then sometimes these people will go quickly and get another body, and we call these "yoyos"--they just sort of yo-yo back and forth. I would say that over half of the beings on this planet have done this. It's very difficult to break it. With a yo-yo experience you make your great plans and your scenario and all your general plans of what you want to experience, so that if you die and then you yo-yo back, you go back to the same blueprint. And that old blueprint gets all tattered and torn and you have 16 lives living the same personality.

Setting It Up for the Next Time Around

Question: Exactly when does the soul enter the body?

from Li Sung

There are various practices, but very often the soul will keep an eye on a body, perhaps occasionally going to see if it is developing properly, and then at the time of birth (or as birth approaches) it will join the body and help guide it through the birth canal, for this is a very intricate process. And if the body is imperfect, very often the soul will choose to leave and there will be self-termination or miscarriage.

The soul may enter the body after birth. We are not aware of any time limit, as such. You see, the body is able to function in a purely mechanical way without the soul being present. But there must be a soul present before there can be emotion. And the emotion experienced by infants at birth is very great. The attachments made with mother and father are very great. And for this, the soul must be there.

It is like your new automobile. Before gasoline is put in the engine, everything is ready; it merely needs the spark of energy to get going.

In what you call "crib deaths," often the soul has had second thoughts. The soul believes it has chosen the wrong body and it has lost its nerve to continue with the rigors and challenges of life, and so it chooses instead to leave quietly and perhaps to incarnate at a later date and more propitious time. And that results in a cessation of breathing of the infant.

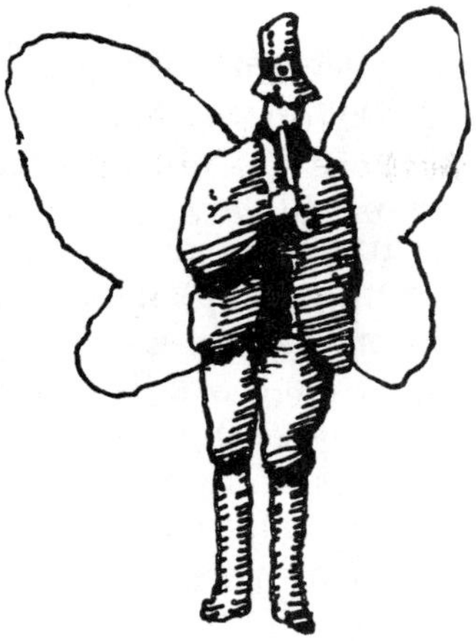

Incarnating in forms other than human

from Dr. Peebles

You are capable of looking at the need for incarnation and suddenly becoming aware, "Well, for goodness sakes, I can have those experiences, the balance that I need, but I do not have to be in a physical body. I have to be influenced by specific beings who are incarnated. I could be in one of those bodies, but there are chances that I could build new karma, or even prolong the old karma." You are able to project (as consciousness) into an event: becoming the consciousness of an event that other people, other beings on this or other planets, need for their growth. You are also able to enter other life forms, yes, *other life forms,* without interfering with your evolutionary process.

As an example: your soul might find that what it really needs most is to learn patience. And to learn that patience, you need to be around specific experiences, events, other souls, but you do not have to interact with them but only to observe, silently. And so you would enter a form, not so that you would have sentience, but so that you would have energy awareness. It could be projected into a rock. It could be projected into a tree.

Now at the very same time, part of your soul might have an incarnation in a physical human

form. But your soul is able to project into that form, such as a tree, to discover and learn patience as it observes other trees, as it observes people climbing it, as it observes a war without being able to influence it, change it, or stop it. Isn't that exciting?

Now friends, did you all understand that experiences, events, have *their own* consciousness, and that there is a soul existing, or a series of souls existing in those events? They are experiencing for their growth. And those of you participating in that event are doing so for your own karmic interchange; but it is an event that must be allowed to fulfill itself or play itself out, not yours to change, not yours to alter, for it is an event of karmic soul consciousness. Most fascinating!

The Spirit Dimension Is a Way Station

from Soli

Your life within the earth plane is a brief period, your time out from life within the spirit dimension. The spirit dimension you might consider to be a *way station*--a place where you go for a little rest and relaxation between your lives of experience in this physical dimension or in other dimensions beyond the physical plane.

What is the difference between the spirit plane and the physical plane? It is one of vibration, one of density, one of lightness and denseness. You, within the physical dimension, are used to dealing with heaviness--with denseness, with slow vibration. Everything is energy and vibrations. The vibrations that you deal with upon the physical plane are low frequency. Those objects that you feel to be solid are simply low-frequency energy coalescences (for want of a better word) that your senses pick up or respond to as being solid. They are not, of course; there is no such thing as a solid in the way that you think of it. But that is how your subconscious mind, your senses, perceive that frequency, that vibration of energy.

It is well known by scientists now that energy is matter and vice versa, as put forward by your great scientist Einstein. Well, within the spirit planes it is far more obviously so.

First and foremost, your thought form creates your reality wherever you are. Your environment (what you see, feel, hear, taste, touch around you) is a projection of your belief system, of what you have stored within your subconscious mind. Thought forms, within the planet earth within this physical dimension, take time to manifest. Those thoughts that recur are those that have the major impact upon your life, upon your environment, upon what you see around you.

Now when you move into the spirit plane, when you make your transition from this to the spirit life once again, you do not have that density of matter holding you down, dragging you down in a sense. Your thought form becomes instantly your reality.

It is important to realize that you are *not the individual that you think you are.* That individuality (that subconscious mind, that projection/belief system that you have) is but one aspect of yourself, your higher self, one aspect. You have many others, some occurring in the same instant and time within the same dimensions, some occurring in previous times, future times--all of them being you in different aspects, your higher self experiencing with different outposts, as if it were, with connections to them all. And so you, as a personality, are but one outpost of your higher self, experiencing. All those experiences come together. You begin to integrate with your other selves, your other lives. You begin to re-coalesce as a spiritual entity so you ultimately know once again your total spiritual beingness.

This does not mean that you stop having experiences. Part of your higher self may very well wish to have another experience within the physical dimension and so you, as that part, will return

There are those who leave the Earth plane firmly believing that they will meet St. Peter at the Pearly Gates with choirs , angels, and golden harps playing. They believe this so strongly that this is exactly what they find when they make their transition.

and experience again. Your own higher self, once you have experienced those things that you need within the physical dimension, will coalesce with other higher selves to form yet higher entities.

And so, what is life like for us within the spirit plane? Once you get used to not having a physical body (as it were) solidly around you, life can be very similar to that within the earth plane. There is much less negativity, although some is carried forward by those leaving the earth plane and other dimensions. The negative emotions carry through, creating difficulties sometimes between individual spirit entities, but much less so.

Speech is non-existent. We communicate instantly by thought form. Perception is different. We do not perceive objects in the same way as you do with your physical eyes. It is rather the perceiving of a vibration, a light. This is extremely difficult to describe, for you do not have the experience to understand the words that we bring forward. Each of you, my friends, we see as a light. We see the aura, the colors that you are. We recognize you by color. We can understand who, where, and what you are doing by the color of your aura.

And so, all within the earth plane is color and vibration and we see it in that way. And in the same way, we recognize other spirit entities within the spirit planes by vibration, by color, and by light. When we wish to communicate closely together, to commune together (as you might very well within the sexual union, for example), we, within the spirit planes, coalesce entirely. It is as though one individual walks completely *into* the other. All experiences of one are known by the other. It is a total melding, total understanding and communion. It is a great delight for us. We have our times of fun, and joy, and party--of relaxation. It is not all work and growth and evolution. Just the same as in the earth plane, there are times for relaxation and joy.

More about what it's like in the spirit dimension

from Enid

The first thing I want to tell you about the spirit world is that *it* is All That Is. *This* is the spirit world! You are living in the spirit world. There is no other world than the spirit world. Everything in the world is spirit and everything that the world is made of is made of a wonderful spirit. But you see, if you can approach life and living with the whole idea that everything is spirit and that everything is made of spirit and that everything is made of love and that love is what spirit is, then there is only one element, and that is *love.*

So when you ask what is life is like in the spirit world, you tell me because you're living in it!

You're living in a wonderful spirit world. You're living in a wonderful theater with all kinds of drama going on and all kinds of wonderful experiences going on. And if you look back through your life and if you close your eyes --remember all of the ups and downs and the big things that happened--you'll realize how rich all that experience was. You can't really recall pain, only the experience.

So as we live in our spirit world (and we live as spiritual beings, which is all we ever can be) we pretend we are bodies and we pretend we are cats and all kinds of things. But this is for fun, this is experience, this is to teach us things about life that we don't know.

You are an infinite beingness.

You are an infinite beingness. However, when you look at the fact that you are an infinite beingness and that the person next to you also is, you can see that you're not separate in your heart. Put yourself close enough together like your fingers so you can see how you're not separate. Understand that you're always your own self--you never become a part of some big blob and lose your identity. Well, you'll lose your identity as *this* personality. You'll have it tucked away in your filing cabinet somewhere and you'll take it out and look at it and say, "Wasn't that cute! I loved that!" And you'll put it back.

But for all practical purposes, your inner beingness has no edges to it. And it has no top and it has no bottom. It has no end at the beginning, in the front, and no end at the back. So you are an *infinite beingness*. Every being is an infinite beingness. Now the infinite beingness has a lot of things going on, in fact, too many things going on to put all attention and energy into one little tiny speck of a world such as this. It sticks a big toe in and says, "Well, I'm going to enjoy the water with this big toe!"

And the whole body can feel this. So you (in a sense) are a big toe of your inner beingness--wiggling in the water and enjoying itself. But the whole of your inner beingness is enjoying this experience. Understand that if all the energy were placed into this world, it would immediately "implode" and be no more. So you can only put tiny little fingers or toes in this world; otherwise the inherent energy in a beingness is far too concentrated and intense to be placed in one place.

from Zoosh

How many times have you been told that we are all one; we are all one consciousness; we are all one being? Understand that we are, indeed, all one. There is no separation whatsoever; there is only an illusion. To understand this better, understand that the cells in your finger do not have any particular understanding that they are cells within a finger operating a muscle, tissue, bone or whatever. They do not have the consciousness to know that they are cells within a finger, and yet your finger functions as a part of your hand, as a part of your arm, as a part of your body.

And yet, would you say that your finger is a separate entity unto itself, that each cell is a separate entity? In a matter of looking at it, you might say that each cell is, indeed, separate. And yet, despite this, together they function very nicely as a finger and as a hand and as a body and so on.

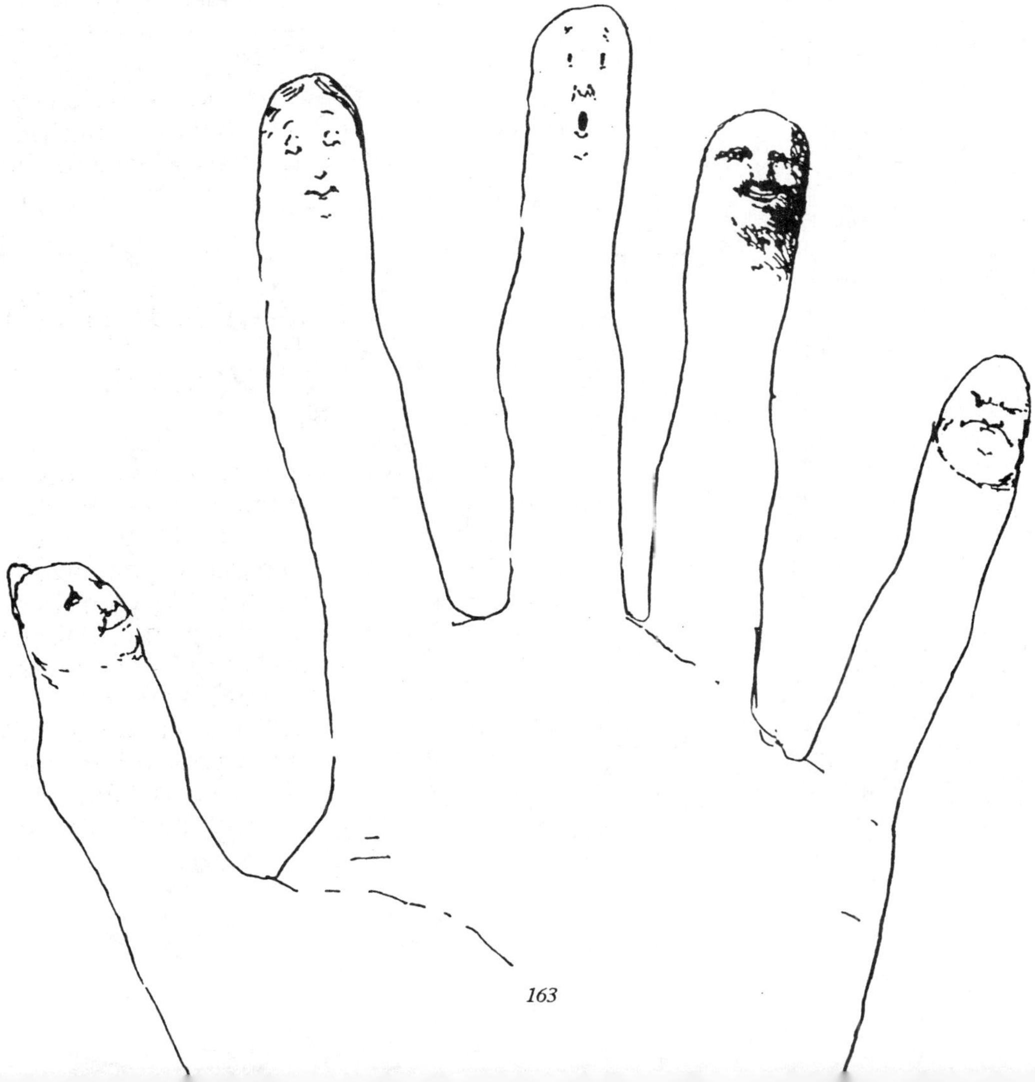

Each of you is a cell in the All That Is.

In your body, there are millions and millions of cells just as there are millions and millions of souls and light bodies in the universe. They are all cells, in that sense, in a massive body of consciousness.

from Li Sung

Our minds, if you wish to call them that, on both sides, are made up of energy and create a world of artistry much as an artist creates a world or much as a dreamer creates a world. And, therefore, we do not spend a great deal of time looking through the peepholes of eternity to see what our brethren on Earth are doing. This vision works because it excludes the vast eternity and focuses on only one tiny peephole. And this focusing of consciousness happens when we see (for we do not have the physical eyes) with our psychic or ethereal eyes which are created by our consciousness. And this, the etheric vision, is far superior to your physical vision; one can penetrate all eternity.

It is important to realize that, although you may not have awareness of it, your spiritual being exists already on our plane and that at times (mostly during dreams or when your physical mind goes into a daze) your spiritual mind takes over and often visits here, for there is much to be understood, much wisdom to be drunk from the well, and much kindness to be furnished from our side.

Question: Are there "black hats" (bad guys) on the spirit side?

from Li Sung

Well, the diversity of realms is quite considerable and we do not have knowledge (personal knowledge) of all other beings, for they are so numerous. However, it is true that in different areas, or you may wish to call them different dimensions, there are souls who have common experiences and

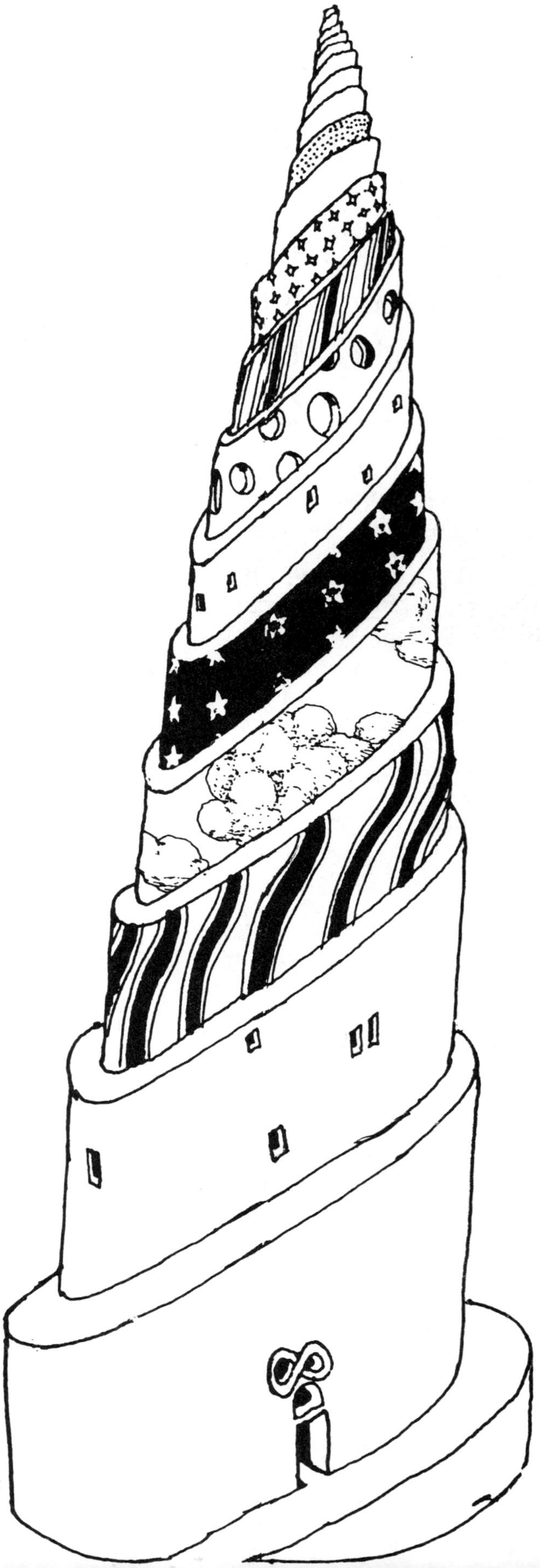

common points of view. And you could term some of them "bad." They are persons who (on the physical plane) were unable to learn and who made the transition to our world in violence, guilt, and revenge. And so they seek out their own. We have not seen them in our own places; we have not wished to. But we are told that there are such here.

You may consider our world as a vast apartment tower. There are many thousands of levels and each level corresponds to a level of vibration of the spiritual being. Souls who tend to be on the same wavelength congregate together and create their worlds together. And then there are the above and the below-related ones. And there is also some trouble between them, yes, much as you have here on Earth. But we do not travel about much; we do not visit thousands of levels away.

Now, on most levels they have schools and universities, and these are very active pursuits of many. And there is (in a sense) a graduation and moving on to a higher level. You must realize that when we say high or low, we do not mean necessarily better or worse. It is as different as when you go from your high school to college. One is not better or worse than the other--only more advanced.

And so, there is a transition of souls from one level to another--they wish to learn. You see many, however, who are waiting for their return to Earth and give this much thought and planning. Oh, and they concoct various scenarios or plans about their next lifetime and this is given much play. For every lifetime that is lived on Earth, there are perhaps ten planned on our side of which nine will never happen.

We have as much time as we wish (for we are creating it) and therefore we may study as much and long as we wish. It becomes, for some souls, a matter of great preoccupation.

Some souls stay here for thousands of your years to undertake vast study programs. And then when they are to be born into the world, they have no conscious memory of this. But there is, in their unconscious, a vast reservoir of knowledge that they may tap or channel, and they may seem very wise although they have not studied in your world.

Sex after death

from Soli

The male/femaleness is very much an identity of the earth plane. It is here (as in other dimensions) less well defined. The maleness and femaleness on the earth plane have grown farther and farther apart over the millennia, and this is a question of thought form of those within the earth dimension. The more you concentrate on the differences between the sexes, the more that you have genetically different bodies, therefore creating different experiences and lives. It is because you have such a strong belief system in the difference between the sexes that the thought has created the genetic pattern. As always, first comes the thought, then comes the reality.

Now when you first make your transition, you carry through your identity from the earth plane, including the maleness and femaleness, the beliefs within your subconscious mind. And so when you first move into the spirit plane, you still are male-female or whatever it was you were.

However, once you have had those lives upon the physical dimension that you wish to have, then those male-female principles re-merge together to become one yet again. It is not only male and female. Very often, spirits will have experiences in more than two aspects within the earth plane: three, four, five, sometimes even more. In other dimensions, you will split yourself into several--many, many more than five or six different aspects--and carry on similar experiences. It might be said that in some dimensions you have 33 sexes.

It is as if you had an apple. You split it down the middle and pull the halves apart and you said, "Oh, my goodness, on the left I have the positive and on the right I have the negative." You push them back together and lo, you have the whole apple again.

And so yes, the maleness, femaleness, this differentiation, the positive and negative, is far less marked within the spiritual dimension, especially for those who have evolved and have had many lives and gone beyond the necessity for that maleness and femaleness.

The society upon the earth plane is going to be dealing far less with male and female, and much more with understanding of the male within the female and the female within the male, a much greater understanding of the *similarities* rather than the *differences*. A far more androgynous society is coming about. You do not see it yet, but it is beginning and is very much a part of the New Age--the Age of Aquarius where there is far less concern about differences between individuals and far more *understanding* of the similarities.

Spirits never sleep

from Master Adalfo

We talk about a day in the life because you understand a day, but we are not bound by 24-hour time slots because there is no time where we are. We only conform to time when we are working with you. And we do not sleep, so we do not have problem of hours wasted, so to speak. Not really wasted for you, but it would be a waste for us to simply lie down for nothing. We have *nothing* to rest.

We are constant energy. We do not go through all things you go through like getting up and eating breakfast and things like that. So our day is a day of work and study and play--enjoyment. But none of those is a separate thing. Work and study and play are all alike. They are all the same. So we spend however much time is the right time to spend doing a particular thing.

For example, I will be spending some time with my instrument (channel) this afternoon (during taping). It would be possible for me also to be spending the same time elsewhere. Since we are only an energy body, it is possible to be in more than one place at one time.

I am often available for my instrument to talk to me, but not all the time. Sometimes I have gone to a meeting. Sometimes we do have meetings where we discuss new plans, things that we would like to encourage you to be doing. We would not have to have meetings either; we could do it telepathically. But we do have meetings or get-togethers. We enjoy one another's company and we do have things which appear to be material if that is what a spirit or soul wants.

So we have people here with gardens. We have people here who cook. We have people here with houses. It just depends. If a spirit or soul wants something, then it can be created, it can happen. And that way is a way of working on karma also. There are many different planes of dimension. In some respects they are uncountable. There is an understanding of people on planet Earth that there are *only* so many, and they give them names and that makes a nice, orderly existence. People on Earth need to have that order (like a filing cabinet) where Master Adalfo fits and where everybody else fits. To us that all seems quite funny.

Who Does What on the Spirit Plane

from Dr. Peebles

The spirit guides and teachers have many, many different roles. You all have master teachers. Just to be born, you have one, two, or three master teachers. And these are beings who are always with you. But you are not always aware of them until you evolve, until you expand, until you develop. Your master teachers are there to give you philosophy and spiritual psychology. They are there to encourage you always toward the best. They are equal to your conscience.

They give you an inspiration once. If you are turning wrong, according to your own chosen pathway, your master teacher will be there, and will say, "Turn the other way." And if you say, "Oh, no, I'm not going to do that. I'm too busy," they're not going to force you. They do not have that right. They just observe, for they do not care if you do your growing in one life or 15 lives. They know you will do your growing, and they will still *always be there.*

Your master teachers will do nothing according to your demands.

Your master teachers will only give you that which your higher selves have already agreed upon before entering the physical density.

You cannot make deals with your master teacher by saying, "I want this kind of master or that kind."

This is not your choice, dear ones. Your masters will be decided upon long before you enter the physical density. And often your master teachers have been with you for lifetime after lifetime. You cannot say, "Oh, I don't like that master. I don't like this one over there. I prefer a Tibetan rather than an African." No, dear ones, they will not listen. You were assigned to them, they were assigned to you by choices made long before you entered the physical density.

You all have what I would call gatekeepers, spirit guides who are to keep you protected from the darker forces, the negative forces, the earthbound, who keep imposters from the spirit world away from you. But they also cannot interfere with your free will. If you open yourself up to just anyone on the spirit side, your gatekeepers do not have the ability or the right to keep away from you those that you have attracted.

If you start attracting the spirit world and say, "Well, come on over, whoever's there. Just come on and get me," you have taken away the directives of your gatekeepers. You must live in such a way that your gatekeepers can do their job. You must live light, you must live affirmation, you must live so that only those of the higher levels will come to your gatekeepers. Ask permission, and then they will come in. If you open yourself up to anything, your gatekeepers are still there, but you have taken away their opportunity to do their job.

from Master Adalfo

Gatekeepers are the ones who *protect* the connection between the physical body and the astral body. They do not go around doing what some people suppose guardian angels do, which is to protect you from everything like falling off a cliff or a car accident. A gatekeeper's job is to protect what you call the silver cord, which is simply the connection of energy between the physical body and the astral body.

When you leave your physical body, for example, when you dream at night, or when you practice mediumship, as people do all the time through daydreaming (what they have really done is to leave their physical body), you have to be able to get back; otherwise you would be dead. The physical body can only go so long without any being in it because there is nothing to sustain it. So they are there to keep that connection so that you know how to get back in and to assist you in getting out. They may occasionally assist in astral travel as well. Some of those jobs they do automatically. Some of the jobs, such as mediumship, they will do only if you request it, if you make statements about what it is you desire. You might say, for example, to your gatekeeper, "I want only this person to come in," and they will honor it if they are told. They will not honor it if you do not tell them anything.

from Dr. Peebles

You all have healers, spirit guides, who are assigned to healing. They will not take away your experiences, but they will take away your fear *if you allow them.* They will take away your anger if you *allow them*. They will take away the pain if you will allow it, but you cannot say, "Take it away, take it away." If it was your experience, they must allow that, but they are there to give you the courage and the strength, the character to have your experience with dignity, with grace.

Often you will see people in the human body who have tremendous pain, discomfort, or deformity, but they have an ability, they have a strength that always makes them joyfully happy. They find a way to be creative or artistic through all of their pain. It is because they have kept a willingness to be open to the healers, knowing that the healers will not take away their experience, but will help them *through* their experience for themselves and for all others concerned, all who are observing on the physical and non-physical sides.

You have guides of intuition. Your intuitive guides are the ones who will inspire you with your clairvoyance, your clairaudient development. You say, "Well, I'm going to develop my psychic abilities." Dear ones, you do not develop your psychic abilities, you *allow yourself* to channel the insights, the inspirations of your intuitive guides. Oh, but you don't all like that. You say, "Oh, well, I want it. I'm going to do it, I'm going to do it." Dear ones, you do it *with* the guides, but you don't do it yourself.

This is a *collective venture,* and you must eventually discover the trust, discover the maturity to allow yourselves to work with the spirit. Open your chakras, open your psychic bodies. This will help the intuitive guides be there more actively, but you must take the final step of opening your minds willingly to let them *work* with the tools and the facilities that you have developed.

Often you will hear people say, "My guides and my teachers are always with me. They are my guardian angels." This is not quite accurate. Your guides and teachers, even your masters, are perfect souls who followed an attraction and entered the cycles of birth and death. They are evolving in the same processes as you, but they are not guardian angels.

from Master Adalfo

Angels are great light bringers, and when you teach your children about having guardian angels, that is a lovely thought and it is even true: a being of light who is always with you to shed light when you feel you have none.

And you can ask, "Dear one, please bring me a one-hundred-watt bulb now; I am feeling like I am in darkness."

from Hilarion

Every human soul born into incarnation on the Earth has a specific guardian whose primary function is literally to guard the incarnated personality from any harm that is not part of the "plan" or path of the individual. This guardian function is especially important in the childhood years, although the guardian's duties do not cease until the particular life is completed. Now, for many individuals, the

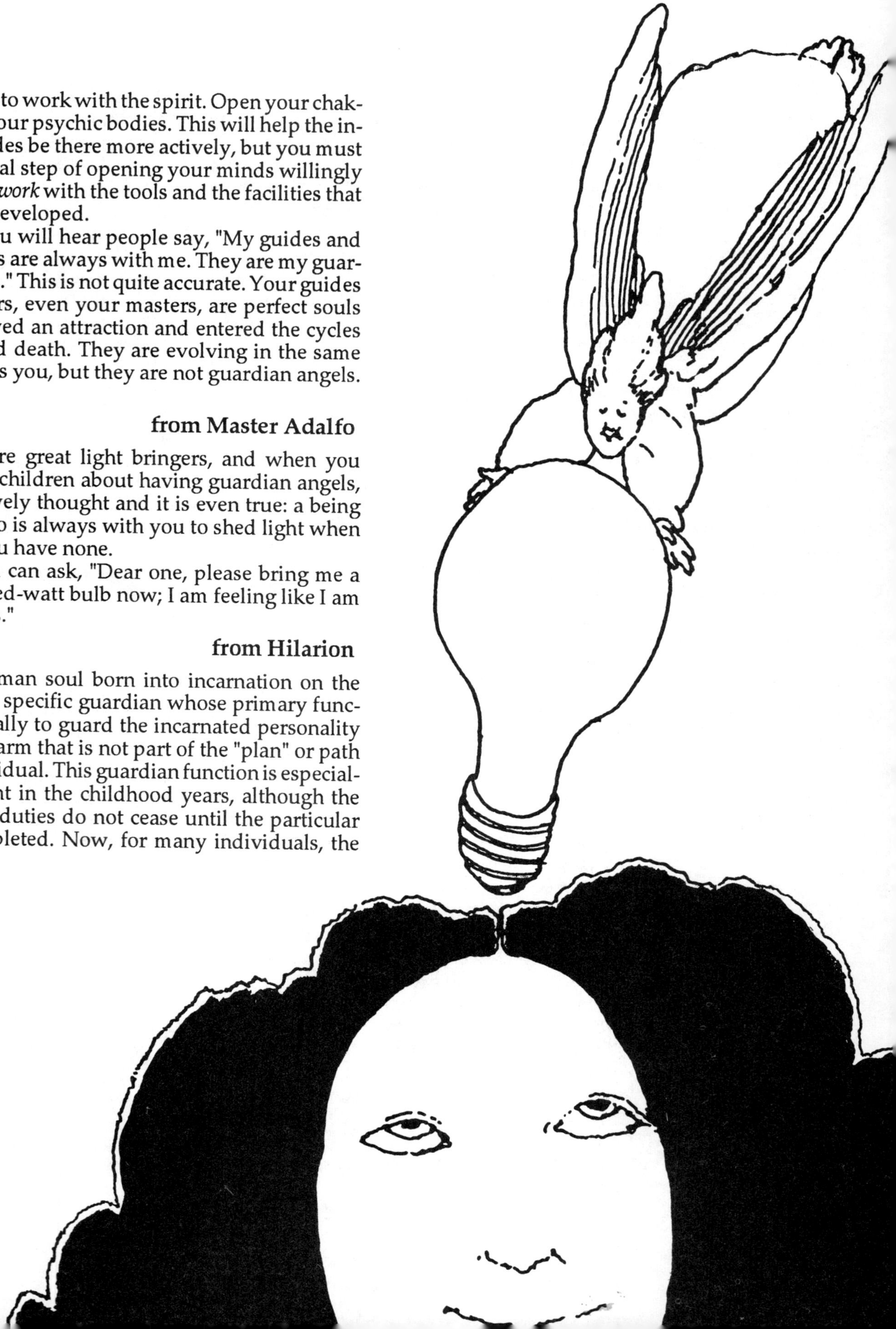

same guardian continues through a long string of lives. There are many human souls who have had the same guardian in every life they have lived.

The guardian is invariably a being belonging to the angel group of entities, specifically the portion of the angel group that did not participate (or not significantly) in what has been termed the "Temptation," which took place many millions of years ago on the Earth, and resulted in the first straying of human souls from the path of spiritual unfoldment.

The guardians have volunteered to fulfill these duties until mankind can, through its own efforts, rise to that level of spiritual achievement at which it is no longer necessary to reincarnate into the material level of being. Each guardian has *great love* for the human soul in its charge. Indeed, the love of the guardian angel is so great that the human would be totally overwhelmed by the vibration of it if the angel were to direct his or her entire affection at the human consciousness all at once.

There are many stories told about how this person was miraculously "saved" in a car crash, how another survived drowning against all odds, and so on. You may be absolutely certain that, in all such cases, the guardian angel had a great deal to do with the "miracle."

It is not usual, in the present phase of humanity's pilgrimage, to allow the guardian angel to speak directly to the consciousness of his or her human charge while that being is in incarnation. While there are a few exceptions to this rule, they are infrequent. It is part of the angel's challenge to continue to serve in this special way without actual interchange with the human at the mental level. Such restriction, however, does not apply to others of the helpers.

from Soli

We don't even like the word "angels," because it has such a religious connotation for you--of little winged beings floating down to be around you. That which you would call angels are energies assisting the growth of the earth dimension and other dimensions. They are what you might call high level guides and teachers. Again, no judgment is implied in that concept of level. They are expressions of energy that are beyond physical existence, who have not had physical lives on Earth. They do not intend to have physical lives on Earth. They are not caught up in the cycles of birth and death in any way. They are specifically there as part of your creation and all of energies' creation to assist you from afar. They work with energies in a totally objective way.

You have, within your earth plane, a concept of love that is very controlling, a concept of love that says, "If I love you, I am going to look out and make sure that you do this, that, and the other thing just the right way. I am going to make sure that this and that happens within your life, and then you're going to do things for me." But love from the spiritual perspective is totally objective, totally unconditional. It is ruthless.

No one on the spirit side, my friends, cares what you do on Earth except those who are very close to you in vibration and have that same feeling. But the highest frequencies of vibration and energy, of those whom you call angels, do not care what you do on Earth. Their love is unconditional, totally nonjudgmental. If you call upon their energy, their vibration, they will do what they are created to do, and it may not necessarily be what *your ego wants.* They are not there to make your life easy, to make your life one of peace and happiness, for that is your own decision. It is your own prerogative to create peace and happiness within your own life. They are there to assist you with energy balance when you call upon them.

You see, my friends, many within the spiritual path of growth on the Earth at this time believe that the path forward is toward a place of total peace and ease and calm where everything is perfect (in the sense that you understand the word perfect), where your life is totally easy. That is not the spiritual way. The spiritual way is to take the experiences of life and *transmute* them into their highest vibrational frequency, to create the peace and happiness within you regardless of what is going on around you. It is not to have beings come and *change* the external circumstances so that you can be peaceful, for then you would be a victim of happiness, just as you feel you are a victim of being depressed or a victim of others around you who create your depression. *You are not ever a victim.*

So your purpose (if you would call it purpose) in life is to transmute every experience into its highest

form, its highest frequency. If you will find the joy and happiness of any circumstance in life, it is yours and yours alone to create that. There are guides who *will assist you* to do that, such as your joy guides and others who are around you. They will not do it for you and they will not change the circumstances around you to make you happy. They will help you find the happiness *within* you. This will *transmute* the circumstances around you. That is a very big difference. They are also quite subtle in many ways.

Those that you would call angels (what we would call *energy balancers*) are there to help you understand more of your creative power within yourself, of how you are relating to your external circumstances. They will protect you, yes, but they will not protect you from those things within your life that you have set up as your experiences. They will not prevent those experiences within your life. But generally when you ask for protection, you are asking protection from the ego perspective. The ego is saying, "I don't want to experience anything that is bad or anything that I define as being bad. I don't want to experience that. Guides and teachers, prevent anything bad from coming into my life." But your guides and teachers and the angels will most certainly *not prevent* such experiences.

Those very experiences are the things that you need in order to grow and evolve within your being. That's why you came into this life. That's why you set them up. The angels will not prevent or change that probability pattern for you. They will help you understand it. They will help you transmute the energy of it. They will help you keep extraneous aspects of other people's probabilities away from you, to some extent, as long as that doesn't interfere with others. They are highly objective, totally objective. They do not care about you in the sense that you use the word care. They will do what you ask to the extent that they are able, to the extent of their abilities (and their abilities are very narrow in that way).

Your guides and teachers, on the other hand, sometimes can be persuaded to the point of interfering and creating changes in your life beyond that which is, as you might say, best for your growth and evolution at that time. They can be persuaded, out of their feeling for you, to interfere. However, there is no way to get the angels to so interfere. They are totally objective in that sense. They do not have that same connection with the Earth as your guides and teachers.

from Dr. Peebles

Now, there are warrior angels, but they do not create war. The warrior angels go in front of you and when you invite them, they will clear a path. But if you say, "Clear the path because I am frightened. Clear the path of that one over there and that one over there," they will not do that because those that are there might well be there for your experience. It is yours to use the power of the warrior angels within your own heart and being without shirking your responsibilities to avoid experiences and confrontations.

When you call upon the teaching angels, it is not the same as calling upon the masters. When you call upon the teaching angels, they give you a lesson. But they do not give you the lesson that you are asking for. Seldom does that happen. They give you the lesson that your *soul is ready for.* You can say, "Oh, teaching angels, I wish to understand reincarnation." They will give you an experience that will make you understand reincarnation if you look at it from a soul perspective. The majority of you are incapable of doing that while in the physical body. So you must be very clear and very loving and very focused in specifically calling upon the angels. And in your own beings, in your own minds, keep separate your relationship to the angels from your relationship to your guides and teachers.

You will never be an angel, but you are already a guide.

from Hilarion

There are not many souls presently in incarnation who have what we would term "teacher" entities assigned to them. Actually, what happens is that there is a kind of fraternity of teachers at higher levels, who perform the teacher function for a number of incarnated human souls who are at a level where they are capable of assimilating what the teachers have to impart. While one particular teacher may habitually "talk" to a given soul, this is not to say that the teacher is restricted to dealing exclusively with the soul in question.

Consider the relationship presently taking place, for example, with this source, the entity Hilarion, who has been chosen to be the higher focus for this particular channel due to the vibrational similarities between the instrument (M. B. Cooke) and the source. Other teachers could have assumed this function, but the confluence of vibrational energy would not have been as great. This would therefore have restricted the amount and quality of the information we would have been able to pass.

By the same token, the source Hilarion is by no means restricted to this particular channel. There are many conscious and unconscious channels with whom this source is in active contact. The greater percentage of these is made up of unconscious channels, through whom it is admittedly harder to work, in general. However, a great deal of new information is being placed into the Earth realm through these secondary channels, and the benefit to humanity that has come through their efforts has been enormous.

What we are saying, then, is that teachers, as such, are not tied to individual souls to the same degree that one finds with guides and guardians. Furthermore, even though the total number of teaching entities is small compared to the numbers of guides and guardians of humanity, they are enabled to deal with and through a large number of people at once. This means that each and every human soul in incarnation could receive this kind of direct teaching guidance at virtually any time, simply by *asking* for the help, and by *opening* their mind and consciousness to what is given in response.

As with anything of a spiritual nature, it is sufficient to ask for the help, and it will be given. There is a law at a very high level which requires this to be so.

Ready when you are, ready when you're not

from Dr. Peebles

If you are walking in your physical density and are not *consciously* pursuing communication with the spirit guides and teachers, they do not go, as you would describe it, on vacation. They might take a coffee break at times. But they are always there. They always give you the exact same amount of guidance and inspiration. But the guides and teachers really do not care if you listen. They get you anyway. It is you who will become aware of it. There are some who will go for years before suddenly one day they say, "There is something out there." They have to open the door; the Spirit doesn't open it for them. The Spirit is not suddenly more intensely there. They are just more intensely aware of the guides and teachers who are *always there.*

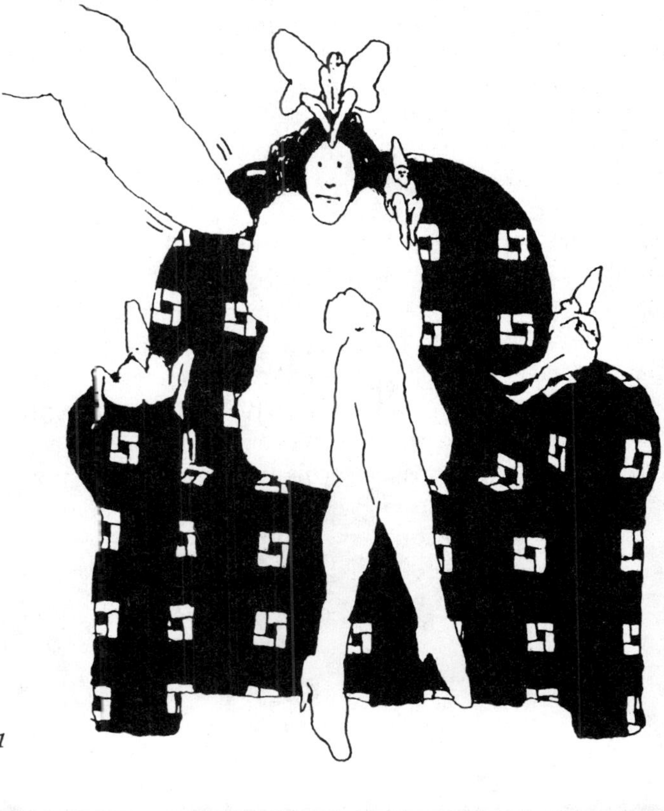

There are some who enter the body and get so caught up in their experiences that they don't quite follow their path. But something in them keeps them always very, very ethical until one day they might be standing on a street corner and someone throws a rock and hits them in the head, and they become instantly in touch with the spirit. That experience was motivated because they were ready to take on the experience that they came into their life to have. Now another being would stand on the same corner and say, "Oh, I saw that one last year get hit by the rock. Here you, go over there, throw the rock, hit me," and then would leave the body because they are trying to force that experience.

Question: Are there guides and teachers for the entity Earth?

from Dr. Peebles

The spirit guides and teachers are not limited to humans. Animals have guides and teachers. Some of you have animals who are your guides and teachers from the spirit side. The planet Earth is a consciousness. Existing on the planet are what some call nature spirits, others call deva. They are vibrational presences. There is the deva of the tree, of the mountain, of the clouds, of the water. There are nature spirits of minerals. There are deva of healing, and these all work with the consciousness known as the planet Earth. There is a hierarchy of deva assigned to the planet Earth who help transmute negativity. They don't take negativity away, they just transmute it. They give options. And whether the options are taken or not by individuals is not at all important.

The deva are not shaped like humans. They are lights. They are energies. They are vibrations. They are frequencies. They do not have reincarnation. Now, they are not created in the same fashion as angels. But the deva are energy forms, not entities. The human does talk to the deva. The deva talks to the human. It is not a form of guidance. It is more a form of inspiration. It is more a sensual communication. The deva nature spirits are very sensual. They stimulate energy and vibration. Guides actually

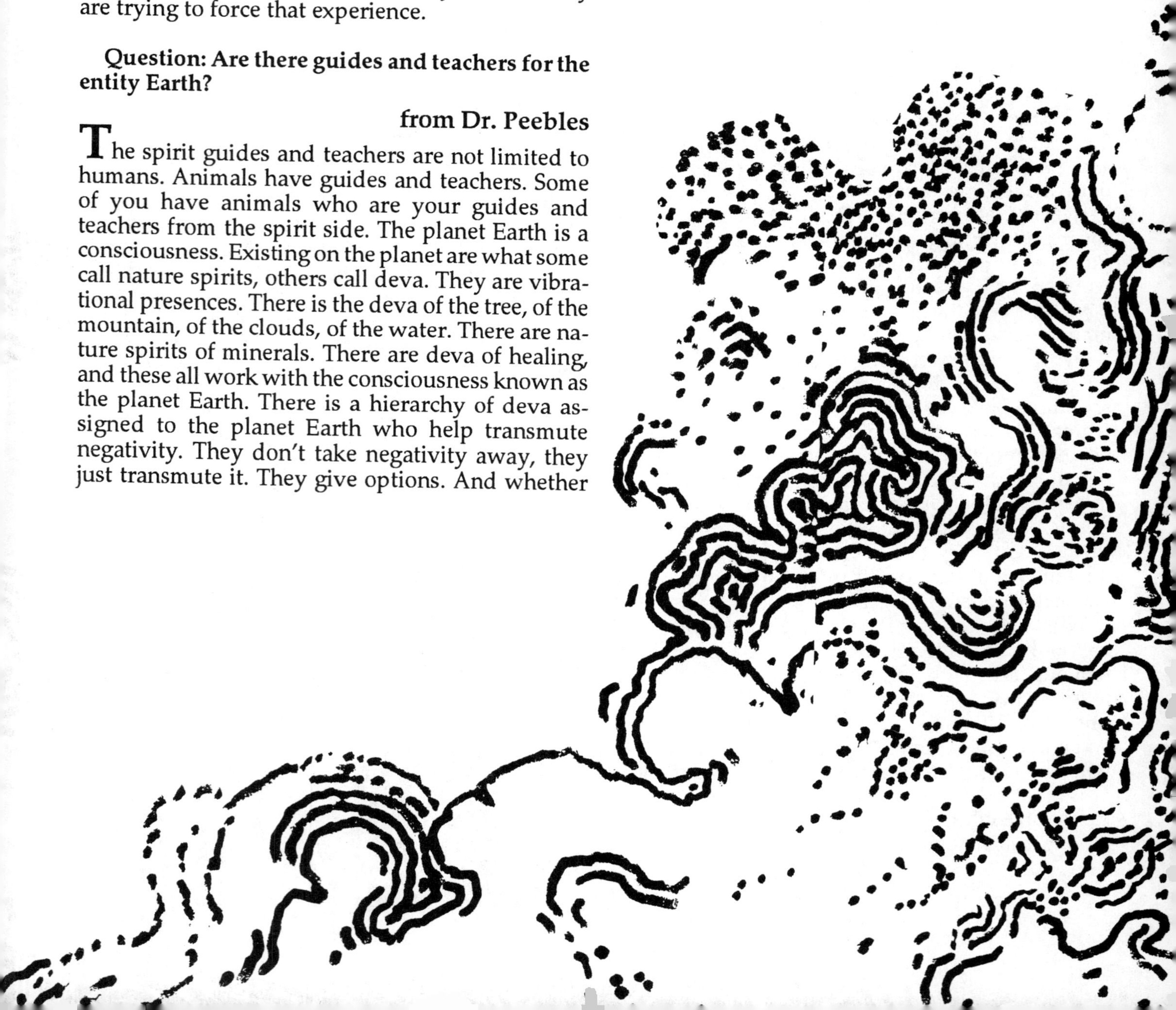

guide you. If you were blind, for example, the guides would take you by the hand and lead you. The deva would stimulate you to turn, to lift.

from Abrham

Nature is a rule of life. And you all abide by that rule of life as long as you are setting foot upon your Earth. That rule is service. And you all use nature in every way you can by allowing nature to serve you well. You can also say that nature is the grand spirit guide because you always allow nature to guide you through your life.

You all *listen* to nature, you *pay attention* to nature, you *talk* with nature. You have your own nature communications taking place within you all the time. And when you place your focus of attention within nature, you become a portion of the consciousness of nature, and in that way you are serving nature back. And you are completing a cycle--not only a cycle of reincarnation, but a cycle of communication and a cycle of service.

Once you complete the cycle and realize the totality of the cycle, you then meet your own death, and you find then that your death is nothing more than one more birth.

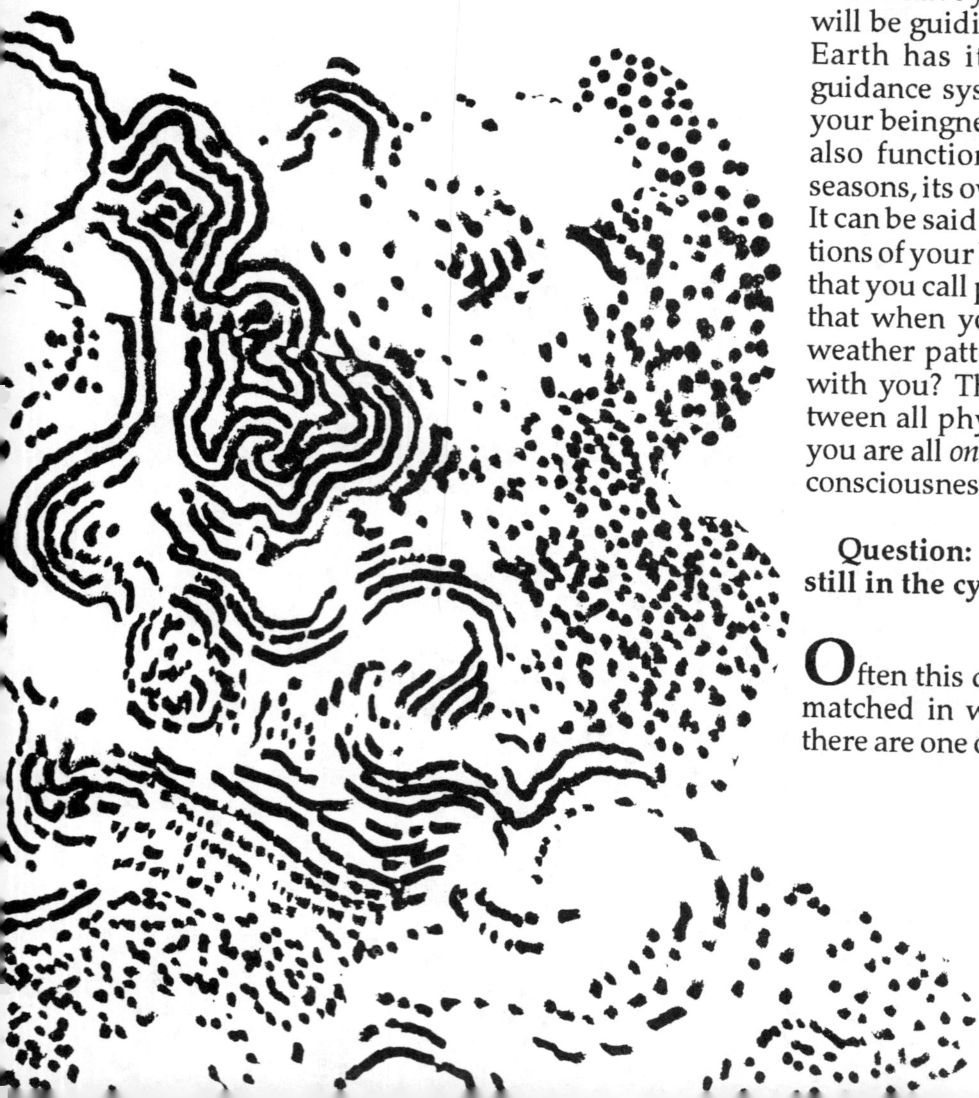

You have your own guidance system. You always will be guiding yourself throughout all your lives. Earth has its own guidance system. As your guidance system will function within all levels of your beingness, your Earth's guidance system will also function that way. Your Earth has its own seasons, its own climates, its own senses of weather. It can be said that your Earth's seasons are the emotions of your Earth being played out in a grand form that you call physical reality. And have you noticed that when you change your own emotions, your weather patterns also seem to change right along with you? There is a co-creation taking place between all physical people and your Earth because you are all *one* consciousness, and you are all *of* one consciousness.

Question: Do we serve as spirit guides while still in the cycles of incarnation?

from Hilarion

Often this does take place, but again the guide is matched in wisdom to the "charge." And usually there are one or more principal guides who have the main responsibility. Normally, a human soul still caught in the cycles of rebirth into the physical plane is permitted to act only peripherally as a guide to another--a kind of apprenticeship which is meant to allow one soul to set aside karma through service to another.

It is far more common for humans, when between incarnations, to study spiritual matters at one or more of the various wisdom schools of the higher levels. Even those who believe that they are comparatively "advanced" in their spiritual understanding will find that there are many things they have not properly grasped, and will readily wish to attend the higher schools during the between-life phase. Here we are talking about those who have pursued a spiritual path while on the Earth.

The vast majority of humans, who die without the faintest inkling of what lies ahead for them, are not able to benefit from attendance at the higher schools, and instead spend most of the between-life period sloughing off undesirable proclivities and attitudes that they have acquired during earth life. This procedure takes most of their energy, with little left over for serious study.

Communicating through channels/mediums

from Dr. Peebles

Human beings who become channels of the spirit know long before they enter the physical density that they have the potential, that there is a possibility, that they will live according to their chosen life path. And so it is already assigned, already agreed upon that the guides, the masters, will be there. And so you do not come into the light taking a chance. You come into the light knowing there is always the probability of becoming a channel. Some come in knowing that they have no possibility of that for that life, but they still have with them masters who will channel through them if *ever* they become a channel in this or another life.

For example, William, as a higher self, knew that he would be channeling, not just myself, but some of the others. I, for instance, am not a master. I have another lifetime coming. But there is a master who does speak through him. There are other masters who have spoken through him. Channels not only allow their own guides, teachers, and masters to speak. A channel allows self to be open and then the gatekeepers of life allow through the masters who would like to come.

Each and every living being is interconnected. You are existing in each and every person around you. You are existing in people whom you have never even seen. And they are in you. We are connected very specifically. And on the spirit side there is no time and space as you know it.

And so there are direct channels. Visualize them as ribbons. I am connected to some of them very succinctly. I am also available to all who call upon me, who enter a frequency that connects very much like a radio. When you get a certain frequency, a certain density, I am able to be there. But others on the same frequency are also able to be there. And so it is important to have your gatekeepers so that the imposters cannot be let in.

There are those who will say, "I am on the same frequency. I'm going to call myself Dr. Peebles just to get in there and have a good time." And so it is all a collective, a frequency connection. It is a ribbon connection. It is a channeled connection.

For you are responsible to me. I am responsible to you. And so, with the collective karma, we are magnetized one to the other. And there are billions upon your planet. Many of those have no magnetization to me, none. And so they will not even know my presence even when standing right next to me. But they would know of the presence of another to whom they are magnetized.

It is difficult for the human mind, caught in its physical density, to comprehend. It's on this dimension, this plane, that those connections are very simple and very basic. Though you count billions, those billions are very specific densities, qualities, vibrations, and magnets on the astral and on the spirit side.

Working with Spirit Guides and Teachers

Dial-a-spirit

from Li Sung

There is a group of scientists on our side who are working on this very interesting development. They have made some strong progress in this and are waiting now for the development on your plane of more sensitive valves or transistors so that there is heightened sensitivity in the apparatus. For it would be necessary for the apparatus to extend into our dimension somewhat. And it will work only in the presence of human mediums or those with great psychic energy who are then able to energize the device. So there will not be one in every home, but it will be a research device for those who are dedicated to learning more wisdom from us. But you will see that there will be progress made on this later.

We feel one process may soon (within 20 to 30 years) be developed in which what you call an "average" person may sit in a room that has been energized with psychic power, electrified so that he becomes extremely receptive to our world and is then able to perceive us in form or hear us speak. There are those skeptics in the world who say, "Oh, he will be able to see spooks." But this device will increase his sensitivity and raise his vibration level temporarily. He might even be able to perceive much in our world. And this device is being worked on by those on our side who are *inspiring* scientists on your side to assist them in working out the details.

Question: Do chemicals or specific foods like mushrooms help to increase communication between our worlds?

from Li Sung

There is difficulty with the chemicals. The ingestion of hallucinogens opens the door to the unconscious, and many fears and many imaginations come running forth, which may be mixed sometimes with the perceptions of our world, so it is hard for you to decide which is which. There is no control and there is no way to slow down the flow of information so that you are able then to study it and to perceive what it is. There may be flashes of vision, of insights in these hallucinogenic trances, but they are not dependable.

But, as you may suspect, if it is possible to open the valve of the mind through drugs, it may also be possible to open it through a more sophisticated technique. The most sophisticated of these is a human medium--the one who is able to alter his or her level of being sufficiently to become aware of messages from our dimension, and also occasionally to see us as we would appear to them.

With great love for the earth plane

from Soli

Many individuals who have had experiences within the earth plane have great love for it. Such entities recognize (once they have left the earth plane) the growth, the change; recognize what they have experienced; recognize the beauty that they had within the earth plane; recognize that the way forward for all entities is to learn that they are God, that the way lies within and not without.

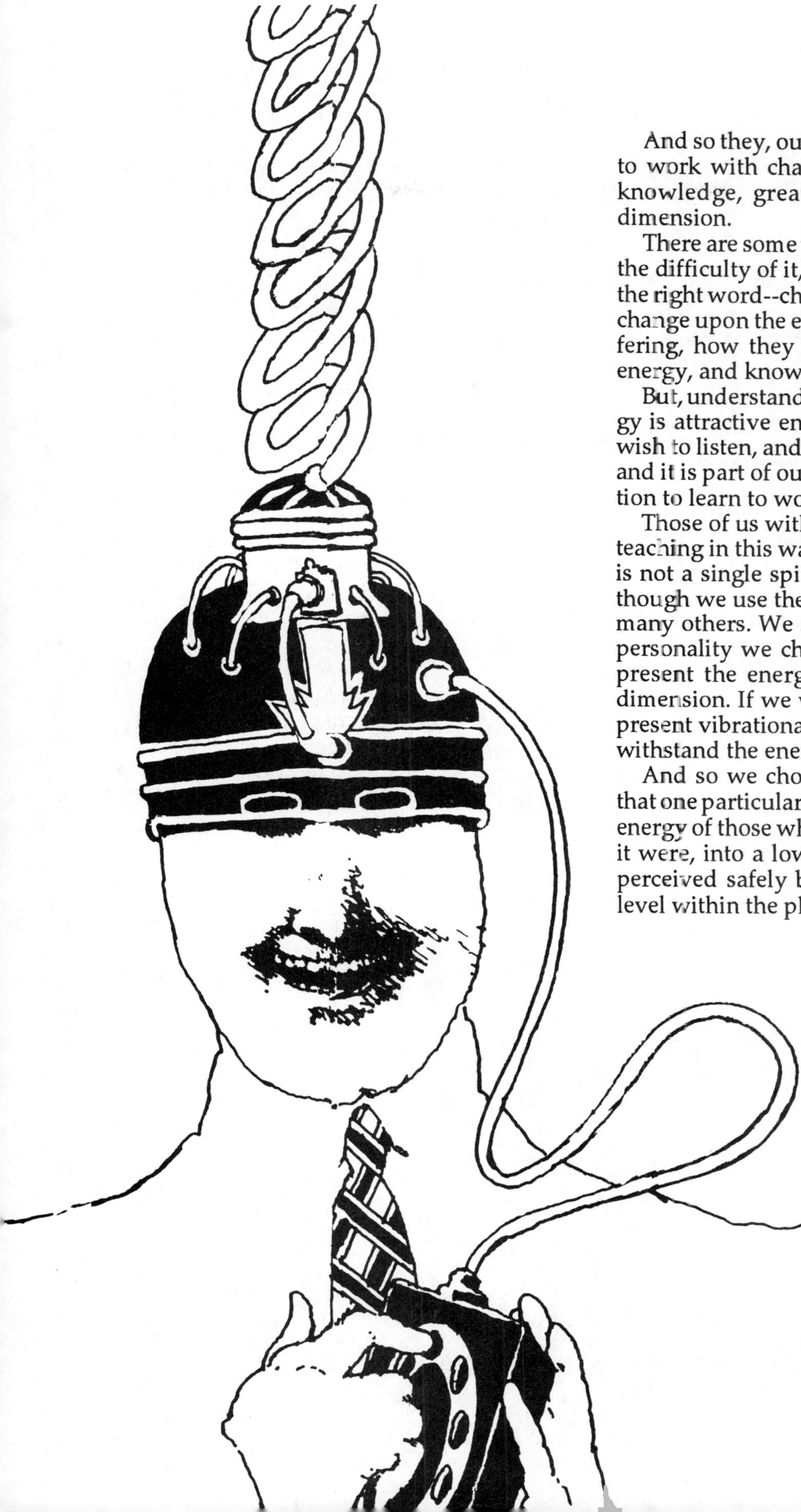

And so they, out of great love, decide and choose to work with channels, bringing forward greater knowledge, greater energy within the physical dimension.

There are some who choose such a task rather for the difficulty of it, rather out of--amusement is not the right word--challenge to see how they can effect change upon the earth plane without directly interfering, how they can bring forward information, energy, and knowledge.

But, understand that we can only work if the energy is attractive enough to draw those who would wish to listen, and so there is challenge within that; and it is part of our growth, experience, and evolution to learn to work in that way.

Those of us within the spirit dimension who are teaching in this way (through channels), each of us is not a single spirit. We are not individuals even though we use the names Soli and Dr. Peebles and many others. We are not *that* individual. That is a personality we choose by which to be known, to present the energy to those within the physical dimension. If we were to present ourselves in our present vibrational state, you would not be able to withstand the energy.

And so we choose, as a transformer, a lifetime that one particular spiritual entity has had. Then the energy of those who are teaching is transformed, as it were, into a lower vibrational level so it can be perceived safely by those of a similar vibrational level within the physical dimension.

The Story Corner

The butterfly

from The Eternals

A butterfly was soaring through the air, floating and gliding, when it looked down and saw its reflection in a pure, clear mountain stream. The butterfly, seeing its reflection, was astounded by its own beauty, and said, "I must come closer and see this wonderful sight." The butterfly rode spirals of wind downward, and the closer it came to the mountain stream, the more enchanted it became with the reflection which it saw. The closer the butterfly came to the mountain stream, the more beauty it thought it saw as it gazed at its own reflection. The butterfly came all the way down to the water. When it touched the water its wings became wet. It could not fly. It began to drown!

The butterfly struggled in the stream among floating debris. Mud, twigs and leaves floated by the butterfly as it struggled to stay afloat. Then the butterfly found a rock, an clung to it. It crawled and struggled until it came forth from the water.

The butterfly laid upon the rock to rest. The sun shone down upon it. Its wings began to dry, and soon the tired butterfly regained its strength. It raised its dry but tattered wings and began to fly. It soared upward from the rock. It looked down at the stream and saw its reflection. Seeing its reflection the butterfly thought of the horrors that it had encountered. Then, soaring, it thought of beauty, the wonder in the original place where the butterfly had dwelt in the air. It said, "The heavens are my home. There shall I dwell."

And, so it is with life. We are but as butterflies that have become enchanted and fallen to the material wherein we struggle and fight to climb upon the rock to dry our wings that we might again soar within the spiritual.

You Are the Endless Sky

from Bartholomew

The Divine speaks with many voices on your planet. And one should not, in my estimation, fall into judgment of which is best, or which is better. It is simply a matter of which one resounds most deeply within your physical being, lights up your mind, gives you hope for clarity and a possible awakening, and a way to fly Home.

The purpose of this message is to tell you that you have made a misidentification. You have identified yourself with the clouds that pass to and fro in the sky, but you are, indeed, the *sky itself.* The clouds, according to this tradition, are all of the points of duality--love and hate, war and peace, rich and poor, etc. You know the dualities well, and these are the clouds that pass through you, about you, and hopefully out of you and on their way.

What would be a way to perceive this old truth in a new way? Every thought and action that you have accumulated on the earth plane, as a human consciousness, still remains present. All of the mass events, and all of your own personal events, go together to form a vortex of power and energy that keeps revolving around the globe. There is such a thing as energy in motion, and this energy continues to circle your globe, which is why you can say there is such a thing as "world karma," or a "world idea." Since the beginning of humanity's journey here, all of these positive and negative ideas and actions, and all of the rules and regulations that have come down through the ages can still be found here.

When you begin any spiritual path, you also begin to magnetize your own energy field. In doing this, you draw to you all of the accumulated truths and untruths associated with that particular system. Unfortunately there is no way to filter out the untruth and just leave the truth shining by itself. Energy is energy and you cannot put rules on it. So when you begin an "ascent to the mountain peak" through a certain tradition, you magnetize yourself in line with that particular consciousness. People follow different traditions and become aware and awake in different ways. So the job is how to love past all of the clouds and to simply love from the vast sky.

When we speak about the truths in Vipassana, or the Zen tradition, what are we speaking about? Those monks came to know, through a very austere method of meditation, that there was no personal "I" moving through lifetime after lifetime, accumulating karma, etc. What they found instead was amazing. If they sat quietly with enough determination, yet ease, they found the dualities would rise and, if they persevered in their quiet watching and nonjudgmental attention, *they would also leave.* Hatred, anger, resentment, and all of the emotions, arose in their consciousness. But, by quiet contemplation of them, making no judgment about what they felt, they realized those emotions drifted out of their awareness and, lo and behold, something else arose.

The monks sat there long enough to see it was very difficult to allow only light and love into their awareness, because right on the back of those wonderful feelings almost always would come what you would call "negative ones." As the weeks, months, and years drifted by, they came to the knowledge that they had misunderstood something very simple. They had mistaken themselves, the sense of who they were, for those emotions, for the passing clouds. They were always trying to decide, "Is this a cloud I should allow to enter me? Is this a good cloud? Is this a bad cloud? Is this cloud right? Is this cloud wrong?" The struggle, as they tried to sift through these different layers, showed them that the rules they had been trying to follow were of no help. Some came from the Indian tradition, which is interesting, but rather complicated because of the rules one must follow.

So these first monks had quite a job of it, trying to follow the rules, be quiet, and become enlightened. They struggled to rid themselves of all negative thought and feeling and enter into a state of bliss. They found they simplified their lives to such a point that all they did was eat very little and meditate all day. Therefore there wasn't much opportunity for negativity to come rolling in. Make no mistake, these were real warriors of their time, but nevertheless they were finding there was something essentially missing when they left their peaceful caves of isolation. Back into the township they would go to buy their bag of rice, and, lo and behold, they might get jostled or a shopkeeper might give them the wrong change or tell them to leave because they smelled so bad. Then, unless they had truly reached a clear state of awareness, up would arise the duality and away they would go again!

Is it possible to keep the negative away from your consciousness? Is there anything you can do to so purify yourself that you will never have a negative thought, never perform a negative act, but always think in loving kindness? I am sure you have tried to, because it is part of the path. Be honest about your own success. How much have you succeeded?

You are wonderful and amazing people and I see in your consciousness a tremendous amount of true striving, a desire to awaken, to have loving kindness and Christ Consciousness in your hearts. So we have to ask: if you do not, is it because you are not good enough or don't try hard enough? I would like to suggest something slightly different for you to consider.

Is it not possible that the goal is to become aware of the same thing those courageous monks observed so long ago, that you, through objective observation of your own life, can come to see that you are something *through* which the positive and negative poles of this planet move? They come to you! Is it possible that all of the energy which has been revolving in its own pattern around the globe comes down to you, enters you, and exits? And that the job, perhaps, is not to keep the doors shut, to keep the negative out, because in so doing you also deny the positive?

There is a doorway to awareness in each individual and it is either open or closed. When it is open, anything moving through, around, or in this planet will be welcome to move through you and out. Allow it to happen. Practice and you will begin to develop the feeling of *space* within you. This is why in our Vipassana workshops we teach strong warriors to sit and watch, to walk and watch, to eat and watch, to simply give them an opportunity to begin to *feel* that space and to understand what inner space really means.

There is a doorway to awareness in each individual. It is either open or closed.

On a physiological level, you know there is a lot of space within and around the cells. You are filled with space. It is that space which reflects the knowingness of the vast sky. It is exciting to watch the thunderclouds as well as the beautiful clouds move through you, because you will realize *experientially,* not mentally, that something is present other than the motion of the clouds. Do not trap yourself by trying to categorize that feeling. Do not label that "otherness" God. There is always something the mind would like to grab onto and feed back to you, so you can worship it and be safe. The moment you worship something else, duality is present. Worship implies *two*--that which is being worshipped and the one doing the worshipping. The moment that separated thought arises in your consciousness, you are off the track.

This other feeling, this knowingness, this awareness that begins to arise in you, if consistently paid attention to, will tell you directly all you need to know. The way to the Divine is often through patience, a quality that is very difficult on a busy planet where people are always *doing* something. The reason we keep maintaining that some kind of dedicated practice of meditation is helpful is because of the following.

Inside the space of your body and inside the space of your psyche, there is a power and awareness that, *when paid attention to,* begins to calm down your entire system, take the edge off your pain, and stimulate a sweet feeling within you. It is called "belief."

Until the moment you *feel* the Divine, you are only someone *trying* to believe. The moment that you, with awareness, let this spatial quality move within you, you will experience the hope that says, "It is true. God exists and exists in me." Do this enough and God becomes a reality because the space is so much vaster than the concept in your mind.

It is at this point that confusion will arise. All of your concepts and ingrained beliefs about what God wants and requires from you--that He will love and accept you--crash up against the reality that *GOD IS!* Now that you *believe,* you also experience *fear.* What if it isn't true? What if God isn't really there? In that moment, the fear becomes so overwhelming that many people turn to religion in the *hope* that the rules will make them safe.

When this duality faces you, what do you do? You do the very same thing you have been doing to get to the point of God-awareness in the first place. You become very, very big, because you are holding in your consciousness two things: God and fear. The immensity of God and the immensity of your fear. At that point, many people start to wobble. Just stay with it. Laugh if you can, watch the fear, feel the God-Self, feel the feeling of the fear you have just found which you believe you cannot possibly get rid of. At that point, you have to become very big to encompass both.

When I had this experience, it fit into the category of what you call "the dark night of the soul." I decided that the only way out was to stop struggling and allow the forces of "dark and light" to fight it out themselves. I finally realized I could not do it. With my limited understanding, I had no hope of ever settling anything between these two amazing powers which were struggling for victory in my consciousness. Every time I would move toward one, the other seemed to get larger and larger, and the first one farther and farther away. So then, being a warrior, I would try the other side, hoping to reverse the process. You see, I was trying to trick God into deciding for me. This went on for what seemed like a long time.

What was the outcome? I was sitting there filled with depression, then light, then depression, then light, wobbling! Back and forth. But then, one day, opening my eyes and looking out, I saw an endless sky, and it happened at that moment the sun was setting. I saw reflected on one of the cloud clusters an immense golden light, representative, I thought, of the golden side of me. Equally powerful, a dark, gloomy, thundering black cloud was present next to it. I sat there watching, even to the end projecting all of who I was out there. And as I watched,

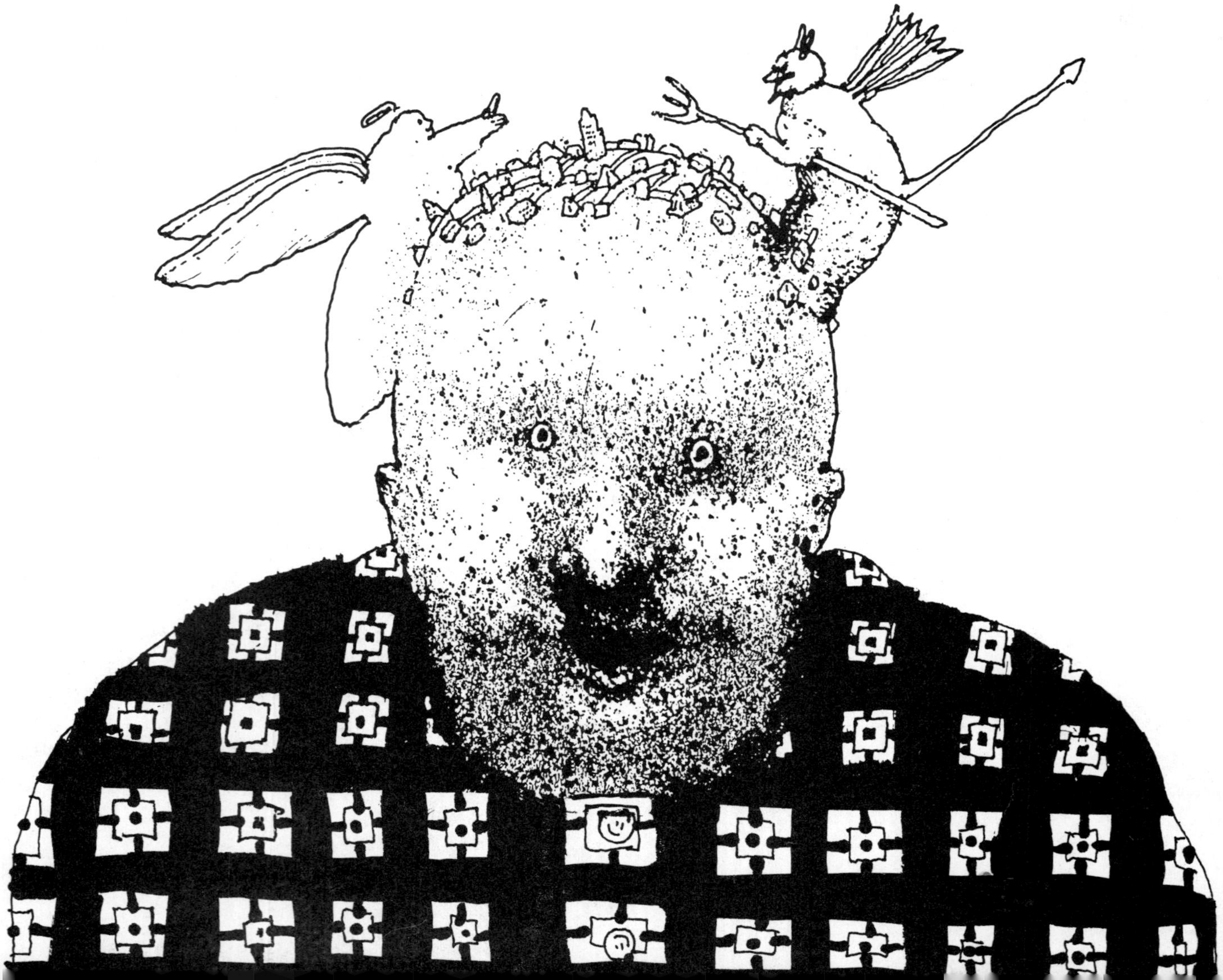

both of the clouds began to disappear. In those moments, as I kept staring at both of them disappearing, I saw the dark evening sky *coming through them.* Then suddenly, as in the great Zen stories, a brick dropped and enlightenment happened. In my case, the clouds disappeared and awareness was present.

I tell you this because I believe with all of my being that you can follow this same pattern in your present life. Begin to experience *yourself* as the vast sky and observe the endless clouds moving through you. When you are paying attention to your thoughts, you will see clearly that they rise and fall, and there is a space between them. You are *not* one continuous, chattering mind. When you look for spaces, when you begin to identify with the sky and abandon what I call (with humor) the neurotic tendency to pay attention to the clouds, you will begin to get a sense of how incredibly vast your consciousness is.

You do not have to destroy every cloud to see the sky. All you have to do is keep remembering that *you are the sky.* And you can do that because it is true! Since you have misidentified yourself in the first place, you have the capability of re-identifying yourself. You thought yourself into this and you can think yourself out of it!

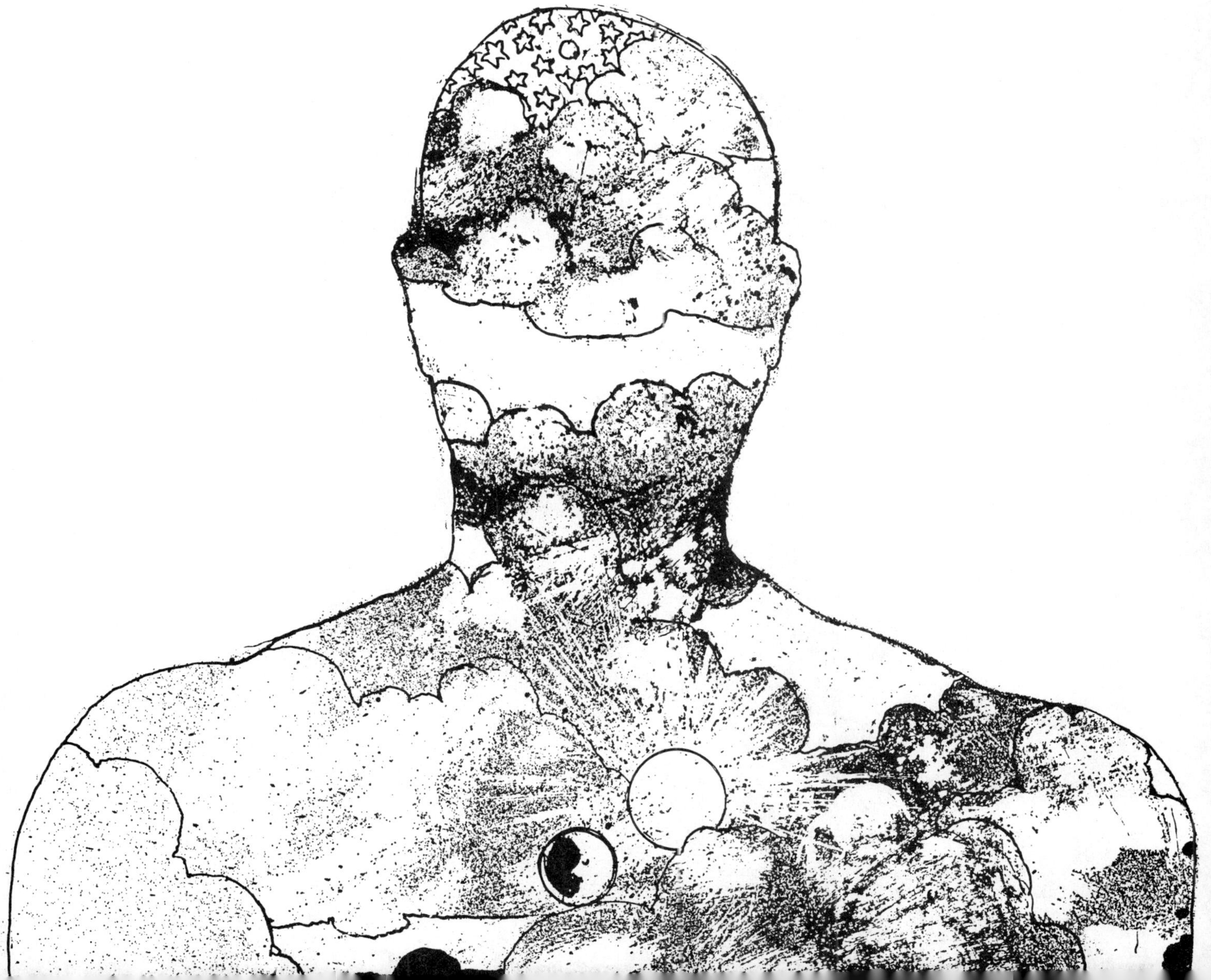

You are not *of* all the polarities you think you are. You do possess them in some measure, but they move *through* you. You will never, ever clean up your clouds sufficiently, my friends. There will always be a little dark one that you can't quite get at. There will always be one somewhere that you can't quite reach.

So, what again to do? Just continue what you are doing, but with a slight shift. Start feeling yourself as the vast sky, and let the clouds do what they do. The winds of karma do blow, and I advise you not to try to get them to blow the way you want them to. Karma is an energy form that pushes the clouds around in your particular sky. All you have to do, my friends, is start re-identifying yourself, dropping the belief that you are a limited, polarity-pulled consciousness, and commit deeply to being the vastness that you are. Any other concept of yourself is a limitation.

You are not the actions you perform any more than the figures on a screen projected in a movie are the screen itself. The most incredible holocaust can be projected onto that screen and it will remain unchanged. The most wondrously uplifting statement can be shown on the screen and it still remains unchanged.

Concentrate on who you really are
and you will know!
There is no other solution,
my friends.
You cannot
clean up
your clouds,
and you don't need to.

You are changeless.

You are eternal.

The rest
is
your illusion.

Spirit Teachers & Channels

All channels and spirit teachers who have contributed to this book offer a wide variety of services and related learning tools. Some may be reached through addresses given below. Others wish to be contacted c/o *Spirit Speaks*, P.O. Box 84304, Los Angeles, CA 90073.

ABRHAM, as channeled by Thomas P. Massari (a channel since 1972), lived during the time of Atlantis, in the Mayan civilization, and during the time of Jesus. Tom, also a certified hypnotist, has created four lines of highly empowering self-help tapes, including *Subliminal Motivation, Hypno-Sleep, Self-Hypnosis,* and *Subliminal Motivation for Children.* For information on channeled workshops with Abrham or Genesis Reflection Self-Help Tapes, contact Genesis Reflection, P.O. Box 4111, Simi Valley, CA 93063, (805) 581-2241.

BARTHOLOMEW, as channeled by Mary-Margaret Moore, has been speaking from a vaster field of awareness for over ten years. Although "living" in New Mexico, Bartholomew conducts workshops throughout the country, as well as accompanying seekers to other places around the world. Information on over 400 informal tapes of meetings may be obtained from Dr. John Aiken, 920 Annette St., Socorro, NM 87801. Two books, *I Come as a Brother* and *From the Heart of a Gentle Brother*, are available. For information on the books or Bartholomew's scheduled lectures, travels, etc., write to High Mesa Press, P.O. Box 2267, Taos, NM 87571.

DR. PEEBLES, as channeled by Rev. William Rainen, was last incarnated in Scotland. After years of medical practice in England, he came to the United States to research the philosophy behind illness and accident. The founder of the Universal Life Alliance, William travels extensively, conducting seminars and lectures focused on the study and practice of psychic development, communication with all life, and the practice of spiritual interaction. Dr. Peebles is available for lectures and private or group sessions, and he answers written questions with taped responses. Contact c/o *Spirit Speaks.*

DONG HOW LI was a spiritual counselor and philosopher, last incarnated as a Tibetan monk in the Nepalese Himalayas of 600 B.C. From 1982 through 1986, Master Li expressed himself through trance medium Allen Page. Since completion of their work together, their respective evolutions have proceeded independently. Allen presently offers private consultaions and classes, facilitating the discovery and integration of one's Self in one's life. He may be reached at (818) 766-6334 or by mail at P.O. Box 2151, Toluca Lake, CA 91602.

ENID, as channeled by Iris Belhayes, was last incarnated in the 1840s and speaks in an earthly manner with an Irish brogue. Iris and Enid have published a book, *Spirit Guides*, available through ACS Publications in San Diego or your local bookstore. Iris teaches Yohti healing techniques which she channeled from the beingness Octo. She also offers spirit guide sessions in which you meet your own guides and teachers. Contact c/o *Spirit Speaks.*

THE ETERNALS, as channeled by Daniel Clay, describe their energy as being "the force of life itself." Daniel is part of an organization called Ageless Expressions, whose purpose is to seek spiritual information and guidance to help both the individual and mankind. He is featured in two books, *Developing Your Psychic Ability* and *Journey Within: Past-Life Regression and Channeling.* Daniel offers full individual readings (physical, mental, and spiritual) as well as group channelings. For additional information please contact Daniel at Ageless Expressions, Box 100, Troutdale, VA 24378, (703) 579-4061.

HILARION, as channeled by Maurice B. Cooke, has been identified in theosophical writings as one of the seven masters responsible for various phases of Earth's development. Hilarion serves as the source for a major series of books and other teaching material. For more information, or for a free catalogue, please write to Marcus Books, P.O. Box 327, Queensville, Ontario, Canada L0G 1R0.

JOHN, as channeled by Gerry Bowman, lived in Israel 2,000 years ago. In Los Angeles, John can be heard Sundays at midnight on KIEV Radio, 870 AM. John conducts seminars and workshops nationwide, and offers private sessions by phone and in person. John also has 21 audio cassettes, and two powerful videos taped live on Mt. Shasta. Contact John through the Freewill Foundation, P.O. Box 1135, Concord, MA 01742, (508) 369-6533.

KUNDA, as channeled by Marcella Daniels, is a higher helper assisting in humanity's spiritual awakening. Kunda has never worn the veil of human limitation and offers greater soul awareness and understanding. She is a collective intelligence committed to man's cosmic development through universal teachings. Some of her teachings are available on cassette and in booklet form. Marcella channels the Kunda energies for group-sponsored events and is available for lectures and workshops through the Crystal Light Centre Inc., Box 1946, Rockford, IL 61110-0446, (815) 968-0422.

KYROS, as channeled by Sandra Radhoff, has never been expressed in the physical. Sandra has been channeling for 17 years and is one of the founders of Universalia, a Colorado-based group which creates a bimonthly newsletter, *The Universalian*. Sandra writes for several New Age publications. Her channeling is frequently reprinted in many New Age magazines and newsletters. She is currently preparing a collection of Kyros material for submission to publishers. Contact c/o *Spirit Speaks*.

LI SUNG, as channeled by Alan Vaughan, lived 1200 years ago in Northern China. Alan's major TV appearances include *Donahue, Merv*, and *20/20*. He is rated America's most successful psychic predictor by the Central Premonitions Registry. He is former editor of *Reincarnation Report* and *Psychic* magazine, author of five books, and holds an honorary doctorate in parapsychology. He has been teaching psychic techniques for 20 years and teaches channeling classes and seminars. For information on consultations and tapes, contact Alan at 3015 Glendale Blvd., #600, Los Angeles, CA 90039, (213) 666-9735.

MASTER ADALFO and **CRYSTAL MOON RUNNING**, as channeled by Rev. Carol Simpson, were, respectively, an Atlantean priest and an Arapaho woman. Carol is a trance medium and teacher, and also serves on the staff of the Healing Light Center Church in Glendale, California. She offers private and group trance consultations, mediumship development classes, laying-on-of-hands healing, pastoral counseling, and nondenominational ceremonies. Carol may be reached at P.O. Box 7023, Northridge, CA 91327-7023, (818) 360-3786.

RAHMA, an ascended master, is channeled by Salli Lou West, who has written a book, *BE: The Joy*, with computer files from Rahma. Salli Lou does workshops and private sessions with Rahma and also offers crystal healing for energy balance both in private and group settings. Contact her at 546 Onate Place, Santa Fe, NM 87501, (505) 983-9550.

ROBBYN AND HIS MERRY BANDE, as channeled by Karla Spitzer, consist of energies who are focused on planetary, social, and political change through friendly and fun spiritual enlightenment. As masters of healing through compassion and humor, the Bande's catchphrase is "Laughter is the best healer." Their wit and wisdom is available for the frank and fulfilling growth and healing of accelerated personal change. For information on mail, phone, or personal appointments, write c/o *Spirit Speaks*.

RAMTHA's teachings, as channeled by J. Z. Knight, have been excerpted from the following publications of Sovereignty: *Ramtha: An Introduction* (copyright 1988) and *Ramtha Intensive: Change, The Days to Come* (copyright 1987). These works may be purchased from your local bookstore or directly from Sovereignty. For information about books, audio cassettes, and videotapes presenting the teachings of Ramtha, write to Sovereignty, P.O. Box 909F, Eastsound, WA 98245, or call toll free, 1-800-654-1407.

SOLI is channeled by Neville Rowe, a graduate engineer who has been involved in psychic development for over 15 years. Soli is a composite of entities responsible for guiding the evolution of the Earth and the solar system during the transition to the New Age. Neville specializes in past-life regression (which empowers others to contact their own inner wisdom and guidance) and teaches consciousness-raising classes. He is available for private and group consultations in person or by phone. Tapes are available. Contact at P.O. Box 11218, Phoenix, AZ 85061, (602) 242-9537.

SPIRIT, as channeled by Michael Francis, describes self as Universal Spirit/Universal Consciousness in action. Formerly with the A. T. O. M. Center in Anchorage, Alaska, Michael left his physical body in spring, 1988.

TING-LAO, as channeled by Kris Topaz, expresses his personality as an Oriental philosopher. Kris is a staff healer at the Healing Light Center Church in Glendale, CA, where she offers consultations with her spirit teacher on physical, emotional, mental, and spiritual levels. Kris lectures, performs pastoral services, and teaches mediumship development. Both she and Ting-Lao speak English and Spanish. Contact c/o *Spirit Speaks*.

ZOOSH, as channeled by Robert Shapiro, is a nonphysical being from Alpha Centauri, the nearest star to our sun. Bob has been a self-employed channel/author since 1978. He receives communications from energy personalities and sources outside of his immediate knowledge, designed to expand the horizons of those with whom he works. He has given thousands of private consultations as well as workshops and seminars around the country. The author of the channeled book *Allies*, a collection of messages from off-planet beings, Robert is available to speak or channel for your group, fair, college, or expo. He also has tapes available. To inquire about the availability of telephone consultations with his spirit teachers, write or call Robert at 130 Castle Rock Rd., #67, Sedona, AZ 86336, (602) 284-9582.

Some of the material in this book was previously published in the following issues of *SPIRIT SPEAKS* magazine:

Issue #1 *Reincarnation: Your Plan*
Issue #2 *Earth Changes: Past, Present and Future*
Issue #3 *Create Your Own Reality: One Day at a Time*
Issue #7 *Life in the Spirit World*
Issue #13 *Channeling Your Higher Self: Finding the God Within*
Issue #17 *Spirit Guides and Teachers: You Are Never Alone*

(For information on the availability of these magazines, please write to the publisher; address given on page 192.)

Some material in this book was excerpted from *AIDS: From Fear to Hope*, published by New Age Publishing Company. This 6" x 9", 267-page paperback contains guidance and wisdom from ten spirit teachers, all of whom have contributed to *Life: Before, During, and After*. Available at $9.95 from New Age Publishing, P.O. Box 01-1549, Miami, FL 33101.

Companion Publications from SPIRIT SPEAKS

Our purpose, as a publishing company, is to share guidance, wisdom, and wit from the spirit dimension. We view this information as a valuable tool for personal growth when applied to all aspects of daily life. The *Celebration of Discovery* series is constantly being expanded to share the broad points of view from a wise group of spirit teachers. Each book focuses on one topic and is fully illustrated by Emmy Award-winning artist Gary Lund.

Vol I in the
Celebration of Discovery series

HEALING THE WHOLE PERSON,
THE WHOLE PLANET

is a landmark publication. For the first time ever, a group of spirit teachers focus their attention on the multiple aspects of illness and health. They share expanded perspectives relating to the mental, emotional, and spiritual misalignment which can manifest as disease. They discuss how and why we use illness as a means of vital communication between us and aspects of our more consciously-aware selves. They also comment on the wide variety of treatment probabilities including techniques of communication to help us better understand the "why" of any illness from the common cold to AIDS. Fully illustrated, 192 pages, $12.95. Available now in bookstores or by mail order (see form on page 192).

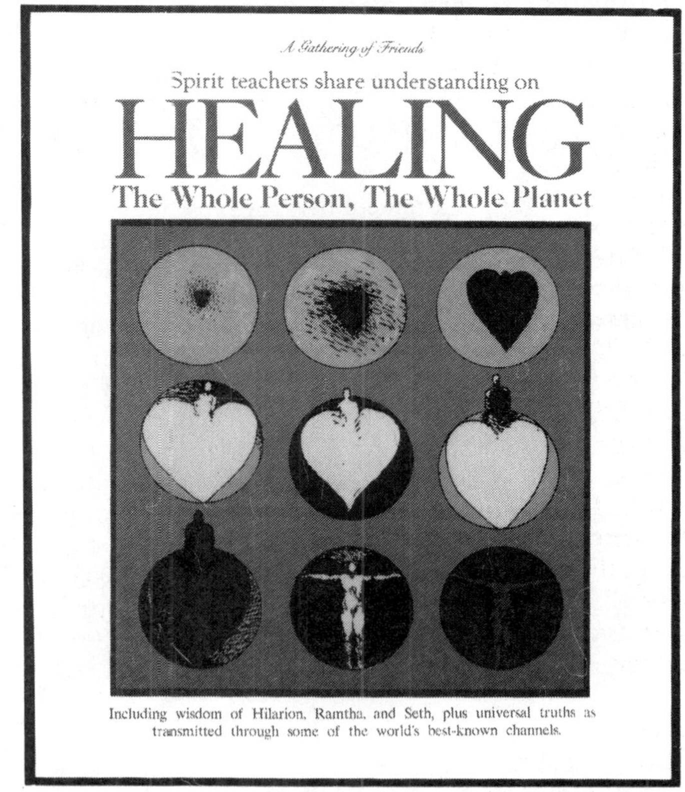

Available in May, 1989, Vol III

RELATIONSHIPS: MINE, YOURS, OURS, AND THEIRS

How we relate to ourselves and to other people is one of the most puzzling and rewarding issues in life. Like all *Celebration of Discovery* books, the focus is on self-help as the contributors explain the process of selecting life situations and relationships. The dynamics of emotions which occur between people are discussed, along with suggestions for building rich and lasting relationships. Our spirit contributors discuss love and sexuality, soulmates, relationships between parents and children, between men and women, and homosexuality. Fully illustrated, 192 pages, $12.95. Available in bookstores in May, or by mail order (see form on page 192).

Introducing *SPIRIT SPEAKS* Magazine

SPIRIT SPEAKS is the source for much of the material in this book and the other *Celebration of Discovery* books. This bimonthly magazine is a unique self-help publication which addresses your deepest concerns and needs. Each 80-page issue focuses on a specific topic such as love, power, health, dreams, sexuality, the planet, etc., sharing guidance, wisdom, and wit from 15 well-known spirit teachers, including many of those you have just met in this book.

Published since 1985, *SPIRIT SPEAKS* features spiritual psychology which encourages readers to consider applying broader, universal insights into all aspects of daily life. Our readers tell us that as they shift their perspectives, they experience new feelings of relaxation, happiness, and personal power. The spirit contributors teach that, despite occasional evidence to the contrary, life, *for all people* is meant to be filled with joy and success. You have the power to make it so.

May we suggest that you give yourself the gift of increased understanding by subscribing to *SPIRIT SPEAKS* today? Thank you.

Order form
SPIRIT SPEAKS magazine
_______Free information about *SPIRIT SPEAKS* magazine
_______Sample issue (postage included) $4.55
_______1-year subscription (6 issues) $20
_______2-year subscription (12 issues) $36
_______1-year subscription, Canadian or foreign, $26

CELEBRATION OF DISCOVERY book series
_______*HEALING THE WHOLE PERSON, THE WHOLE PLANET* $12.95 +$2 postage
_______*RELATIONSHIPS: MINE, YOURS, OURS AND THEIRS* $12.95 + $2 postage
_______Sales Tax (for California residents only) $.84 per book
My check for __________ is enclosed.
Send to:
Name____

Address____

City______________________________State________Zip________

Please send your order to **SPIRIT SPEAKS, P. O. Box 84304, Los Angeles, CA 90073.**
For further information, please call (outside of California) 800-356-9104. California residents, call (213) 826-9197.